The Origins of
Western Warfare

HISTORY AND WARFARE

Arther Ferrill, *Series Editor*

The Origins of Western Warfare

Militarism and Morality in the Ancient World

Doyne Dawson

WestviewPress

A Division of HarperCollinsPublishers

History and Warfare

Copyright © 1996 by Westview Press, A Division of HarperCollins Publishers, Inc.

Published in 1996 in the United States of America by Westview Press, 5500 Central Avenue, Boulder, Colorado 80301-2877, and in the United Kingdom by Westview Press, 12 Hid's Copse Road, Cumnor Hill, Oxford OX2 9JJ

A CIP catalog record for this book is available from the Library of Congress.
ISBN 0-8133-2940-X

The paper used in this publication meets the requirements of the American National Standard for Permanence of Paper for Printed Library Materials Z39.48–1984.

10   9   8   7   6   5   4   3   2   1

Contents

PART FOUR
THE CLASSICAL LEGACY

The Origins of
Western Warfare

Introduction

Strategy, like morality, is a language of justification.
—Michael Walzer, *Just and Unjust Wars*

During the 1980s I taught military history to many Army ROTC cadets at Boston University and the Massachusetts Institute of Technology, while working as a volunteer for several peace organizations in the Boston area. I was not surprised, but was still bemused, by the inability of these two groups to understand one another's language. I had been vaguely aware that there are two vocabularies for discussing warfare, the moral and the strategic, but I had not realized that they ran on such separate tracks. The peace activists, except perhaps for some extreme pacifists, seemed willing to allow the strategic vocabulary its place, so long as it remained subordinate to their own criteria in high-level decisions. The military professionals, except perhaps for some extreme hawks, seemed willing to allow moral discourse its high place, indeed preferred to keep it high upstairs where it could not intrude into military life except in the form of the occasional chaplain's lecture on "military ethics," which would be confined to rules of practical conduct. The two groups did not seek to abolish one another. They ignored one another, especially the intellectuals on both sides.

A common justification for this mutual indifference was that the language of strategy is pragmatic and tough minded, fit for the harsh necessities of war. This assumption could serve both sides: to claim for strategists an autonomous sphere of action ("All's fair in love and war") or to limit that sphere ("War is too important to be left to the generals"). But it was clear that the two vocabularies everywhere overlapped—and not clear that the one was more pragmatic than the other. I made some attempts to lecture to peace activists on concepts of strategy and to cadets on the philosophy of war (not "military ethics"). They listened patiently, and I eventually con-

ceived the idea of writing the present book, which is dedicated to the many
intelligent and idealistic people I met in both camps.

The schism I have described is reflected in the scholarly literature on warfare. For the past two centuries the just war doctrine has been the preserve of
theologians and jurists, and strategy, the property of soldiers. All these
groups—not just the soldiers—are professionals concerned primarily with
practical issues. So far as the world of "pure" scholarship is concerned, the
study of war has been an orphan, but those who approach it from a background in philosophy are usually drawn to the moral vocabulary, and those
who come to it from the social sciences and historical scholarship tend toward the language of strategy. There is little crossover between the two traditions, hence no truly comprehensive history of the theory of war has been
developed. We have many historical studies of the just war doctrine, all concerned primarily with Christian theology and its continuation in international law. There have been some historical treatments of strategic thought,
usually beginning with Carl von Clausewitz, sometimes with a nod to
Machiavelli. The classical antecedents of both traditions are generally acknowledged and generally ignored—a procedure that severs their common
roots, perhaps to their mutual satisfaction, and sometimes obscures the history of their own doctrine. Machiavelli may be called the greatest philosopher of war, but he has generally been anathema to the moral party and unintelligible to the strategic.[1]

In this book, I offer a short account of classical theories of war and imperialism as an attempt to bridge this gap. This study is organized around the
following three major themes:

> The moral issue: warfare as an instrument of justice, human and divine.
> The international issue: warfare as an instrument of foreign policy or
>   *raison d'état.*
> The constitutional issue: warfare as an instrument of internal policy.

1. *War as an Instrument of Human and Divine Justice.* Until recent times,
warfare was generally assumed to have a certain place in the cosmic order,
assigned to it by divine or natural law, which both justified and restricted it.
Under this rubric, we may distinguish two different doctrines, the "just
war" and the "holy war."

The phrase "just war" usually designates a body of Christian teaching that
did not reach its fullest development until the sixteenth century, but I use
it here for something far older: the all-but-universal human assumption that
wars are entirely justified, and requisite, when fought to resist wrong. Such a
just war might easily become a just hegemony or empire, as we will see later on.

The holy war, or crusade, is a just war on a cosmic scale, fought not only
to redress particular wrongs but to restore order to the world. In practice it
is often difficult to distinguish the just war from the holy war. This is so be-

cause the just war is often described as a sort of minicrusade undertaken on behalf of the public welfare, and the holy war retains much of the rhetoric of the just war, as it is still a matter of defending rights and resisting wrongs. But once we begin to think of infidels or barbarians as constituting an offense against God or Nature merely by their independent existence, the language of the just war changes its meaning. The doctrine of holy war, like that of just war, reaches its full development in sixteenth-century Christian theology, but both have their classical precedents.

Premodern thought about the ethics of warfare is distinguished by the absence of two important theories that today dominate discourse on this subject. These are defensism and pacifism.

The traditional just war must not be confused with "defensive" war. This is a common misunderstanding. The distinction between aggressive war and defensive war is modern. The traditional just war was supposed to be "vindicative" rather than "defensive." It was always necessary to have a just cause for war, which meant simply that one had to be able to claim to be the victim of wrongs. These wrongs might include insults as well as injuries, for honor had to be defended as well as land. Often it was felt that there was a moral obligation to redress the wrongs of one's neighbors as well, which provided a ready excuse to intervene in their affairs. Given a just cause, there was rarely any objection to becoming the aggressor, in the sense of striking the first blow. The failure of philosophers and theologians to ban aggression made it easy for theories of just war to become theories of just hegemony or just imperialism, then for these to become holy crusades.

As for pacifism in the modern sense, it literally did not exist. Premodern thinkers were not all militaristic by any means, but they were almost all "bellicist."[2] They assumed warfare was a normal and natural feature of the world, to be accepted fatalistically like any other great force of nature. It is easy to find in premodern thought expressions of bitter antiwar sentiment that is often mistaken for pacifism. But these Stoic and Christian complaints about warfare are not political programs; they are the equivalent of complaining about the weather. Only toward the end of the eighteenth century did any appreciable number of serious thinkers begin to entertain the hope that war might be abolished. The emergence of pacifism and defensivism in the age of the American and French Revolutions created a great watershed in the intellectual history of warfare.

2. *War as an Instrument of Foreign Policy.* I mean here the theory known as *raison d'état*, or *Staatsräson*, a phrase that entered European languages in the sixteenth century, when the word "state" was acquiring its modern sense.[3] The concept designated a set of principles about interstate behavior often associated, then and now, with the name of Machiavelli. Within the purview of *raison d'état*, the world of interstate relations is assumed to be anarchic, composed of competing political units, each of which is pursuing its own interest. Each is assumed to be justified in such pursuit because the "state" is the only

possible moral community. The interests of larger moral communities, such as are assumed in the just war and holy war doctrines, are ignored. Each state is assumed to be capable of identifying its own interests, but since the preservation and strengthening of the state is basic to all other interests, the competition is basically about power for its own sake. War, if consonant with the legitimate interests of the state, is assumed to be a legitimate instrument of state, indeed, its primary instrument in dealing with other states.

This theory has been the dominant philosophy of war since Clausewitz. But it is older than Clausewitz and older than Machiavelli. We do not find the doctrine stated so explicitly before the sixteenth century because only in a Christian society did it become necessary to formulate it in that self-conscious way. But what was called *raison d'état* in the sixteenth century was simply a systematic statement of an attitude encountered everywhere in the cherished Greek and Latin authors. Greek historiography and oratory are suffused with it. It has never been put more succinctly than in the Melian dialogue of Thucydides. The Romans tended to hide it under a veil of moralisms, but Machiavelli could pick out its hard outline beneath the mellow prose of Livy, and later in the sixteenth century, the name Tacitus became practically shorthand for *raison d'état.*

The contemporary strategic vocabulary of war is derived from this tradition, and its roots are classical and neoclassical; the contemporary moral vocabulary, however, comes from the just war tradition and has been heavily influenced by Christianity.

3. *War as an Instrument of Domestic Policy.* There is widespread agreement among anthropologists, as we will see in the following chapter, that primitive warfare, whatever other functions it may have served, had the important function of enforcing social solidarity. Among the Greeks and Romans, this function was quite conscious: They assumed warfare had major effects upon the internal constitution of the state, and much of their thinking about warfare focused on this aspect of it, particularly on an ideal that I will call "civic militarism." This was the military side of what was known as "republicanism" in early modern Europe. Republicanism essentially meant the belief that the best constitution—meaning the mode of organization within a society—is composed of a body of self-governing citizens whose primary duty is to defend their "republic," which in the ancient Mediterranean world was always a small city-state. Martial values were cultivated among the citizens not only because they were needed to defend the city but also because they were highly valued in themselves as a main source of citizen virtue and loyalty. This is genuine "militarism," not just bellicism; it assigns positive social and ethical value to the process of war for its own sake, regarding it as the means and measure of cultural development. I call it "civic" to distinguish it from other types of militaristic culture, such as the primitive militarism to be discussed shortly or the modern nationalistic type, with which we are all too familiar.

The militarism of the classical city-state was always associated with a peculiar type of military equipment and tactic: heavy infantry in a close formation, whether Greek phalanx or Roman legion, relying on direct shock combat. In the ancient Mediterranean, this type of formation and its accompanying ideology were never institutionalized in any social environment but that of a free city. The ideology was responsible for a certain glorification of warfare in Greek and Roman literature and imparted a peculiar spirit of aggressiveness to military ideals and practices. The simple fact that a formation of heavy infantry could be most effectively used in attack bred a tendency to settle wars by a single decisive battle. Among the Greeks, the preference for offensive tactics did not usually imply a preference for offensive strategies; but among the Romans, it normally implied both. This cult of the offensive was one of the most important military legacies of the classical world.[4]

Today, this may seem one of the more dubious classical legacies. But many have found it difficult to resist this heady combination of civic freedom and military glory. In the republics of Renaissance Italy, the classical vision of an armed and militant citizenry was revived and found its philosopher in Machiavelli. The republican dream soon faded before the realities of the monarchic sixteenth century, but the vision of a disciplined conquering army endured. When Captain John Bingham, who had fought the Spaniards in the Low Countries, translated the *Tactica* of Aelian in 1616, he thought it useful to explain to his readers in his preface why the ancient ways of war were superior:

> The Treatise . . . containeth the practise of the best Generals of all antiquity concerning the formes of Battailes. And whereas many hold opinion, that it sorteth not with the use of our times, they must give me leave to be of another mind: Indeed our actions in Warre are onely nowadays and sieges oppugnations [sic] of Cities; Battailes wee heare not of, save onely of a few in France, and that of Newport in the Low-Countries. But this manner will not last alwayes, nor is there any Conquest to be made without Battailes. He that is Master of the field, may dispose of his affaires as he listeth; hce may spoyle the Enemies Countrey at his pleasure, he may march where he thinketh best, he may lay siege to what Towne he is disposed, he may raise any siege that the Enemy hath layed against him or his. Neither can any man be Master of the field without Battaile; in ordering whereof, that Generall that is most-skilfull, seldome misseth of winning the day; experience of former times cleares this.[5]

By "experience of former times," he means much more than Aelian and the other classical authors on the art of war, for the cult of battle, like much else in the classical military tradition, had been passed down chiefly by the classical historians, primarily through the examples of the great commanders. All educated Europeans knew that Alexander and Caesar had won their reputations by seeking out the enemy, bringing him to battle, and annihilating him.

We are still familiar with the problem of warfare as a component of the international system and with war as a religious and moral question. Machiavelli and St. Augustine can still speak to us directly on those issues. But warfare as a constitutional problem tends to be ignored in modern thought, and the civic militarist version of it has no real equivalent at all in the modern world. It lost its allure some two hundred years ago, when the more enlightened thinkers of Europe and America grew suspicious of the fierce militancy of the ancient citizen ideal and turned to a more peaceable and commercial model of republicanism. Today, when political scientists speculate about the relationship between war and the constitution, they do not ask which constitution will be most successful at waging war but rather which will be most successful at avoiding it; and the effects of militarism on society, if mentioned at all, are generally assumed to be deleterious.

Such, in outline, is the plan of the book. Something more should be said about its geographical limitations. I have restricted myself to the Western world for obvious reasons: the need to reduce the subject to manageable proportions, the thinness of reliable scholarly literature on many nonwestern military traditions, and my lack of the linguistic equipment to study these further. But some attempt must be made to address whether there *is* a distinct Western tradition of military thought.[6]

Other ancient civilizations had their literatures of war, but they seem to have been heavily dominated at most times by religious and cosmological theories. The attempt to put warfare in its place within a universal moral order was an important motif in the Western tradition at all times, as I have recognized by making this the first of the three main themes of this book. During the Middle Ages, this theme dominated practically all thinking about warfare in Europe. But the civilization of the Indian subcontinent, before it came under Western influence, seems to have lived in the Middle Ages almost always; and the civilization of the Far East, most of the time. In both traditions, military thought was generally dominated by a learned nonmilitary elite—in India, a priestly caste; in China, a scholar bureaucracy—whose main concerns about warfare were these: to interpret it within a mythic cosmological framework that would not admit the legitimacy of separate warring states, to plant ritual proscriptions around every phase of the art of war, and to keep the military elites of their societies safely under the thumb of Brahman or mandarin.

Nonreligious theories of war can appear in such cultures, but they do not become continuing traditions, or if they do, they are thoroughly subordinated to the ruling ideology. Ancient India produced the treatise called *Arthashastra,* attributed to Kautilya, a minister of the Mauryan empire in the third century B.C. who has often been compared to Machiavelli for his cold-blooded acceptance of *raison d'état.* But the Brahmans reasserted their control and eventually succeeded in subjecting the Hindu warrior caste to what would appear to be the most fantastically elaborate and strategically crippling code of ritual warfare to which any military tradition has ever submitted.

In China, however, military thought achieved a much more significant breakthrough. During the Age of the Warring States (403–221 B.C.), there developed a remarkable tradition of military literature that left us the Seven Military Classics, the basic texts used in imperial examinations for military office in China into the twentieth century. One of these works, the *Art of War* attributed to Sun Tzu, has been well known in the West since the eighteenth century and has enjoyed a popularity denied to any of the ancient Western treatises on the art of war. The precocity of the ancient Chinese military literature is undeniable, but it is sometimes exaggerated because we tend to compare it to the classical Greek and Latin treatises on the art of war, such as those by Aelian and Frontinus, which resemble the Chinese works in literary form. This comparison is misleading. The Greek and Latin treatises on the art of war are indeed a disappointing body of literature when compared to their ancient Chinese equivalents, indeed, when compared to almost anything. The major contributions of the Greeks and Romans to military literature are not to be found in these jejune tracts; they are to be found in historiography. If we are to compare the military thought of the ancient Mediterranean and ancient East Asia, we should include their historical literatures in the comparison, for China, alone among ancient societies, developed independently something like the Greek tradition of narrative history about war and high politics. A comparative study of classical Far Eastern and classical Far Western historiography is one of the great cross-cultural subjects awaiting a competent scholar—a role to which I cannot aspire, owing to the limitations mentioned above.

Chinese military thought was precocious and remarkable, but it did not last. After the establishment of the Han dynasty, the martial tradition was increasingly subordinated to the ideology of the Confucianist elite, whose major traditions were antimilitary. The realpolitik of the Age of Warring States had no place in later Confucianist political philosophy, which was centered on the ideal of a peaceful universal empire reflecting the order of heaven: The military bureaucracy always had its place but was increasingly subordinated to the civil bureaucracy: The heroes of imperial China include no equivalents of Alexander or Caesar: The Seven Military Classics were kept alive only because they were assigned a strictly compartmentalized place in Chinese culture, as required reading for military officers, and were generally forbidden to everyone else.

Finally, even in the great age of Chinese military thought, there seems to have been no equivalent to what I have termed civic militarism, and there was little trace of the decisive-battle ideology that went with it. In fact, the Seven Military Classics have always impressed Western readers because they do *not* exhibit the preoccupation with the offensive that has been a continuing feature of Western thinking about warfare. Rather, they emphasize the importance of gaining victory with as little fighting as possible:

> Attaining one hundred victories in one hundred battles is not the pinnacle of excellence. Subjugating the enemy's army without fighting is the true pinnacle of excellence. Thus the highest realization of warfare is to attack the enemy's plans; next is to attack their alliances; next to attack their army; and the lowest is to attack their fortified cities . . . Thus one who excels at employing the military subjugates other people's armies without engaging in battle, captures other people's fortified cities without attacking them, and destroys other people's states without prolonged fighting. (Sun Tzu 3 [trans. Sawyer, 161])

This is far removed from the thought world of Captain Bingham, not that he represents the acme of European military thinking or that his passion for decisive battle is the only counsel to be found in it.

There is something distinctive about the Western tradition of warfare. No other civilization developed a continuing tradition of military thought independent of religious and social control, no other gave rise to such dynamic patterns of warfare. Belief in the just war is worldwide, but outside the West we find little trace of *raison d'état* and no civic militarism. These were legacies of the Greeks and Romans, and until around 1800, European thought on matters of war and peace was dominated by the classical authors. The classical tradition did not lose its grip on Western military thought until the early nineteenth century, when the influence of the classical historians was finally replaced by the new "scientific" history of Georg Barthold Niebuhr and that of the classical treatises on the art of war, by the new "scientific" military thought of Antoine Henri Baron de Jomini and Clausewitz. In the final chapter of this book, I will attempt to summarize the continuing influence of this tradition. But first, we must look at its primitive roots.

Notes

1. W. E. Kaegi, Jr., "The Crisis in Military Historiography," *Armed Forces and Society* 7 (1980), 299–316, mentions among the topics neglected by military historians "the place of military strategy in intellectual history," and "the influence and perhaps tyranny of Graeco-Roman precedents and precepts on European and American ideas and practices in the art of war and military strategy." He offers a list of military authors who were so tyrannized, from Machiavelli to Guibert. One notices the list includes no one after 1800 except Ardant du Picq. Kaegi remarks, "Historians have seldom given much critical scrutiny to military strategy, let alone to how it is formed or how it might relate to other forms of human thought, in particular to historical assumptions." He thinks that the historical study of strategy practically ended in 1967 with the last edition of Basil Liddell Hart's *Strategy,* after which the subject fell to the metahistorical approaches of the nuclear strategists. Since this article appeared much has been done to fill in the gap between Machiavelli and Clausewitz by the revised edition of *Makers of Modern Strategy: From Machiavelli to the Nuclear Age,* ed. Peter Paret (Princeton, 1986), and Azar Gat's *Origins of Military Thought: From the Enlightenment to Clausewitz* (New York, 1989).

2. A term coined by Michael Howard, used by Martin Ceadel in *Thinking About Peace and War* (Oxford, 1987).

3. It did not, however, find a generally accepted equivalent in English, as witnessed by the English translation of the title of Friedrich Meinecke's *Der Idee der Staatsräson in der neueren Geschichte—Machiavellism: The Doctrine of Raison d'Etat and Its Place in Modern History,* trans. Douglas Scott (New Haven, 1957).

4. One of the many contributions of Hans Delbrück to the history of warfare (*Geschichte der Kriegskunst im Rahmen der politischen Geschichte* [Berlin, 1900–], trans. W. J. Renfroe, Jr., as *History of the Art of War,* 4 vols. [Westport, Conn., 1975–1985]) was to propose that there have been two basic forms of warfare, the strategies of annihilation and of exhaustion. Victor Hanson in *The Western Way of War: Infantry Battle in Classical Greece* (New York, 1989) argues that the first of these is peculiarly Western and can be traced back to the ancient Greeks. This idea is now reaching a wide audience through John Keegan's *A History of Warfare* (New York, 1993), whose master thesis is the contrast between nonwestern traditions of limited warfare and a Western tradition, derived ultimately from the Greeks, of "the face to face battle to the death." I agree, though I think the version of this tradition that most influenced later Western culture is Roman rather than Greek.

5. *The Tactiks of Aelian,* trans. John Bingham (London, 1616), dedication. This debate often became a quarrel between the ancients and the moderns, with the ancients on the side of the offensive. Compare Geoffrey Parker, *The Military Revolution: Military Innovation and the Rise of the West, 1500–1800* (Cambridge, 1988), 6, 16.

6. The most useful attempt at a general theory on the relationship between war and religion known to me is J. A. Aho's *Religious Mythology and the Art of War: Comparative Religious Symbolisms of Military Violence* (Westport, Conn., 1981): Aho supports the view that there is a significant difference between Western and non-Western traditions, the latter being more dominated by ritual codes of behavior and less prone to "Machiavellianism." The Chinese classics have now been translated with full commentary in another volume in this series, *The Seven Military Classics of Ancient China,* ed. R. D. Sawyer (Boulder, 1993). I have also profited from an unpublished doctoral dissertation, C. C. Rand's "The Role of Military Thought in Early Chinese Intellectual History," Harvard University, Department of East Asian Languages, 1977.

Developments in the Islamic world have been too little studied to permit generalization. In medieval times, Muslim culture was strongly influenced by Greek philosophy, had a lively tradition of historical writing that produced the unique historical theories of Ibn Khaldun, and might have had a tradition of military-political literature that escaped the controls of religious law; but if there was such a tradition, it was lost. In early modern times, Muslim religious law did not recognize the legitimacy of wars between Muslims and considered the only righteous warfare to be the holy war between the House of Islam and the House of War, or the infidel world. See the studies collected in *Cross, Crescent, and Sword: The Justification and Limitation of War in Western and Islamic Tradition* (Westport, Conn., 1990), and *Just War and Jihad: Historical and Theoretical Perspectives on War and Peace in Western and Islamic Traditions* (Westport, Conn., 1991), both ed. J. T. Johnson and John Kelsay.

Part One

In the Beginning

We must know that war is common to all and strife is justice, and that all things come into being and pass away through strife.

—Heraclitus of Ephesus, frag. 80 (trans. John Burnet)

Chapter One

Primitive Warfare

What Is War?

In its basic meaning, "war" (*polemos, bellum, guerra, guerre, Krieg,* and so on) is understood to be a specific institutionalized form of human conflict, whose outlines are so familiar that premodern writers on the subject rarely bothered to define it. Modern writers usually define it as an organized, legitimized, lethal conflict between human communities. This form of intraspecific conflict has been extremely common in human history for as far back as we can trace it. But it has taken many forms, and one of the major contributions of modern anthropology is to suggest a distinction of primary importance. There have been two types of "war," or rather, two pure types, with many gradations in between.[1]

There is the warfare of policy, fought between societies that have centralized political organizations, a major function of which is to determine the policies, or *raisons d'état,* for which wars are fought, as well as the "strategies" of war and "tactics" of battle needed to implement those policies. This is the warfare of societies that have reached or approached the advanced technical stage we call "civilization."

But a different kind of institutionalized, sanctioned, and often deadly conflict is common among small decentralized societies. It does not include anything that could be described as a clear policy, because these groups lack any organization capable of formulating one. They fight "wars" for purposes of their own, and at least their *articulated* motives are likely to strike us as private and personal rather than public and political. Their wars seem as devoid of strategy and tactics as they are of policy; because they are conducted according to such rigid conventions, they resemble some elaborate game, sport, magic, or other ritual more than the rational political operations described as wars by people describing themselves as civilized. Most readers of this book probably have sufficient acquaintance with anthropology to appreciate the importance of ritual in primitive cultures and to understand how difficult it is to separate ritual from the culture itself. Primitive warfare is a ritual practiced for its own sake; "civilized" warfare is an adaptation of that pattern to serve as a political instrument.

Most of this book will be concerned with the political wars of advanced literate societies and the ways those societies interpreted the business of war, especially their attempts to interpret the cluster of ideas mentioned above—policy, strategy, tactics—and to fit all this into their value systems and views of the world. But at the start, something must be said about the primitive ritual out of which such wars of policy arose. A better understanding of the assumptions and values of the most primitive warriors may throw some light on their calculating descendants. Although in the West "civilized" warfare has made a heroic effort to free itself from the influence of social structures and develop a clear theory of *raison d'état*, it continues to be more determined by culture and less by policy than we often assume.

Practices of Primitive War[2]

The Maring people of the New Guinea mountains continued their traditional practices of war into the 1950s, when the Australian government more or less put an end to these practices. These are among the best-reported of all primitive wars, and their elaborate ritualization has drawn much attention from anthropologists.[3]

The Maring live in farming communities containing a few hundred people each. Once or twice in a generation such a community would go to war with its neighbors, for reasons to be considered shortly. They distinguished two main phases of warfare, the "nothing fight" and the "true fight," which were performed in that order. When a "nothing fight" was declared, the men of the two quarreling groups met by appointment at a designated clearing in the forest, where they formed two opposing lines and fired arrows at one another at a distance from behind large fixed shields, doing little damage. At this stage, the disputes that had started the affair might be settled by negotiations shouted across the battlefield or through negotiation by members of some neutral group with kin on both sides. Meanwhile, both sides had made a show of force and had had an opportunity to size up one another's capabilities and determination. These activities might go on for weeks.

If negotiations failed, the conflict might escalate into a "true fight," a much more serious and bloody affair using hand-to-hand weapons that could continue sporadically for weeks more, during which time taboos barred all intercourse between the warring groups. Even a "true fight" was strictly bound by convention. Before it began, the shamans would set killing quotas, and as soon as the warriors met their quota of slain enemies they would be ready for a truce. Every serious casualty caused a long interruption in the fighting to perform appropriate rituals—of burial, on the one side, and purification, on the other. Rarely was anything resembling a strategy or tactic discernible on the killing ground. Apparently the usual objective was simply to keep fighting until the enemy's allies grew tired of the business and went home, whereupon the depleted enemy could be routed by a charge. In the event of a rout, or even with the expectation of one, the entire defeated community might flee precipitately from its territory, but the victors would not occupy the vacated land because they considered all the enemy's possessions taboo. The routed group might come back years later and reclaim some of its land, but if not, land could eventually be annexed by the victors, after the proper rituals had removed the taboos.

These wars were rituals enclosed in ritual. Every war was preceded, accompanied, and followed by complicated magic and taboos intended to accomplish certain objectives: secure victory, make the warriors invulnerable, curse the enemy, place sanctions around the rules of war, set killing quotas, make peace, bury the dead, and purify warriors of the blood of the slain so that their ghosts would not cause trouble. The Red Spirits, ghosts of ancestors killed in war, presided over all martial affairs and sought victory for their descendants.

It seems that the most significant practical effect of all this ritualization was to preserve the gradual, multiphase character of the war process and prevent premature or unnecessary escalation. Serious fighting, if it came at all, had to be preceded by many rounds of symbolic confrontation that allowed ample opportunity for arbitration. Redistribution of territory, if it happened at all, came long after the end of serious fighting and appeared in some cases to have required the acquiescence of the defeated community.

Chivalrous though all this sounds, we should not forget the primitive warfare could become deadly. The Maring sometimes suffered heavy casualties during a rout. One routed Maring community was said to have lost in a single day twelve men and six women and children, out of a total population of two hundred and fifty. Nor is all primitive warfare restricted to the sort of chivalrous multiphase process described above. Despite their devotion to ritual, the Maring sometimes resorted to tactics of ambush and raid with the intent of killing and despoiling as many of the enemy, of every age and gender, as they could; and such tactics have been widely reported from primitive societies the world over.

But ritualization has also been widely reported. Earlier Western observers of primitive warfare were often misled because they failed to realize that what they were observing was only one stage in a process more complex, in some ways, than "civilized" warfare. Many primitive wars struck them as a kind of Homeric comic opera, as an excuse for warriors to put on paint and feathers and yell insults at one another from a safe distance. But they may have seen only a "nothing fight"—the innocuous initial phase in a ritual cycle that was as long-drawn-out, cautious, and procrastinating as that of the Maring. (There do seem to have been cultures, like that of the native Californians, where warfare rarely went beyond that stage.) Others observed wars of conquest and occupation that seemed no different from their European counterparts, without realizing that in truly primitive warfare, such an outcome is rare and perhaps accidental.

Such was the repertoire of primitive warfare. What was it all about?

Causes of Primitive War

The Martial Values

Perhaps the most striking difference between truly primitive and truly modern warfare is that the former seems normally to be fought not for materialistic interests but rather for "honor." The commonest reason that primitive people give for going to war is to take vengeance for offenses.

Why is this not a perfectly adequate reason? Primitive people who belong to the same descent group and form a community have sanctions against intragroup violence; neighboring communities with kinship ties can usually settle their disputes through arbitration; but if a man is wronged by someone from an unrelated community, there is no nonviolent recourse, so he has to call upon his kinsmen and start a "war." Any perceived insult or injury will do as a reason. The Helen of Troy theme is recurrent: A woman has been seduced or abducted, or a bride price has been paid and the bride not delivered, or vice versa. According to Napoleon Chagnon, longtime observer of the warlike Yanomamö of Venezuela, practically all Yanomamö wars arise initially over women. Other disputes may involve accusations of malicious magic, for primitive people tend to attribute all misfortunes, including natural death, to the withcraft of an enemy. Then again, retribution may be demanded for deaths in earlier wars, generating a long series of wars that go on until all blood debts have been paid. When a mutual hostility has gelled between two communities, it is likely to become permanent because it prevents intermarriages and kinship bonds, leaving no way to resolve grievances except war.

In a culture where these affairs of vengeance assume an important place, every male (for war is everywhere the exclusive prerogative of men, for reasons we will consider shortly) is primarily occupied with honor. Warlike societies invariably encourage an intense status competition among males over honor: Honor can be preserved only by demonstrating one's readiness to avenge wrongs, will be lost irretrievably by failure to take vengeance, and can be enhanced by the accumulation of war trophies such as heads, scalps, ceremonial titles, and prerogatives. In an extremely warlike culture, martial honor and glory are normally the only means by which men can acquire prestige among their fellows. Obviously, the need for prestige can become a cause of war in itself, and the cult of male aggressiveness makes war more frequent: Ambitious warriors will always be looking for wrongs to avenge, and in turn, frequent warfare will intensify the competition among warriors to demonstrate their bravery. Revenge and prestige are mutually reinforcing.

We may refer to this self-reinforcing complex of motives for war—revenge and prestige, honor and glory—as the "martial values." They are easily recognizable from one society to the next. When a culture has thoroughly routinized them, raising virtually all its males to think of themselves primarily as warriors whose central interests in life are revenge and prestige, we may call such a pattern "primitive militarism." The majority of the primitive cultures known to anthropology seem to have militarized themselves to a greater or lesser degree. Anthropologists have studied some half a dozen examples (lists vary) of societies described as "peaceful," or perhaps better, as "relatively peaceful" or "minimally warlike," in that they do not practice war except in immediate self-defense, and the martial values seem to play no routine part in their culture.[4] Apart from these dubious exceptions, whose significance we will consider later, it is not clear from the anthropological record that any primitive cultures in recent centuries have been altogether free of militarism.

Therefore, the original form of warfare seems essentially what it purported to be: an institutionalized method of conflict management for settling disputes with people outside the community. There is no obvious way to distinguish such wars from the feuding between kinship groups that goes on today in many parts of the more or less civilized world. As has been noted, some anthropologists prefer to call these affairs "fights" or "feuds" rather than "wars."

But surely there is more to these "judicial" or "social" combats than meets the eye. There is a public aspect to the process that seems to justify the phrase "primitive warfare." We have seen that the self-reinforcing character of militaristic culture makes men resort to this particular method of conflict management far more often than would otherwise be the case. Nor are honor and glory the absolute and self-evident imperatives that they always purport to be: Primitive warriors are notorious for "forgetting" wrongs for a long time, that is, until they find it convenient to "remember" them, and it is difficult to believe their fellow tribesmen are totally oblivious to the manipulativeness of this. It is easier to explain the popularity of militarism if we think of it as a public action, not merely as a sort of violent civil suit for the settlement of private torts. In fact, it is easy to see how these fights benefit the entire community, not just the influential men who start them. Men who are quick to react to wrongs gain prestige for themselves and their kindred, and communities led by such men gain prestige among neighboring communities. Those who have won such prestige are less likely to be molested. A reputation for militarism is a great deterrent. There are also more intangible advantages: Militarism promotes solidarity and cooperation, so that the warlike are likely to have an edge in any competition with the unwarlike. Some awareness of these advantages is implicit in the readiness with which a private grievance is taken up by an entire community. The martial values, for all their costs, are readily accepted because they bring easily perceived benefits to the whole people. Even the grisly trophy collections cherished by primitive warriors may protect the community by their deterrent effect, especially if severed heads are staked outside the village to greet visitors, as was the custom of the Northwest Coast Indians.

The culture of militarism has always had this double effect: It confers immediate benefits upon certain powerful individuals (in primitive groups, those seeking vengeance for their personal grievances) and at the same time brings long-term benefits to the whole community by deterring potential enemies and imposing solidarity. In more advanced forms of warfare, the interests of the leadership and the interests of the community tend to diverge, but in a primitive community there is rarely any serious conflict between these objectives. The men who started the war always take a leading role in the fighting, which may consist of little other than the Homeric duels of these heroes.

Revenge war always serves two social functions, one external and the other internal: It deters external enemies, and it promotes internal solidarity. These are the primitive roots of civilized society's "moral" and "constitutional" theories of warfare, respectively.

Competition for Resources

The martial-values complex may seem an adequate explanation of the phenomenon of primitive warfare, but some anthropologists look for more, and their views should be considered.[5] They hold that the common articulated motives for primitive war—revenge and prestige, honor and glory—are not to be taken at face value, as they are chiefly pretexts for materialistic motives arising from the competition for territory and economic resources. Success in war, it is argued, can bring substantial material benefits even at the most primitive level, and the warriors cannot be unaware of this.

There is much to be said for this view. Even in Paleolithic times, warfare probably had certain territorial implications. If Paleolithic hunter-gatherer cultures resembled recent ones, then they did not usually have fixed territories with definite boundaries, but they did have a sense of identification with a locality; it would have been obvious to them that some localities were far richer in game than others and that the number of hunter-gatherer bands any locality could support was strictly limited; and they may have needed access to specific places like water holes and fishing sites. Very primitive groups do not seem to have been capable of anything that we would describe as conquest, but they were capable of displacement: They could deny the use of territory to others, and by frequent warfare, they could induce a neighboring group to move out of a favorable territory.

Furthermore, there is no doubt that the territorial and economic effects of warfare became more important in Neolithic times. Recent primitives, most of whom are culturally Neolithic, usually claim that they fight wars for honor and sometimes deny outright that they ever fight for land, but their actions, and sometimes their words, suggest that competition for food resources—land, water, game, fish, trade goods—is also an important factor. In the scant recorded history of primitive warfare, favorable territories are known to be theaters of frequent warfare, and many cases of population displacement are known. Sometimes the declared motives of revenge and prestige seem no more than palpable pretexts for the acquisition of territory and goods—I have already mentioned the selectiveness and manipulativeness of the primitive memory for insults and injuries. The Munducuru headhunters of Brazil say that they fight only to acquire heads (i.e., for honor and glory), never for land; but the anthropologist W. H. Durham has argued that they really fight to eliminate competitors for their main game animal, which is the peccary, and that this motive is partly conscious, for they express it in their own symbolic terms by saying that a warrior who collects enemy heads has pleased the spirit of the peccary.[6]

But can these motives be clearly separated? One of the insights produced by the new anthropology of war is that primitive warfare tends to fall into a multiphase pattern: It starts as a ritualistic duel with few casualties and then, if the dispute is not settled by arbitration, gradually escalates into more serious hand-to-hand fighting and sometimes into murderous raids and ambushes. The motives can change from one stage to the next. The usual proximate motive is revenge, for the social uses described above, but there is probably always some awareness of the possibility of gaining material resources eventually. It seems misleading to suggest that the one motive is a pretext for the other; rather, they are aspects of the same thing. War trophies are valued not only for their prestige but also for the perquisites of prestige. According to Tacitus, the Chatti of ancient Germany had an elite warrior society distinguished by the cropped hair and rings of the warriors who stood in the front rank of battle and otherwise did nothing because their tribesmen gave them all they wanted. They had brought the tribe honor and, probably, land. A Sioux who had earned the right to wear the warbonnet could enter any tepee and demand food. He had won his band glory and, probably, horses and buffalo.[7]

A human group is an adaptive mechanism that reacts when threatened to preserve its subsistence, security, and spirit. The ritualism of primitive warfare prevents any clear separation of those interests.

Hobbes or Rousseau?

When and how did this pattern arise? Modern theories of warfare have been bedeviled by the question of whether warfare is innate or invented, a product of nature or nurture, a subject for the biologist or the anthropologist. This controversy has sputtered on ever since the Enlightenment, when the two contrary positions were given classic expression by the philosophers Hobbes and Rousseau.

Neo-Rousseauism received a boost during the International Year of Peace in 1986, when an international conference of natural and social scientists at Seville University issued the Seville Statement on Violence, modeled on the UNESCO Statement on Race, which has since been endorsed by the American Anthropological Association, the American Psychological Association, and other professional organizations. The scientists were concerned to "challenge a number of alleged biological findings that have been used . . . to justify violence and war" and to affirm that "biology does not condemn humanity to war," and they specifically condemned the following propositions:

> IT IS SCIENTIFICALLY INCORRECT to say that we have inherited a tendency to make war from our animal ancestors . . .
> IT IS SCIENTIFICALLY INCORRECT to say that war or any other violent behavior is genetically programmed into our human nature . . .
> IT IS SCIENTIFICALLY INCORRECT to say that in the course of human evolution there has been a selection for aggressive behavior . . . [8]

In spite of their confident tone, some of the Seville scientists may have sensed that they were on the defensive, for in fact there did not exist in 1986 a genuine consensus on these questions, either among scientists or the general public. Soon after this statement was published, a poll revealed that 50 percent of American college students believed war to be "intrinsic" in human nature.[9] And since then in both the academic and the popular press, there has been a decided revival of speculation that many aspects of human nature are genetically based, including personality, intelligence, sex differences, and sexual orientation.

In the twentieth century, the Hobbes-Rousseau controversy has become largely a war of the faculties, with biologists (including many biological anthropologists) on the side of Nature and most cultural and social anthropologists in the camp of Nurture. In recent years, each side has produced its own grand theory about the functions of primitive warfare. Despite their contrary premises, these grand theories are in some ways strikingly similar. By "function" they do not mean the conscious motivations and intentions of the human actors, like the functions I have discussed in the preceding pages. Rather, they mean a very long-term causal factor to which the human participants are oblivious. The current version of neo-Hobbism calls itself "sociobiology"; the most influential neo-Rousseaist theory calls itself "cultural ecology."

Sociobiology: The New Hobbes

In the 1970s, there emerged a new field of biological research that aimed to apply recent advances in evolutionary theory to animal (including human) social behavior. It was in fact a revival of the social Darwinism of the nine-teenth century and might well have called itself neo-social Darwinism but preferred the label "sociobiology" because the older social Darwinism had become widely, if somewhat unfairly, associated with racism, eugenics, and militarism.[10]

The evolution of warfare is a central problem in sociobiological literature, as it was to the earlier social Darwinists. In brief, leading sociobiologists have argued that every human group has a natural tendency (often described as "ethnocentricity," a term coined by the old social Darwinists) to close its ranks against outsiders and display hostility to them, thereby cementing the loyalties of the group and deflecting aggression away from it; this ethnocen-tric and xenophobic tendency has a genetic base that has evolved by natural selection. The tendency is adaptive, because a group that displays it will have an obvious advantage in competition with other groups for resources of every sort. Furthermore, once this pattern of in-group amity and out-group enmity is established, it will tend to perpetuate itself, spread, and escalate; it will set up a chain reaction, forcing all other groups to adapt to the militaris-tic pattern or else be pushed out or absorbed. Some sociobiologists have called this chain reaction the "balance of power," borrowing a phrase nor-mally used for the modern system of international relations and suggesting thereby that the familiar Machiavellian game of power politics has very primitive roots. It has been proposed that the evolution of war passed through three stages:

1. Primitive hominids formed small bands for defense against predators, developing a high degree of group cohesion, male bonding, and male aggressiveness.
2. Hominid bands turned increasingly to the hunting of game, for which these cooperative and aggressive tendencies proved advantageous.
3. At some point, the primary purpose of group organization became defense against *other* bands of the same species, followed by the balance of power and escalation in group size and organization to achieve a margin of safety.

Somewhere in this progression came the invention of lethal weapons, whose physically and psychologically distancing effects made it easy for man to kill members of his own species, and sufficient cognitive ability developed to distinguish "us" from "them"—to contemplate the significance of the Other and to decide upon his elimination.

Sociobiology offered a powerful and persuasive synthesis, incorporating the latest research in biology and anthropology. The original Hobbesians, and even some social Darwinists, had thought of warfare as an expression of egotism, which made its place in evolution difficult to explain; but the sociobiologists explained it, rather, as a supreme expression of altruism, stressing its cooperative rather than its violent aspects. They avoided the determinism associated with older biological explanations. They did not talk about blind "instincts," but rather about flexible neural pathways activated by environmental triggers, using metaphors borrowed from the computer industry. They knew differences between cultures must be overwhelmingly the result of cultural evolution and were not biological. They ascribed to the genes a probabilistic rather than a deterministic influence, setting limits on the evolution of cultural patterns and biasing them in certain directions. It is untrue to say that they thought biology had condemned humanity to war, in the words of the Seville Statement (whose authors had sociobiology primarily in mind). They did not think warfare was any longer adaptive or beneficial and thought the ethnocentric tendencies of human nature could be overcome. Nevertheless, they did think that at one time warfare had generally been adaptive in a Darwinian sense and that the genes that pushed it had been selected by evolution. They suggested plausible links between the evolution of war and the evolution of hunting and linked both these quintessentially male activities to the ubiquitous primitive institutions of male bonding and male supremacy. In the 1970s, the new synthesis appeared to receive support from reports that male chimpanzees practice organized hunting of small animals and conduct lethal raids against neighboring chimpanzee bands; if the latter activity was not war, it looked uncannily like it.

Cultural Ecology: The New Rousseau

Despite the sociobiologists' disclaimers of political implications, the new synthesis immediately raised a storm of protest, mostly from scholars with left-wing views, who assumed that to suggest that anything in human nature is biologically based must imply some sort of determinism with reactionary political effects. Sociobiology ran against well-rooted intellectual habits, for twentieth-century social science had been ruled by the hypothesis called "cultural determinism," which holds that almost everything in human culture is a product of learned behavior. This attitude was especially entrenched among cultural anthropologists. For decades, influential anthropologists like Margaret Mead and Ruth Benedict had spread the doctrine that culture is an autonomous and extremely malleable entity untouched by hereditary influences. Some extreme formulations of this view left the impression that "culture" is a sort of blank slate upon which anything might be written. Mead made this explicit in a 1940 article entitled "Warfare Is Only an Invention—Not a Biological Necessity."[11] Notice the assumptions of this title: Warfare has to be *either* biologically determined, which makes it a "necessity," *or* culturally determined, in which case it is *only* that, a sort of "historical accident" (Mead's phrase) persisted in, apparently, from force of habit. The same assumptions underlie the 1986 Seville Statement on Violence.

In fact, the mounting ethnographic data made it difficult by the 1940s to believe in the original Rousseauist view that primitive peoples are inherently peaceable. But the data did seem to support the view that primitive warfare was an innocuous sort of game or ritual or judicial mechanism that was not really "war," and this became the neo-Rousseauist orthodoxy. I have argued here that this distinction between primitive and complex warfare is essentially correct, though I think some of these scholars underrated the seriousness and public purpose of primitive warfare. In any case, to make such a distinction is to raise the obvious question of how the complex political type of war developed out of the primitive practice. If anthropology rejected the idea that war was a product of biological evolution, then anthropology had to show it to be the result of cultural evolution. A cultural theory of the evolution of war was badly needed. By the 1970s, one had been produced, just in time to counter the ambitious claims of the sociobiologists.

The new theory, perhaps best represented by the writings of Marvin Harris, is often described as "cultural ecology."[12] In brief, it holds that primitive warfare is a mechanism for population redistribution: It corrects environmental imbalances by scattering human populations over a wider area than before, thereby reducing pressure on the land and at the same time creating buffer zones that serve as game sanctuaries. Some have gone further and suggested that warfare not only redistributes population but reduces it, not by killing off young men (whose fertility is demographically almost irrelevant in a polygynous society) but by killing girl babies: We are told that militaristic societies prefer to raise warriors and therefore have high rates of female infanticide.

At least some cultural ecologists suggest that these environmental benefits are not just accidental by-products of warfare but are in some fashion—which seems to me none too clear—the ultimate *cause* of the whole process. At such moments they sound very like their opponents. Like the social Darwinists and sociobiologists, they speak of warfare as a major instrument of evolution, only rather than biological evolution, they mean cultural evolution—a selection of norms and practices rather than genes. They suggest warfare may be compared to the agonistic territorial displays found in some other animal species that are said to function so as to ensure optimal population dispersal. If so, perhaps it accounted for the worldwide distribution achieved by *Homo sapiens* even in the Paleolithic. After Cain rose up against his brother Abel and killed him, he went away and dwelled in the land of Nod, east of Eden (Genesis 4.8–16).

The ecological thesis lends an ingenious new twist to Rousseauism. It emphasizes the gap between primitive war and "real" war. It makes primitive warfare a beneficial institution, not only for the human race but for the environment. It is a pacifistic evolutionism, whose dominant metaphor is not survival of the fittest but the maintenance of an equilibrium. It allows us to admit the universality of war without feeling trapped by it, for modern war can serve none of these ecological functions and seems wholly dysfunctional. And if we can no longer visualize primitive man as dwelling in Eden, at least we can imagine him in Nod.

This has been perhaps the most influential anthropological paradigm for explaining primitive warfare for the past twenty-five years, but by no means have all anthropologists accepted it. There are serious problems with this seductive thesis, and in one respect it seems weaker than its sociobiological rival. Cultural anthropologists have long tended to reify "culture," speaking of it as though it were an independent variable that is somehow superorganic, endowed with enormous power to mold the minds and hearts of individuals, yet receiving no input from these individuals who carry it on. The cultural ecologists carry the reification of culture to extremes and, in addition, tend to reify ecology. In some formulations of this theory, a blind force called Culture seems to play at random upon human norms and practices in much the same way that the blind force of Nature, in Darwinian theory, plays upon genetic variations. But biological selection rests on a generally accepted body of Darwinian theory. There is no such theory behind cultural ecology, and this deficiency makes it difficult to imagine how ecosystems express their "needs" and how cultures respond to these. Survival of the biologically fittest is one thing; survival of the ecologically balanced is rather harder to believe in.

A Critique of Grand Functionalism

I suggest, however, that there are weaknesses common to both these grand theories, two of which may be fatal. First, there is the "boundary question."[13] It makes no sense to talk about functions unless we are clear as to who and what they are functional for. The grand theories assume warfare is functional for the society that practices it and speak of primitive "societies" as if these were unambiguously definable in extent. But in fact the boundaries of primitive societies are notoriously fuzzy—witness the trouble anthropologists have had in defining the word "tribe." The smaller and more primitive the group, the vaguer and more anarchical its boundaries. The most primitive groups known to us follow a nomadic pattern sometimes called 'fission and fusion"—they wander about in small open groups that constantly split and merge. Warfare must always benefit somebody, so if we keep changing our definition of "society," it is always possible to say warfare has been beneficial to society. This seems a particularly hard problem for the sociobiological thesis, because in current Darwinian theory the process of natural selection for inclusive fitness can only work within a small group of closely related organisms that is clearly demarcated from other groups of the same species.

Second, neither of the grand functionalist theories seems to take adequate account of the element of historical accident in evolution (whether biological or cultural). Many events take place not because they are "functional" in the sense of being a successful adaptation to anything, but simply because of the history of previous events. In the past, evolutionary theories (both biological and cultural) have tended too often to assume that traits must be adaptive simply because they have been around for some time and to invent "Just-So Stories" to explain why these traits must be functional and beneficial to the society, which is especially easy if we are none too clear about the boundaries of the "society." This method seems more treacherous in dealing with cultural evolution, because the speed with which human cultures can change gives great power to history and the accidents of history, quite independent of biological and environmental forces. Warfare would appear to be a process peculiarly under the control of history, rather than biology or ecology, because of the obvious tendency of a militaristic culture to perpetuate itself and to eliminate its rivals. Once the war pattern gets started, it will continue of its own momentum, so how could it always be good for the environment? Often it must go on until it has reduced population far *below* the carrying capacity of the land. Sometimes, by accident, it may produce the beneficial environmental effects described by the cultural ecologists; but this is an effect, not a cause.

It seems obvious that a prominent cause or function of warfare is militarism and that a prominent cause or function of militarism is warfare. In the current state of our evidence, it seems wise to reserve judgment as to the existence of grander functions.

Cultural Darwinism

In any case, do we really need the grand theories? We have seen that the phenomenon of primitive warfare can be adequately explained in terms of the conscious motivations of its makers, and perhaps these are all we need to explain its evolution.

There is a growing awareness among anthropologists that the processes of cultural evolution resemble those of biological evolution and can also be explained in Darwinian terms, without any sociobiological implications. There is a process of cultural selection that mimics natural selection, though in a rapid Lamarckian fashion that is largely conscious and deliberate on the part of the actors. "Culture" is not a reified abstraction, nor is it a blank slate. It is a public code of symbols that is constantly changing because it receives continual input from individuals who seek to change it for the most Darwinian of reasons—to promote the survival and reproduction of themselves, their kin, and their culture.

Human behavior, in short, is for the most part probably neither Nature nor Nurture, but Nurture imitating Nature. This is not to deny that all culture has a genetic base. The human capacity for culture has itself evolved through natural selection, and it is natural selection that makes cultural selection imitate it. But that means that at some point, culture has taken over from nature. The sheer speed of cultural evolution makes it unnecessary to postulate a genetic basis (and improbable that there is one) for most cultural adaptations. Some of these adaptations may indeed have been influenced by genetic factors. It is possible that there exists in human nature some hereditary tendency toward ethnocentricity, in-group amity and out-group enmity, and, perhaps, male bonding. But if so, it is rather easily controlled and manipulated. It does not condemn us to either war or peace unless our culture decides to program us in one of those directions. Extreme Hobbesians, who always talk about the "universality" of warfare, tend to ignore its equally obvious flexibility. The introduction of the horse into the Great Basin of North America did not automatically turn all its inhabitants into fierce mounted warriors: It had this effect upon the Comanche and the Ute but had the opposite effect upon their neighbors, the "Digger" Indians. Among modern peoples, none seem more pacific than the Swedes and the Swiss, but not many centuries ago, their ancestors had a different reputation across Europe. Under pressure, a culture may switch from extreme militarism to its opposite with the alacrity of Japan after World War II. Primitive cultures can do the same: So many headhunters have become peaceful farmers in recent years that the data bank on primitive warfare is now practically closed.

This hypothesis has been called "cultural Darwinism," "Darwinian cultural theory," or "evolutionary anthropology."[14] It assumes that the primary means of cultural evolution is the rapid, easily diffusible, collective, and sometimes rational and calculating selection of norms and values to promote the survival and reproduction of the members of the culture. It does not imply that *all* cultural change is adaptive in this Darwinian sense. Much change is purely accidental; much of it, especially in the more complex societies, is coercively imposed by the authorities and is maladaptive from the point of view of most of the population; much of it is the result of cultural lag, the persistence from force of habit in practices that were once successful adaptations but are no longer so. Still, it implies that a great deal of the time, culture must be kept on track by the collective interests of individuals acting deliberately. They may receive some help from nature at times, but we can rarely know this, and we should probably cease our obsession with the question. It is past time to bury the Nature-Nurture controversy and its false dichotomies. Warfare is essentially a cultural invention, but it is not "only" an invention. We may be glad biology has not condemned us to war, but if culture has done that instead, we have gained little. A depoliticized Darwinism, open to the fact that cultures evolve by adaptation, may be the most useful intellectual framework now available to address the problem of the origins of war.

The Evolution of Primitive War

Let us begin with a methodological observation. We know far less about the prevalence and frequency of prehistoric warfare than one would think from reading many military histories, which give the impression that primitive tribes are almost constantly at war. The fact is, we know practically nothing about the war habits of the great majority of primitive peoples, even in recent times. An inventory complied at the Polemological Institute of the University of Groningen lists 100,000 known primitive cultures, about most of which we know nothing but the name and location (often, the former location, as they are now extinct), with no evidence as to whether they were warlike or peaceful. An ethnographic survey of the Amazon Basin in 1910 listed 485 distinct tribes, of which about 40 were said to be "warlike" or "fierce," or some such description, and 20 were reported to be "peaceful." Nothing was known about the remaining 400 and nothing ever will be.[15] The great majority of the recent primitives that we know anything about have been very frequently at war. This is as true of hunter-gatherers as it is of agriculturists. A recent survey of hunter-gatherer societies concluded that over 60 percent of the groups included in the sample went to war *at least* once every two years.[16] But we need not assume that what is true of recent hunter-gatherers is necessarily true of the Paleolithic peoples. Some of the recent hunter-gatherers included in these samples were equestrian or fishing cultures, which are modes of life prone to warfare. Most of the known primitives had already come into contact with civilization or had been living in the hinterland of civilization for some time, and such contacts have almost always raised the level of military activity, especially in North America.[17] We should admit we simply do not know what the "normal" degree of warlikeness was among prestate societies, even in recent centuries, before they came into contact with states.

If Hobbesians make much of the notorious "savagery" of primitives, Rousseauists make all they can of the handful of "relatively peaceful" cultures that I have just mentioned. Their existence certainly shows that warfare is not a universal norm, but no one ever literally thought it was. To say something is "innate" does not mean it goes on all the time. Others have argued that there are no truly peaceful cultures, for upon examination, it turns out that so-called peaceful societies like the Bushmen and the Eskimo have gone to war in the past, and their current pacifism is the result of defeat and isolation. There does seem to be a correlation between simplicity of social structure and unwarlikeness. But perhaps the extremely small and simple societies that have survived into the present are unwarlike because they have been marginalized, and they may not be typical of the simple human societies that existed in the Stone Age.[18]

Nor can archaeology tell us much about warfare before the Neolithic, from which there are indeed abundant traces (it is said the earliest *conclusive* evidence of warfare is the great stone wall of Jericho, which was built circa 8000 B.C., clearly not for the purpose of keeping out wolves). But what we really need to know is whether war existed in the Paleolithic and if so, of what sort. Hunting societies do not usually distinguish weapons of war from those of the hunt, and spearheads do not reveal their targets. It has been said that a high percentage of the known human fossils, including those of early hominid species, show *possible* signs of human violence, but this evidence now seems thoroughly inconclusive.[19] Besides, there may well have been times during the Ice Age when more than one hominid species inhabited the same area, a possibility that raises intriguing questions about our definitions of "homicide" and "war."

With these considerations in mind, let us attempt to reconstruct the evolution of warfare. There have probably been several major breakthroughs, of which the first and most decisive was surely the invention of culture itself. Doubtless this was preceded by a long period of preadaptation. Lethal intraspecific aggression is not so uniquely human as was once thought. We know now that social predators like lions, wolves, and hyenas engage in deadly combats to guard their territories from members of their own species and that male chimpanzees cooperate not only to hunt small game but under certain circumstances to attack individuals from other chimp bands.[20] Among living species, the social predators are closest to early hominids in social organization, and the chimpanzees are their closest genetic relatives. During the millennia of preadaptation, our sociobiological evolution, building upon such habits as these, eventually endowed us with a highly flexible capacity to develop fierce ethnocentric conflicts. At some point there came language and culture, along with sufficient cognitive ability to clearly distinguish group from group and express the concept of "revenge." At this point the ancient animal patterns of instinctual behavior developed into the conscious practice called "primitive warfare." People were categorized as friends or aliens, and offensive behavior from aliens was likely to be met with organized retaliation. Honor and glory came into the world.

Unfortunately, nothing is more mysterious than the origins of language and culture. Some think that a fully human language and the capacity for rapid cultural adaptation did not emerge until about one hundred thousand years ago with the evolution of *Homo sapiens sapiens;* and others believe that these abilities had a much longer prehistory.

A second major turning point was the rise of big-game hunting, long considered a clue to the rise of war. But its chronology is as mysterious as that of language. Most anthropologists now think of *Australopithecus,* and even early *Homo,* as Man the Scavenger rather than Man the Hunter. Some think big-game hunting may have developed as early as *Homo erectus,* more than 1 million years ago; and others believe it did not appear until *Homo sapiens sapiens* did, a mere one hundred thousand years ago. Some kind of hunting society could have predated language. There may have been a long and slow evolution in which hominids, who at first lived by gathering plants, scavenging dead animals, and hunting small live animals, gradually learned the art of hunting larger ones. However it happened, adaptation to the hunting life must have brought with it the following changes: increased territoriality (not focused on occupation of land but rather on control of food resources to guard them from other bands, in the fashion of the social carnivores); a premium on male bonding and male leadership; a trend toward larger, more stable, better organized bands; and more intergroup conflict.

Why hunting and warfare are male monopolies is not clear. The male advantage in physical strength and the female occupation with child rearing would of course suggest this monopoly, but do these factors explain why the monopoly is so exclusive? All one can say is that the gender-based division of labor—women gather and care for infants, men hunt and go to war—is pervasive in the known hunter-gatherer cultures and clearly has deep roots in human nature, whether these are genetic or cultural or some combination of the two.[21]

Several considerations, however, prevent us from supposing that Paleolithic warfare, whether it began 1 million or one hundred thousand years ago, was very common or very serious. Among these factors are the puny manpower resources (recent hunter-gatherer bands have an average size of about forty people), the probably frequent intermarriages between bands, and above all, the thin distribution of these bands (a hunter-gatherer band may have a territory one hundred miles across). All theories of primitive warfare have recognized that whether or not warlike behavior is "innate" in human nature, it has to be triggered by competition. When competition reaches a certain level of intensity, it produces a balance-of-power situation in which all groups have to cultivate warlikeness simply to preserve a margin of safety. As Hobbes put it (*Leviathan* 1.13), "From this diffidence of one another, there is no way for any man to secure himself so reasonable as anticipation; that is, by force or wiles to master the persons of all men he can, so long, till he see no other power great enough to endanger him; and this is no more than his own conservation requireth, and is generally allowed." But as a modern anthropologist has said, "In large areas of the world in the past, social inefficiency was so great that the possibilities of effective competition were very limited."[22] It seems likely that the threshold of Hobbes's "State of Warre" was not passed until a late date in human history. The practice of revenge warfare may have helped to account for the wide dispersal of early Paleolithic man, but the same dispersion would have checked the practice of revenge warfare.

Perhaps the final turning point was the intensification of revenge warfare into a balance of power, when primitive militarism became a normal pattern. This stage was probably reached during one of the two great revolutions of late prehistory, each of which brought a dramatic increase in cultural complexity.

The rise of the Upper Paleolithic hunting culture some thirty-five thousand years ago is now considered by many anthropologists to have been a breakthrough in social evolution at least as significant as the better-known Neolithic Revolution. By this time, a fully modern type of man (*Homo sapiens sapiens*) had fully occupied the Old World and may have already colonized the New World. He hunted the biggest game and could have hunted men if he chose. Often he had little choice, for in many areas bands could no longer avoid conflict with their neighbors simply by moving away from them. Population density brought increased territoriality, quasi-permanent settlements, and the ability to store food, which created caches of defensible resources. The sudden flowering of the visual arts testifies to an explosive growth in cultural complexity, richness, and sophistication. And perhaps it was in the Upper Paleolithic that militarism became a common and expected feature of human society.[23]

If not, it certainly became that during the Neolithic Revolution, which began in the Middle East some ten thousand years ago. There appeared fixed settlements dependent on agriculture, with concentrated and vulnerable food supplies and a population density often many times that of the Paleolithic. Archaeological evidence leaves no doubt that warfare of an often lethal intensity was common among Neolithic settlements the world over: Villages were fortified, and burial sites yield an unnaturally high percentage of young males wounded in forearm or skull. The first real missile weapons, the bow and the sling, seem to have been invented around the dawn of the Neolithic; and from the same period come the earliest depictions in cave art of what would appear to be battle scenes. Population growth multiplied opportunities for mutual irritation, while allowing more human and material capital to be allocated to war making, which was now perceived as the protection of a fixed territory. It has even been suggested that the decline of hunting redirected masculine energies into the hunting of men.[24]

In spite of all this, the course of primitive warfare, even in the Neolithic Age, probably resembled an endless cycle rather than a clear line of development. A group might take up the culture of war because of the pressures of competition or because certain of their traditions predisposed them to that solution; and they might later revert to a more peaceable pattern, bridling the prickly martial virtues, settling disputes by arbitration, slowing the escalation of warfare by heaping more and more ritual encumbrances upon it. Until the end of the Neolithic, the option of migration was often open. The "relatively peaceful" cultures, now driven to the ends of the earth, may have been much more common. There was still nothing inexorable about the progress of primitive warfare.

But warfare then began to promote the development of more advanced forms of social organization, simply because these were better at war. There appeared genuine "tribes," networks of villages united by social and cultural ties—ties that included military assistance. In such tribes, famous war leaders might arise, and a very successful war leader might become a "chief." With the chiefs, warfare in the political sense entered history.

Notes

1. The notion that primitive warfare was essentially different from modern warfare was established by the 1940s. In 1942, in *A Study of War* (2d ed., Chicago, 1965)

Quincy Wright estimated that about 60 percent of primitive wars were fought not for economic or political reasons but for what he called "social" reasons (revenge, prestige, sport, ritual) and the more primitive the group, the more "social" its warfare. The distinction was supported by Bronislaw Malinowski, "An Anthropological Analysis of War," *American Journal of Sociology* 46 (1941), 521–550, reprinted in *War: Studies from Psychology, Sociology, Anthropology,* ed. Leon Bramson and G. W. Goethals (New York, 1964), 245–268; by H. H. Turney-High in his 1949 work, *Primitive War: Its Practices and Concepts,* 2d ed. (Columbia, S.C., 1971); and by Joseph Schneider, "Primitive Warfare: A Methodological Note," *American Sociological Review* 15 (1950), 772–777, reprinted in Bramson and Goethals, *War,* 275–283. Schneider concluded that primitive war is "a matter of crime and punishment within populations where systems of public justice are undeveloped. This is not war." This view I find too extreme, but the general distinction has won acceptance. Compare Tom Broch and Johann Galtung, "Belligerence Among the Primitives," *Journal of Peace Research* 3 (1966), 33–45.

2. Anthropological studies of warfare, a once-neglected subject, have proliferated in the last thirty years, as witnessed by the titles listed in *The Anthropology of War: A Bibliography,* ed. R. B. Ferguson and Leslie Farragher (New York, 1988). We still lack a comprehensive and up-to-date synthesis comparable to the older works by Wright and Turney-High, but the collections listed in the bibliography will show the range of recent research. See also the report on a 1990 American Anthropological Association conference by Bruce Bower, "Gauging the Winds of War: Anthropologists Seek the Roots of Human Conflict," *Science News* 139 (6) February 9, 1991, 88–89, 91.

3. Roy Rapaport, *Pigs for the Ancestors: Ritual in the Ecology of a New Guinea People* (New Haven, 1968); A. P. Vayda, *War in Ecological Perspective: Persistence, Change, and Adaptive Processes in Three Oceanian Societies* (New York, 1976); John Keegan, *A History of Warfare* (New York, 1993).

4. David Fabbro, "Peaceful Societies: An Introduction," *Journal of Peace Research* 15 (1978), 67–83, reprinted in R. A. Falk and S. S. Kim, eds. *The War System: An Interdisciplinary Approach* (Boulder, 1980).

5. I refer to the anthropological school called cultural materialism, well known through the writings of Marvin Harris: *Cows, Pigs, Wars, and Witches: The Riddles of Culture* (New York, 1974); *Cannibals and Kings: The Origin of Culture* (New York, 1977); *Our Kind: Who We Are, Where We Came From, Where We Are Going* (New York, 1988). See also R. B. Ferguson, ed., "Introduction: Studying War," in Ferguson, *Warfare, Culture, and Environment* (Orlando, Fla., 1984), 1–81.

6. W. H. Durham, "Resource Competition and Human Aggression: Part 1, A Review of Primitive War," *Quarterly Review of Biology* 51 (1976), 385–415; *Coevolution: Genes, Culture, and Human Diversity* (Stanford, 1991).

7. Tacitus, *Germania* 31. I owe the parallel with the Sioux to Turney-High, *Primitive War,* 146.

8. Reprinted in *Aggression and War: Their Biological and Social Bases,* ed. Jo Groebel and R. A. Hinde (Cambridge, 1989), xiii–xvi.

9. *U. S. News and World Report,* April 11, 1988, 57–58.

10. The most influential sociobiological treatises include Edward Wilson's *Sociobiology: The New Synthesis* (Cambridge, Mass., 1975) and *On Human Nature* (Cam-

bridge, Mass., 1978)—the latter contains Wilson's fullest discussion of warfare—and Richard Alexander's *Darwinism and Human Affairs* (Seattle, 1979), which introduced the balance of power theory. Literature on the sociobiological controversy is vast and keeps proliferating. A survey of recent research particularly relevant to the study of warfare is *Sociobiology and Conflict: Evolutionary Perspectives on Competition, Cooperation, Violence, and Warfare,* ed. J.M.G. Van der Dennen and V. Falger (London, 1990).

11. *Asia* 40 (1940), 402–405, reprinted in Bramson and Goethals, *War,* 269–274.

12. Marvin Harris, "Warfare Old and New," *Natural History* 81 (1972), 18–20, and the works of the materialist school cited here in nn. 3 and 5. For the female infanticide theory, see Harris and W. T. Divale, "Population, Warfare, and the Male-Supremacist Complex," *American Anthropologist* 78 (1976), 521–538.

13. The phrase was suggested by C. R. Hallpike, "Functionalist Interpretations of Primitive Warfare," *Man* 8 (1973), 451–470. Another useful critique of the grand theories is C. A. Robarchek's "Primitive Warfare and the Ratomorphic Image of Mankind," *American Anthropologist* 91 (1989), 903–920.

14. Leading examples of the "cultural Darwinist" approach are Irenäus Eibl-Eibesfeldt, *The Biology of Peace and War: Man, Animals, and Aggression,* trans. Erich Mossbacher (New York, 1979), first published in German in 1975; Robert Boyd and P. J. Richerson, *Culture and the Evolutionary Process* (Chicago, 1985); and Durham, *Coevolution.* These theories are discussed at greater length in my article "The Origins of War: Biological and Anthropological Theories," *History and Theory* 35 (1996), 1–28, copyright © 1996 Wesleyan University. Some of its argument is used here with the permission of Wesleyan University.

15. J.M.G. Van der Dennen, "Primitive War and the Ethnological Inventory Project," in *Sociobiology and Conflict,* 247–269.

16. C. R. Ember, "Myths About Hunter-Gatherers," *Ethnology* 17 (1978), 439–448.

17. *War in the Tribal Zone: Expanding States and Indigenous Warfare,* ed. R. B. Ferguson and N. L. Whitehead (Santa Fe, N. Mex., 1992).

18. Eibl-Eibesfeldt, among others, has argued against the existence of peaceful societies. But see the counterarguments of B. M. Knauft, "Violence and Sociality in Human Evolution," *Current Anthropology* 32 (1991), 391–428.

19. M. K. Roper, "A Survey of the Evidence for Intrahuman Killing in the Pleistocene," *Current Anthropology* 10 (1969), 427–459.

20. See G. E. King, "Society and Territory in Human Evolution," *Journal of Human Evolution* 5 (1976), 323–332; J. H. Manson and R. W. Wrangham, "Intergroup Aggression in Chimpanzees and Humans," *Current Anthropology* 32 (1991), 369–390; and for a "Rousseauist" interpretation of chimpanzee and early-hominid societies, see Margaret Powers, *The Egalitarians, Human and Chimpanzee: An Anthropological View of Social Organization* (Cambridge, 1991).

21. The question of the origins of war is closely linked to the equally controversial question of the origins of gender roles. It is often said that all known human societies are male dominated to some degree, but this depends on our definition of male dominance. Some anthropologists think that any "asymmetry" in gender roles that is oriented to the male principle—whether in division of labor, descent systems, or postmarital residence—implies what Harris and Divale have called the male supremacy

complex (see n. 12 here). For an introduction to this controversy, see Peggy Sanday, *Female Power and Male Dominance: On the Origins of Sexual Inequality* (Cambridge, 1981), 161–183. My own provisional conclusions, which in this limited space must be stated somewhat categorically, are as follows:

1. It is not clear that there has ever existed a culture without gender asymmetry in at least the division of labor. Since men monopolize warfare, they necessarily control external relations, so in this sense there has probably never been a society without a degree of male leadership, except possibly some of the so-called peaceful societies. This does not prevent women from having a degree of autonomy in their own sphere.

2. I prefer to restrict labels like male supremacy and male dominance to the more militaristic cultures that emphasize male aggressiveness and male secret societies and exclude women from decisionmaking in council. There is general agreement that militarism is associated with male supremacy, though even in very warlike cultures this may be more pronounced in myth than in practice.

Ever since Margaret Mead returned from Samoa, anthropologists have tried to find cultures without male leadership. Recently, Maria Lepowsky (*Fruit of the Motherland: Gender in an Egalitarian Society* [New York, 1993]) claimed to have discovered on the island of Vanatinai near New Guinea a "sexually egalitarian society that challenges the concept of the universality of male dominance and contests the assumption that the subjugation of women is inevitable" (vii); she found there neither gender asymmetries nor any exclusively male institutions of significance. These claims are somewhat dampened when one learns that the island was pacified by the British early in this century, and naturally, the end of warfare would have put an end to the principal male-bonded institution, there as elsewhere in Melanesia. The author minimizes this fact by arguing that even in the days of war making "women were not excluded from councils of war or diplomacy or from the battlefield" (75). One does not know what "diplomacy" could mean, but the traditions she relates suggest that Vanatinai women never participated in fighting and appeared on the battlefield only to perform the roles commonly assigned to women in primitive ritual battles—making magic, cheering the warriors, nursing the injured (58ff.). Lepowsky thinks that Vanatinai warfare was defensive rather than aggressive, but she also speaks of these people fighting for "revenge or defense" (74, 292), which raises the suspicion that like many other writers on premodern warfare, she has confused the two notions (see my earlier comment on this issue in the introduction).

22. Hallpike, "Functionalist Interpretations," 467.

23. See W. T. Divale, "Systemic Population Control in the Middle and Upper Paleolithic: Inferences Based on Contemporary Hunter-Gatherers," *World Archaeology* 4 (1972), 222–243; and for a survey of the general problem of the evolution of complex cultures, see *Prehistoric Hunter-Gatherers: The Emergence of Cultural Complexity,* ed. T. D. Price and J. A. Brown (Orlando, Fla., 1985).

24. Clinton Kroeber and Bernard Fontana, *Massacre on the Gila: An Account of the Last Major Battle Between American Indians, with Reflections on the Origin of War* (Tucson, Ariz. 1986).

Chapter Two

Chiefdoms, States, and Empires

The Rise of the Chiefs

Anthropologists commonly use the term "chiefdom" for a primitive culture that has developed a formal social hierarchy in which the war leader holds a unique and permanent rank above all his tribesmen, often with theocratic and redistributive functions as well.[1] Such chiefdoms are familiar in ethnographic literature because they are common in the hinterlands of civilized societies. Among the known examples, the eighteenth-century kingdom of Hawaii may represent the highest point of development. Most of the known examples, like Hawaii, owed much to contact with civilized peoples, who tend to think that such well-organized tribes are more typical of the primitive world than they really are, because the societies in contact with civilized people tend to be like that.[2] In the Neolithic, chiefdoms of this type were probably less common than in historical times, but there is no reason to doubt that they existed here and there.[3] They provided a transitional stage in social development between the tribe and the state.

At the level of the chiefdom, the causes of war become more complicated and the motives for war become separable. We can now distinguish among ideological, economic, and political motives.

1. The articulated motives for war are still revenge and prestige. The difference is that wars are now fought to avenge wrongs *against the chief* and for the honor and glory *of the chief.* Primitive militarism is being replaced by kingly or theocratic militarism, an ideology that continues without much change until the time of Louis XIV.

2. The economic causes of war become more compelling. Genuine conquests and occupations are now possible, so wars can be fought more openly and directly to gain territory. The values of honor and glory may become a pretext, masking a chief's grab for land and wealth.

3. Finally, war becomes an organizational source of power. It is now possible to fight wars simply for political reasons, and the martial values may become a pretext for a chief's grab at power for its own sake.

It has been pointed out in the preceding chapter how warfare, at some early stage in human evolution, escaped from the control of nature and became an instrument of culture. By the time the stage of the chiefdom is reached, warfare has begun to escape from the control of culture and is becoming a political instrument used in the search for wealth and power by a ruler who is no longer responsive to the collective interests of his people. The forces of escalation break loose. Armies, recruited by command as well as consensus, may number in the hundreds or even the thousands, are able to fight formal battles in line, and may be capable of systematic tactics and strategies. A specialized warrior class is likely to emerge, and wherever it does, its extravagant demands for honor and glory multiply the pressures for military escalation. The trophies of honor and glory become more lucrative and now include prisoners of war for slavery, sacrifice, and cannibalism, all of which become additional incentives for warfare. The rituals of war become grand and expensive, and the Red Spirits are promoted to war gods.

The more advanced chiefdoms appear to practice what is today called warfare in every sense, except for the lack of an ideology that permits self-conscious strategic thinking. The history of political warfare should therefore begin with these chiefdoms, except that they have no history. In spite of their efficiency, chiefdoms do not seem to last. Only a bare handful of chiefdoms have ever made the full transition to bureaucratic state. The process of military escalation and political centralization is reversible, and normally, it is reversed. The disadvantages of losing freedom to the chief are as obvious as the advantages of military superiority, so the chiefdom rarely survives the death of the chief, which is likely to be premature. Countless societies may have come to the edge of statehood and drawn back from that brink. Chiefdoms do not last *because* of their efficiency.

If this necessarily hypothetical reconstruction of Neolithic history is correct, then we may conclude that as late as five thousand years ago the essential nature and functions of primitive warfare had not changed, so far as the vast majority of the human race were concerned. The inherent tendency of militarism to escalate was still contained. The occasional attempts to turn warfare into something more dynamic, purposeful, and expansionary had all self-destructed.

The Rise of the State[4]

Although the possibilities of warfare as a source of political power may have been realized in some Neolithic chiefdoms, they could not have been exploited further without the development of political hierarchies exercising routine coercive power. That this breakthrough happened so rarely and in such specialized environments suggests that primitive society had built-in checks on the escalation of war. If it had not, the Stone Age could not have lasted so long, nor would the state have taken so long to rise. When it finally rose, it brought a new kind of warfare, the invariable symptom and perhaps the major cause of early state formation.

This breakthrough occurred independently in only half a dozen places on the earth, all of them regions that were more or less circumscribed geographically and socially. The clearest examples of circumscription are the Nile and Tigris-Euphrates Valleys, both alluvial river systems suitable for irrigated agriculture and surrounded by arid country. In these environmental traps, Neolithic peoples were forced to submit to new forms of social control because they could no longer escape by fission and migration. This process was first consummated in Sumer (now Iraq) between 3400 and 3100 B.C. and was soon after replicated in Egypt. Later, independent breakthroughs took place in the Indus Valley, the valley of the Yellow River in China, in Middle America, and in Peru. (The extent to which all these cases fit the circumscription model is disputed, but these controversies need not concern us here, as our main interest is the Middle East.)

Theories about the origin of the state tend to fall into three categories. There are those who see the early state as an integrating mechanism that responded to the need for efficient management of complicated irrigation systems and brought perceived benefits to the entire society. Karl Wittfogel's "hydraulic" theory about the rise of civilization is a well-known example.[5] These theories resemble the "social contract" theories of John Locke and other early modern philosophers. Other theorists see the early state as a coercive mechanism arising out of internal social conflict; this is a Marxist view, though it has influenced many who are not strictly Marxist.[6] And the third group of theorists emphasizes the importance of external war and conquest in promoting internal consolidation. The role of warfare in the rise of civilization has been pointed out by the Scottish Enlightenment philosophers David Hume and Adam Ferguson, by Herbert Spencer and other nineteenth-century social Darwinists, and by many twentieth-century anthropologists.[7]

But we do not have to chose among Locke, Marx, and Spencer. The theories are not mutually exclusive, and it seems unlikely that any one theory could fit all cases. Warfare plays the largest role in the third class of theories, but practically all theorists, even the integration theorists of the first group, admit that warfare must have been a powerful integrating factor in the rise of the state, provided a supportive climate for it, and was the mechanism by which the state system spread.

Whether or not warfare was essential to the rise of the state, the rise of the state certainly marked a decisive break in the history of warfare—the most important turning point until the gunpowder revolution in early modern Europe, which brought with it a still more potent form of political and military centralization. The *cultural* balance of power, in which most human societies had been trapped for thousands of years, was replaced by the *political* balance of power, which has endured to the present day. The cultural trap had loopholes: People could escape from it by "forgetting" about their grievances when "remembering" them would have been inconvenient, by ritualization, by arbitrating their disputes, by moving away. But there was no escape from the political trap, except in circumstances of unusual geographical isolation like those of Old Kingdom Egypt. The political type of warfare, heretofore an occasional and not particularly successful experiment in human history, now broke free of all constraints. War ceased to be an ancient ritual of earth and became a struggle for power and wealth between ruling groups claiming descent from the gods. They began the progressive elimination of primitive societies and primitive ways of war, a process that today is practically completed.

The sheer scale and pervasiveness of warfare in early states justifies these conclusions about its central importance. All early states had standing armies, all were expansionist, and all engaged in chronic interstate warfare that resulted in fewer and fewer states. In Egypt, with its extremely circumscribed geography, the process resulted almost at once in the unification of the Nile Valley under a single ruler, whose theocratic functions thereafter overshadowed his military functions. In Iraq, much less circumscribed and divided among many powerful city-states, the process of unification took longer and was never permanently successful, and the militaristic character of the state became much more pronounced. Not until the twenty-fourth century B.C. did Sargon of Akkad unite all the cities of the plain into the first hegemonic empire.

This pattern of interstate warfare continued through the Bronze Age. There was a notable increase in scale during the high Bronze Age (circa 1600–1200 B.C.), when civilization spread outside the two original river valleys and there emerged a system of international relations covering the entire Middle East. Another leap forward came in the early Iron Age, when the first true territorial empires arose. The Bronze Age empires, following the model of Sargon, had been loose hegemonial structures in which a conqueror ruled his client states only by threatening them with his army and usually did not rule for long. But the vast neo-Assyrian empire (ninth to seventh centuries B.C.) and the far vaster empire of the Persians (sixth to fourth centuries B.C.) maintained relatively centralized imperial administrations supported by armies that could attempt to provide for the defense of all the king's territories. In the Achaemenid Persian state, warfare reached an apogee that would never be exceeded in antiquity, as far as organizational and logistical capabilities went. The total armed forces of the Assyrians exceeded one hundred thousand men; those of the Persians may have exceeded three hundred thousand. Field armies of twenty thousand men and campaigns extending over hundreds of miles were common features of early Iron Age warfare.

The Art of War in the Ancient Middle East[8]

The earliest depictions of "civilized" warfare, the Standard of Ur and the Stele of the Vultures, both artifacts from Sumer circa 2500 B.C., show spearmen protected by shields standing several ranks deep. They do not look very different from their Neolithic predecessors, except for technical improvements made possible by the invention of bronze: the first real helmets, the first real swords and axes, more reliable spears and shields. In addition to this heavy infantry, there was a light infantry armed with missile weapons. Other than that, there is little that can be said with confidence about the art of war in the early Bronze Age.

We are somewhat better informed about warfare in the high Bronze Age (circa 1600–1200 B.C.). By then the horse-drawn chariot and the composite bow had come into common use, producing a period unique in military history, when civilized armies in the Middle East and the Aegean Basin relied upon a main striking force—some think an exclusive striking force—of chariot archers.[9] The reliefs depicting the Battle of Kadesh in Syria circa 1300 B.C.—the first battle whose course can be reconstructed in some detail—show masses of spearmen drawn up in deep formations, but they seem to be restricted to a purely passive role, such as guarding the camps; the offensive role is left to squadrons of charioteers firing long-range bows.

The age of chariotry came to a sudden end with the sack of the Bronze Age citadels around the eastern Mediterranean circa 1200 B.C. The early Iron Age brought a revival of infantry (or perhaps the first reliable infantry), soon to be joined by the first cavalry, for the Assyrians had mastered the art of riding into battle on horseback. The Assyrian army included the equivalents of all the services known to Napoleon: heavy infantry, light infantry, heavy cavalry (lancers), light cavalry (archers), and in addition, retained chariots, whose function may loosely be compared to that of Napoleon's field artillery.

But the Assyrian reliefs do not suggest that they relied much upon their heavy infantry in an offensive role. They seem to have used charges of cavalry and chariotry to break up the enemy formations, after which their infantry moved in to mop up. Even in the infantry, the archers seem more useful than the spearmen. Later on, the Persians relied still more on archers, both mounted and on foot, and hardly seem to have had a heavy infantry tradition at all.

The conclusion that no ancient Middle Eastern army possessed a heavy infantry capable of effective shock tactics is confirmed by the fact that in later times such tactics were peculiar to the Greeks and were incorporated into eastern armies only to the extent that they were able to hire Greek mercenaries. Some historians think "phalanx" battle was much older than the Greek *polis* culture because they see descriptions of it in the Homeric poems and artistic representations of it in the Middle East as far back as the Bronze Age, which I have already mentioned. These do look like Greek phalanxes, but after all, there is nothing else that any fairly close formation of fairly heavy infantry could look like, and we know of nothing else that *acted* like a Greek phalanx. Putting men in a close formation would not make them capable of the tactics and ethos of Greek hoplites, described in the next chapter.

Warfare in Ancient Religions

This heading may arouse expectations that I can in no way satisfy. The connections between warfare and religion in antiquity are so pervasive and so little explored that they defy generalization, but the subject is of great importance to a study such as this, so the attempt must be made.[10]

What attitudes about warfare are suggested by the common features of primitive religion? The signals are mixed. The constant participation of the spirit world conveys a sense of "bellicism"—of warfare as part of the natural world. At the same time, warfare seems to be regarded, even by the most warlike, as a sort of interruption of normal life. Warriors must be dressed and painted so as to change their personalities. Special ceremonies signal their departure from normal life, and others, their return to it. Above all, warfare requires justification: The constant efforts to secure the favor of the spirit world imply that fighting and killing to avenge wrongs are required by the order of the world. We have seen how the elaborate ritualization of primitive warfare both promotes war and limits it. It is possible to discern in primitive religion the germs of all later philosophical and theological interpretations of warfare, including both *jus ad bellum* (the right to make war) and *jus in bello* (rights in war).

Specific myths about the origins of war are difficult to find because the practice is so taken for granted. Most mythology seems to assume that conflict is simply part of the cosmos and has been so always, among spirits as well as men. Even if there was a primitive dreamtime inhabited by ancestors or gods, these beings fought with one another. Often the cosmos itself must be born in battle, as in the Babylonian creation myth, where the gods fight Tiamat the cosmic dragon and make the world out of her dismembered body.

Sometimes we find myths about a primitive golden age in which there was no war or other strife. This provides an explanation for the origins of war, and the need for such an explanation reflects a sense that warfare is an evil. The curious story of Cain and Abel in the Book of Genesis may in part be a myth about the origin of war. But this primitive pacifism is always very pessimistic. Golden ages are usually lacking not only in warfare but in sickness, old age, and every other evil, and they always ended long ago, leaving warfare to be accepted as one of the inescapable misfortunes of the world we live in. The Xingu River Indians of Brazil—one of the "relatively peaceful" cultures—say that in the beginning, the Sun Spirit created three kinds of people, the peaceful Xinguano, the warlike Wild Indians, and the warlike White Men, and then gave each its own world to inhabit, so that the Xinguano were not bothered by the two nasty breeds. Unfortunately, the boundaries separating these worlds have now been permeated.[11] This myth is unusual in that the golden age continues into recent times. But the myth also contains a realistic acknowledgment that the sphere of peace has always been fragile and is now collapsing.

In organized chiefdoms, the rituals of war take on a theocratic function: The chief is a deputy of the gods, sometimes divine himself, and all warfare has to be explained as an act of the gods, fought for their honor and glory and the honor and glory of their chiefly champion. All warfare must still be justified as an act of righteous vengeance. As shamans once brought down the spirits with magic to help the people avenge their wrongs, so priests petition the gods with sacrifice to avenge the wrongs of the chief.

In the early civilizations religion does not change much in the ideology of war. The rituals of war become more costly and ferocious, and the gods and their myths are more clearly defined by organized temple priesthoods. But all aspects of warfare are still interpreted in the terms of theocratic kingly militarism. The inscriptions of the Assyrian kings attribute all their victories and massacres to the power of Assur, a being far more reliable than the primitive spirits in that he had little use for chivalric conventions and none at all for purification rites.

Here are some excerpts from the ninth-century B.C. annals of King Ashurnasirpal II of Assyria:

> When Assur, the lord, who called me by name and has made great my kingdom, intrusted his merciless weapon unto my lordly hand, (I) Assur-nâsir-pal . . . who has battled with all the enemies of Assur north and south and has laid tribute and tax upon them, conqueror of the foes of Assur . . . when Assur . . . in his wrath had commanded me to conquer, to subdue, and to rule; trusting in Assur my lord, I marched by different roads over steep mountains with the hosts of my army, and there was none who opposed me. . . .
>
> To the city of Sûru of Bît Halupê I drew near, and the terror of the splendor of Assur, my lord, overwhelmed them. . . .
>
> At the word of Assur, Ishtar, and Adad, the gods, my helpers, I mustered my chariots and armies . . . With the masses of my troops and by my furious battle onset I stormed, I captured the city; 600 of their warriors I put to the sword; 3,000 captives I burned with fire; I did not leave a single one among them alive to serve as a hostage. Hulai, their governor, I captured alive. Their corpses I formed into pillars; their young men and maidens I burned in the fire. Hulai, their governor, I flayed, his skin I spread upon the wall of the city of Damdamusa; the city I destroyed, I devastated, I burned with fire.[12]

The ancient Middle East saw the full development of warfare as an instrument of state policy; but as the annals of Ashurnasirpal suggest, the intellectual history of war had hardly begun. The elites of these societies thought about war in ritual and mythic terms similar to those of primitive cultures. In official language, war was always described as an act of the gods. In practice, it must have been perceived as a human act performed for political functions, but none of these societies possessed a political culture capable of expressing such ideas. There must have been a kind of conscious strategy, for there had to be long-range planning behind such extensive campaigns, but the nature of it is a matter of inference. Inference cannot justify the assumption that any of these states had a "grand strategy," or long-term plan for relations with the outside world, or that they ever did any planning beyond immediate war objectives.

In one corner of the Assyrian empire, a peculiar variant of theocratic militarism had developed. Some scholars doubt that the Hebrew people, in the days when they really conducted warfare, had any military practices that differed much from their neighbors.[13] But it is certain that the priestly editors who compiled the Torah in its present form, probably in the seventh century B.C., wanted to believe that their forefathers had practiced a very special form of warfare. The wars of Assur were just wars, but the war of Yahweh was a genuine holy war. The wars of the ancient Hebrews had been expressly commanded by Yahweh as part of his cosmic plan, to clear heathen nations out of the way of Israel, though he allowed some to remain in order to test the Israelites. Yahweh fought in these wars as an active participant and prosecuted them with genocidal fury. "The Lord is a man of war," Moses sang after the destruction of the Egyptians in the Red Sea (Exodus 15.3 RSV). Here is the war code of Deuteronomy:

> When you draw near to a city to fight against it, offer terms of peace to it. And if its answer to you is peace and it opens to you, then all the people who are found in it shall do forced labor for you and shall serve you. But if it makes no peace with you, but makes war against you, then you shall besiege it; and when the Lord your God gives it into your hand you shall put all its males to the sword, but the women and the little ones, the cattle, and everything else in the city, all its spoil, you shall take as booty for yourselves; and you shall enjoy the spoil of your enemies, which the Lord your God has given you. Thus you shall do to all the cities which are very far from you, which are not cities of the nations here. But in the cities of these peoples which the Lord your God gives you for an inheritance, you shall save alive nothing that breathes, but you shall utterly destroy them, the Hittites and the Amorites, the Canaanites and the Perizzites, the Hivites and the Jebusites, as the Lord your God has commanded; that they may not teach you to do according to all their abominable practices which they have done in the service of their gods, and so to sin against the Lord your God. (Deuteronomy 20.10–18 RSV)

The Deuteronomic tradition was the most extreme version of crusading warfare in all antiquity and was to have a profound influence on the Christian world. We will return to it in the final chapter.

In summary, primitive and ancient societies all thought of war as an act of human and divine justice, as the avenging of wrongs. And as a constitutional act, it was the ultimate expression of group loyalty. They did not think of war as a strategic act to carry out purposes of state. That was the unique contribution of the Greeks, to whom we now turn.

Notes

1. E. R. Service, *Primitive Social Organization: An Evolutionary Perspective,* 2d ed. (New York, 1971).

2. R. B. Ferguson and N. L. Whitehead, eds., *War in the Tribal Zone: Expanding States and Indigenous Warfare* (Santa Fe, N. Mex., 1992).

3. In fact, there might have been experiments along this line even in Paleolithic times. This hypothesis provided the plot for *Dance of the Tiger: A Novel of the Ice Age* by the Swedish paleontologist Björn Kurtén (English translation, New York, 1980).

4. *Origins of the State: The Anthropology of Political Evolution,* ed. Ronald Cohen and E. R. Service (Philadelphia, 1978); *The Early State,* ed. H.J.M. Claessen and Peter Skalnik (The Hague, 1978); Jonathan Haas, *The Evolution of the Prehistoric State* (New York, 1982). The circumscription theory I follow here was developed largely by Robert Carneiro in "A Theory of the Origins of the State," *Science* 169 (1970), 733–738, and "Political Expansion as an Expression of the Principle of Competitive Exclusion," in Cohen and Service, *The Early State,* 205–223.

5. Karl Wittfogel, *Oriental Despotism: A Comparative Study of Total Power* (New Haven, 1957).

6. E. g., Gordon Childe, *What Happened in History,* rev. ed. (Baltimore, 1964).

7. The correlation between political centralization and military effectiveness has been emphasized by Wright, H. H. Turney-High, Robert Carneiro, and Keith Otterbein, *The Evolution of War: A Cross-Cultural Study* (N.p., 1970), among others.

8. On this neglected subject, see the bibliography in Robert Drews, *The End of the Bronze Age: Changes in Warfare and the Catastrophe ca. 1200 B.C.* (Princeton, 1993). Yigael Yadin's *The Art of Warfare in Biblical Lands in the Light of Archaeological Discovery* (London, 1963) is valuable both for text and plates, which include photographs of the Standard of Ur and the Stele of the Vultures. Arther Ferrill's *The Origins of War: From the Stone Age to Alexander the Great* (London, 1985) includes a useful survey of ancient Middle Eastern warfare.

9. See the fascinating, if admittedly conjectural, reconstruction of Bronze Age chariot warfare in Drews's *End of the Bronze Age.*

10. I know of no very useful general treatment, but see the material on primitive religion collected by H. H. Turney-High (*Primitive War: Its Practices and Concepts,* 2d ed. [Columbia, S. C., 1971]) and the articles on the golden age, Creation, and related subjects in *The Encyclopedia of Religion,* ed. Mercia Eliade (New York, 1987–).

11. Thomas Gregor, "Uneasy Peace: Intertribal Relations in Brazil's Upper Xingu," in Jonathan Haas, ed., *The Anthropology of War* (Cambridge, 1990), 105–124.

12. *Ancient Records of Assyria and Babylonia,* ed. D. D. Luckenbill, vol. 1 (Chicago, 1926), 139–146.

13. See the discussion by Robert Carroll, "War in the Hebrew Bible," in *War and Society in the Greek World,* ed. John Rich and Graham Shipley (London, 1993), 25–44.

Part Two

Greek Warfare

The rulers must be those who are best suited both for philosophy and war.
—Plato, *Republic*

Chapter Three

The Greek Way of War

Early Greek Practices of War

The unique decentralized culture of the Greeks, which lay on the western flanks of the great Iron Age empires, had developed an oddly archaic kind of warfare. The Persians do not seem to have realized how odd these neighbors were until the beginning of the fifth century B.C., when, in order to avenge insults to their Great King, or perhaps to round off their European frontier (I have mentioned the difficulty of distinguishing strategic motives in ancient empires), they attempted to absorb all the little Greek city-states clustered around the Aegean Sea. Their commander, Mardonius, is said to have given his king the following advice:

> It were indeed a monstrous thing if, after conquering and enslaving the Sacae, the Indians, the Ethiopians, the Assyrians, and many other mighty nations, not for any wrong that they had done us, but only to increase our empire, we should then allow the Greeks, who have done us such wanton injury, to escape our vengeance. What is it that we fear in them?—not surely their numbers?—not the greatness of their wealth? We know the manner of their battle—we know how weak their power is . . . And yet, I am told, these very Greeks are wont to wage war against one another in the most foolish way, through sheer perversity and doltishness. For no sooner is war proclaimed than they search out the smoothest and fairest plain that is to be found in all the land, and there they assemble and fight; whence it comes to pass that even the conquerors depart with great loss: I say nothing of the conquered, for they are destroyed altogether. Now surely, as they are all of one speech, they ought to interchange heralds and messengers, and make up their differences by any means other than battle; or, at the worst, if they must needs fight against one another, they ought to post themselves as strongly as possible, and so try their quarrels. (Herodotus 7.9 [trans. George Rawlinson])[1]

What the Persian finds absurd is the Lilliputian pugnacity of the Greeks: their readiness to go to war and, in war, their readiness to offer battle without attention to elementary strategic or tactical considerations. He exaggerates. As we will see, Greek warfare before the Persian Wars could not have been nearly so common as Mardonius thinks, nor its casualties so heavy. But the historian Herodotus and his audience must have thought this, too, for Herodotus never corrects these impressions. Therefore, this is what Greeks of the late fifth century B.C. imagined the wars of their grandfathers were like. The picture is at once too critical and too idealized, but if we allow for the exaggerations, we can agree with Mardonius and Herodotus that early Greek warfare was distinguished by an unusual taste for violent battle, and we can accept the above as a fairly accurate description of what happened when two Greek cities went to war before 480 B.C. On a level plain, two deep formations of armored spearmen drew up facing one another, packed closely together with big shields overlapping. They collided in a cloud of dust, and there followed some minutes of deafening butchery, the spears of the front rank clashing against shield and helmet, while the files behind them yelled and pushed; then on one side or the other, suddenly the shield wall was broken, the little army scattered, the battle lost.

It requires some effort of the imagination for us to understand why this should seem so odd to a Persian commander. No one now alive has witnessed combat between organized forces using hand-to-hand weapons, for the last vestige of it disappeared one hundred fifty years ago when the bayonet charge became obsolete. We tend to think (assisted by the movies) that direct shock combat of the sort described above was much more common in premodern warfare than it was. In reality, it was always difficult to make foot soldiers seriously engage one another with edged weapons because of their natural tendency to keep out of one another's way. We have already seen that the Persian and other Eastern armies put no faith in heavy infantry assault. The main function of their spearmen was to provide cover for their archers, and battles were won by cavalry and archers with a minimum of physical contact. Only the Greeks had developed a style of warfare that made shock combat inevitable, because their infantry formation was no loose huddle but a tight rectangle (*phalanx*) often eight ranks deep or more, its heavy shields a collective locking device, its sheer depth and weight propelling the men in the front ranks onto the spears of the enemy.[2]

This type of heavy infantryman, called a "hoplite," was recognizable because he was burdened with armor and shield probably heavier than any infantry had ever carried. The style of fighting for which his equipment was designed had been perfected in the seventh century B.C., perhaps at Sparta, so by the time the Persians encountered hoplites in their homeland, Greeks had been warring in this way for some two hundred years. In the course of the Persian Wars, the archaic style of warfare began to change, and by the time Herodotus wrote the first useful descriptions of Greek warfare, the system was almost obsolete. But some of its practices and many of its values lived on to influence the whole classical tradition.

Mardonius and Herodotus were right to emphasize the backwardness of hoplite warfare. It was in some ways a throwback, closer to the practices of primitive tribes than to the great standing armies of contemporary Assyria, Babylonia, and Persia. As in many primitive cultures, warfare among the small agricultural communities of archaic Greece was fairly frequent in occurrence but low in intensity. The frequency of it is certainly exaggerated in Mardonius's speech. Apparently, the later Greeks liked to imagine their ancestors as almost constantly at war, but it is possible that for the average Greek city-state (we should remember that there were more than one thousand of these, with very different histories, mostly lost to us), war was a rare event. We have very little information about Greek wars before the Persian invasions, but we do know much about the traditions of Athens, and it is surprising how little warfare was waged there in the archaic age.[3] When wars did occur, they were always border wars between neighboring cities. Campaigns did not require much planning or preparation because the participants did not aim at occupation but only hoped to damage the enemy by raiding. Tactics were equally simple, hardly distinguishable from strategy, for all fighters were armed alike and battles tended to be conducted according to rigid conventions that gave them the ritualistic character of a duel— one of the things that perplexed Mardonius.

All this reminds us of primitive warfare, and we might be tempted to call archaic Greek warfare a specialized variant of this, surviving in that corner of the world because the decentralized Greek political structure had resisted the formation of large bureaucratic states. But if Greek armies had been no more effective than primitive warriors, Greece would have been part of the Persian empire by the time Herodotus wrote, and Herodotus would probably never have written. What was unexpected and formidable about Greek warfare was its reduction of the process to a single offensive shock tactic.

Causes of Early Greek Warfare

It seemed obvious to Greeks why they had to play by these rules. Their art of war was intensely territorial. As soon as a war started, their land became the military objective. An invading force had to be met and fought at once before it could ravage the cultivated fields surrounding the city walls. The strategy of the campaign, or rather, raid, was to force the defender to immediate combat, which could be accomplished simply by marching onto his fields. The necessity of driving the enemy away at once reduced the defender to the use of a single arm, the hoplite phalanx, and to a single tactic, the hoplite charge, which nearly excluded other methods of fighting. As Herodotus's bemused Persian pointed out, they did not even try to find an advantageous position; nor would there have been much point to that attempt, for the phalanx could charge only on level ground, normally so scarce in Greece as to leave little room for maneuver, and since the hoplites did not bother with supply trains, it was rarely feasible to hold mountain passes against them.[4] Thus, armies met on a level field, as if by appointment. A successful charge was not followed up, for the phalanx was too unwieldy to conduct a pursuit, and siege tactics, though well advanced in the Middle East at this period, were rudimentary in Greece.

Nevertheless the hoplite charge was a terrifying ordeal, and the economic explanation the Greeks commonly gave for it—the need to defend their crops—is not entirely satisfactory. If military tactics are really that controlled by agriculture, then we might expect something like the hoplite style of battle to evolve not long after the first agricultural settlements; yet no other society of primitive or peasant agriculturalists, as far as we know, ever saw the need to submit to any such thing. Their fields were subject to raids, but they do not appear to have thought it imperative to drive the enemy away immediately, and it is hard to find pressing *economic* reasons for the Greeks to have thought so. The normal season of war in the ancient Mediterranean was the summer. An invader might do heavy damage if he arrived just before the grain harvest in early summer, but such timing must have been difficult, and often the precious fields on and for which the hoplites died were dry stubble. An invader could always try to destroy vineyards and olive groves, but the amount of permanent damage that could be inflicted in such a raid does not seem sufficient to force battle upon the defenders. To remain safely within the city walls and harass the invaders until they left must have been at times a reasonable option. Nor is it true that the seizure of land was an ultimate war aim: As will be discussed later, the central agricultural land of a city was hardly ever at risk in war, either tactically or strategically.

Therefore, there must have been some powerful emotive, symbolic, ideological reason for this choice of tactic and strategy.[5] The key to the Greek system of warfare is that hoplites, who had to furnish their own equipment, constituted a privileged minority in the city-state, composing perhaps one-third of the free population, and they were often the only full citizens. Their political and social predominance was based squarely on their right and duty to carry a shield in the phalanx. There was an obvious connection between the role of hoplite and the role of citizen: Hoplites were the citizens in battle; citizens were the hoplites in assembly. It was this style of battle that had endowed small farmers, or the more prosperous of them, with a prestige unknown in other ancient societies, and it had transformed peasants into citizens. No other ancient society had a decentralized political structure based on private property, with landownership distributed among such a large percentage of the population. Hoplites were a landowning class that adopted this offensive style of war, despite its cost to themselves, because their status depended upon their demonstrated ability to defend the soil. Only citizen soldiers of high morale could have submitted to the discipline of the phalanx. They were jealous of their role as defenders of the soil and were reluctant to make much use of slingers and archers, though these fighters were much better suited to the terrain, because they were not eager to enhance the military value of their poorer neighbors. In sum, they accepted all the consequent tactical and strategic limitations for the sake of preserving their leadership.

The intense territorialism of early Greek warfare was more symbolic than material.

Given these premises, the hoplite battle made sense. For both sides, it was the cheapest and quickest way to settle the business. Like no other method of fighting known to antiquity, it ensured that the battle, and normally the war—almost synonymous with "battle"—would be ended by a single, short, savage clash, after which the farmer-soldiers could return to their fields. And this procedure spared lives as well as time. Herodotus greatly exaggerated the casualty rates in early hoplite battles, apparently because Greeks of his generation commonly believed that old-style battles had meant near annihilation for the losers and appalling losses even for the victors. This heroic legend led them to miss altogether the clue to the archaic military tradition: Battles were so short that casualties must have been relatively light.[6] Hoplite battles were supposed to create awe and terror, and their reputation deceived even Greeks into thinking the system more vicious than it really was. In reality, it was vicious mostly to the men in the front rank, and then not for long, for their heavy panoply, worn in the heat of a Greek summer and in the press of battle, kept the fighting short while it increased their chances of surviving it.

The hoplite ideology may be correctly described as militaristic—the original form of what I have dubbed "civic militarism." But it was a defensive and protective militarism, the sole purpose of which was to promote communal esprit de corps. It could not easily be used to justify expansion, like the theocratic militarism of eastern kings or the Roman version of civic militarism to be examined later. The hoplites were tied to their own soil, and their notions of the purposes of war were as limited as their practices of war were offensive. Recently the sociologist W. G. Runciman asked,

> What, then, was it about the Greek *poleis* [city-states] which prevented any of them from breaking out of the evolutionary dead-end up against which they found themselves? If there is any single inference to be drawn from the comparison with Rome and Venice, it is simply that the *poleis* were all, without exception, far too democratic. Some, of course, were more oligarchic than others. But this meant only that their government was in the hands of a relatively smaller number of relatively richer citizens rather than a relatively larger number of relatively poorer ones. In terms of a close concentration of economic, ideological, and coercive power in the hands of a compact, self-reproducing élite, no Greek *polis* ever came anywhere near the degree of oligarchy which characterized the institutions of both Rome and Venice during the period of their achievement of world-power status . . . the ideology of the Greek *poleis* was . . . strongly populist; it was, that is to say, hostile to the concentration of power in the hands of any single person, family, or group except for limited periods and for limited purposes as endorsed by the citizen body as a whole.[7]

As to the *formal* causes that Greeks gave for going to war, we find much the same complex of motives as in the better organized primitive tribes. Some historians have assumed that early Greek wars were normally over land,[8] but that seems an illusion left by the hoplite ethos and its tendency to speak of territory as a symbol for all civic values. Their ritual territorialism actually worked to *limit* conquest: The wars of the *poleis* were less territorial in the economic sense than those of the Homeric kings. It is true that they fought many wars over disputed border territories. The long enmity between Sparta and Argos, at war repeatedly for two hundred years, centered on the disputed possession of a border territory called Thyreae (Herodotus 1.82); but this Peloponnesian Alsace-Lorraine was worth so little as to suggest the fighting was more about honor than land. Other wars arose over thefts that seem more like insults than injuries, as when Sparta in the late sixth century B.C. went to war with Samos because Samian pirates had hijacked both a bronze bowl that the Spartans had sent as a gift to the king of Lydia and a corselet sent by the Egyptian pharaoh to Sparta (Herodotus 3.47). Others began over ritual matters, like the enmity between Athens and Aegina, which originated in an ancient quarrel over certain cult statues (Herodotus 5.82). Whatever the original cause, disputes could easily turn into hereditary hostilities lasting for generations and imparting to warfare the legitimacy of tradition. The world of Herodotus knew that such an enmity was self-perpetuating and that the grievances behind specific wars might matter little. Herodotus spent some time explaining the disputes between Corinth and Corcyra in the late sixth century, which had to do with charges of homicide and slave stealing; but he remarked that the real reason for all the trouble was simply that Corinth and its colony Corcyra had suffered bad relations ever since Corcyra was founded (Herodotus 3.49).

All wars were ostensibly fought for honor, and in all, some material interest was involved. It is likely that people were aware the Spartans had some financial interest in putting down Samian piracy, in addition to the defense of Spartan honor. The causes of war in early Greece, like many of the Greek practices of war, retained a primitive simplicity. The need of a city to protect its honor and its land was obvious, and honor and land were essentially the same.

Warfare in Early Greek Religion and Poetry[9]

The early Greek assumptions about warfare are those found among primitive peoples the world over: Warfare is a natural and inevitable part of the order of things, and when fought to avenge wrongs (but for no other purpose), it is fully justifiable, indeed, it is then a moral imperative and the source of male identity. The poems of Homer and Hesiod, written perhaps in the eighth century B.C., gave these ancient notions permanent literary expression.

As has already been discussed, some primitive cultures had antimilitaristic traditions about a peaceful golden age in the remote past, but this was a passive and fatalistic antimilitarism that accepted war as an inevitable evil.

Among the Greeks, this attitude was represented by *The Works and Days* of Hesiod, which describes a primitive state called the Time of Cronus (later called the "golden age" by Latin poets), during which there was neither warfare nor any other misfortune. The "ghastly action of Ares" (1.146, trans. Richard Lattimore), god of war, is one of the more dramatic misfortunes of the increasingly degenerate times that followed, especially our own time. In later centuries, this Hesiodic myth inspired much antiwar rhetoric, but at least until the time of Erasmus, these expressions never went beyond sentimental nostalgia, because the pessimism of the myth was too plain to permit anything else. In the world we live in, war is as inescapable as sickness and old age.

Hesiod represents the antimilitaristic side of the ambiguous Greek attitude toward war. But much more important as an influence on later war literature is Homer's *Iliad,* the greatest of all literary glorifications of warfare. The epic poem is filled with a tragic sense of the costs of war, expressed in its opening lines:

Sing, goddess, the anger of Peleus' son Achilleus
and its devastation, which put pains thousandfold upon the Achaians,
hurled in their multitudes to the house of Hades strong souls
of heroes, but gave their bodies to be the delicate feasting
of dogs, of all birds, and the will of Zeus was accomplished . . .
(Lattimore trans.)

But the main theme of the epic poet is "the fighting where men win glory" (*Iliad* 4.225). The Homeric heroes live with an absolute imperative, encouraged by the gods, to defend their honor and gain glory. Homer must be held largely responsible for the view that warfare is the noblest subject of literary art and that the highest aim of the artist is to celebrate the martial values.

The Homeric code was, of course, highly individualistic, and it required considerable socialization to fit the later hoplite ethic.[10] Homer portrays a society resembling the more advanced primitive chiefdoms. Every war leader is concerned exclusively with his personal honor and glory, not that of the army, but this society is sufficiently complex and articulated to make it easy for conflicts to arise between these goals, and precisely such a conflict forms the plot of the *Iliad.* The anger of Achilles is a problem endemic in societies at the edge of state formation, when for the first time a gap opens between the motives of the chief and those of his warriors. Likewise, the battle descriptions in Homer, whose gory realism was never matched in classical literature, almost exclusively feature duels between individual heroes, though we catch confused glimpses of masses of troops milling in the background.

But the greatest and most original contribution of Homer to the literature of war was his invention of a narrative form that inspired the precocious Greek historical spirit. Many ancient societies had some kind of narrative battle poetry, but none other produced a poetic medium capable of describing action with the empathy, psychological subtlety, mimetic vividness, and compositional technique of the *Iliad.* The simple fact that Homer portrays Greeks and Trojans with equal sympathy was sufficient to raise Greek narrative forever above the vainglorious boasting and flattery of divine patrons that fill most ancient war literature (compare the annals of Ashurnasirpal quoted in the previous chapter). In some ways Homer bequeathed a straitjacket to later Greek historians, few of whom could break away from his fascination with individual heroics. But without him it is difficult to believe that the analytical attitude toward the past peculiar to the later Greeks could have developed at all.

It turned out to be surprisingly easy to adapt the language and values of Homer to hoplite warfare. This was being done as early as the seventh century B.C., or almost as soon as hoplite warfare appeared. We know it had not yet fully developed at the time Tyrtaeus of Sparta composed his war songs in the mid-seventh century, because these describe a kind of battle in which there is still some room for individual initiative, though what Tyrtaeus describes is not Homeric warfare, either. He praises the valor of the Spartan warriors in the language of Homer, but the Homeric duel between individual heroes has become the mass duel of hoplites:

> Ye are of the lineage of the invincible Heracles; so
> be ye of good cheer; not yet is the head of Zeus turned
> away. Fear ye not a multitude of men, nor flinch, but let
> every man hold his spear straight toward the van, making Life
> his enemy and the black Spirits of Death dear as the rays of
> the sun. For ye know the destroying deeds of lamentable Ares,
> and well have learnt the disposition of woeful War; ye have tasted
> both of the fleeing and the pursuing, lads, and had more
> than your fill of either. Those who abiding shoulder to
> shoulder go with a will into the mellay and the van, of these
> are fewer slain, these save the people afterward. (Frag. 11 [trans. J. M. Edmonds])

In poetry, too, the phalanx meant something of a throwback, as poets now left behind the kingly ideals of Homer and reverted to the celebration of tribal solidarity. In later classical literature, the kingly militarism of Homer was always applied to civic militarism without the slightest sense of incongruity, loaning to the republican ideal its fierce archaic rhetoric of glory, inviting every hoplite to think himself Achilles.

All military traditions and values were thus adapted to the needs of the city-state. In Homer's world, wars were begun to avenge wrongs against the kings: The grievance behind the Trojan War was the typical primitive cause of war, the abduction of a female. But after the rise of the city-state and the hoplite phalanx, wars were fought to uphold the honor of the citizens, meaning especially the hoplite class, and took the form of a duel for the literal and symbolic protection of their land. Individual trophy hunting was replaced by group trophy hunting: In the *Iliad,* a victor would strip his dead enemy of arms and armor and keep those spoils of war, but in later Greece, it was customary for a victorious city to make a collective dedication to the gods of all captured arms.

Every effort was made to secure the favor of the gods with sacrifices, vows, consultation of oracles, and examination of omens. An army made a sacrifice just before the charge and, if the signs were unfavorable, made repeated sacrifices until the desired results were achieved—a custom resembling the most primitive magic in its manipulativeness, requiring an army to drive with it a small flock of goats or sheep on every campaign. An army might hope that the gods would demonstrate their support by appearing on the battlefield, which they seem to have done at least as often as modern generals do, the apparition of the hero Theseus to the Athenian hoplites at Marathon being only the most famous such. And if the ancestral gods failed to bring victory, diplomatic overtures might be made to foreign gods.

But Greek religion was not totally manipulative, and sacrifices and vows were not sufficient to win the favor of the gods. If one hoped for the favor of either gods or men in wartime, one's war had to be just. It had to conform to the unwritten code of usages called "the laws of the Greeks" or "the laws of mankind." In the fourth-century dialogue *Alcibiades I* by Plato or by one of his disciples, Socrates asks the young Alcibiades, who is ambitious to enter public life, how he would advise the citizens on matters of war and peace. What reasons, Socrates asks, do we give for going to war? Alcibiades replies immediately that "we say we are victims of deceit or violence or spoliation." Socrates then asks him if there are any circumstances in which he would advise the citizens to make war on people who are *not* practicing injustice. Alcibiades replies, "That is a hard question: For even if someone decides he must go to war with those who are doing what is just, he would not admit that they were doing so" (109; trans. W.R.M. Lamb). They agree that wars against those who are guilty of no wrong are neither lawful (*nomimos*) nor seemly (*kalos*).

They are aware that, in practice, a different kind of reasoning is possible in warfare and that the routine protestation of seemliness and legality may be a facade. The historical Alcibiades had been one of the most notorious practitioners of such realpolitik. But all think it wise to observe the proprieties. When Herodotus makes his Persians brag about how they have conquered peoples who have never even offended them, that is meant to show the depths of their barbarous impiety. Thucydides, as we will see, has his Athenian politicians speak of war and empire with astonishingly candid *raison d'é-tat*—perhaps in part the historian's artifice, in part a reflection of a real bluntness in Athenian political oratory in Alcibiades's generation. But in any case, even Thucydides's Athenians do not in public altogether forget the need for a just cause. To have a just cause, one must be fighting to resist aggression or to avenge a broken treaty or any other insult or injury against the citizens as a whole. Every war opens with the proclamation of such a grievance, made first to the citizens to persuade them to declare war, then to neighboring cities to ensure their assistance or neutrality, then by official herald to the enemy, and finally to the gods.

The treatise *The General* by the Greek philosopher Onasander was written in the first century A.D., but his advice on public relations would have been intelligible to his countrymen at any time: "It should be evident to all that one fights on the side of justice. For then the gods also, kindly disposed, become comrades in arms to the soldiers, and men are more eager to take their stand against the foe . . . [The general] should call heaven to witness that he is entering upon war without offense" (4.1–3 [trans. Loeb Classical Library]). It was, of course, normally possible to get favorable signs from the gods one way or another, and cases of engagements postponed for ritual considerations are hard to find except among the notoriously superstitious Spartans.

It was not only necessary to have a just cause (corresponding to the *jus ad bellum,* or the right to make war, in the later Christian just war doctrine) but also to observe a rudimentary code of conduct during war (corresponding to the Christian *jus in bello,* or rights in war). Everything connected with the worship of the gods was inviolable during wartime, including temples, sanctuaries, priests, and the great Panhellenic games; the persons of heralds were sacrosanct, and so were defeated enemies, once they threw down their arms and became suppliants; the gods were called upon to enforce truces and treaties; and it was the height of impiety not to allow a defeated enemy to bury his war dead, as shown in the importance of this taboo in heroic legend. Later Greek writers certainly idealized archaic military practice, and the reality could not always have been so chivalrous. But these were rules sanctioned by the gods and universally respected by men, and the need to strengthen the soldiers' faith in divine support put teeth into them.[11]

Rarely are we told which gods they called upon. Usually we hear only that an army sacrificed to "the gods." Ares, the ancient Greek war god, was a cruel and barbarous lout to whom the Greeks, even in archaic times, paid relatively little attention. In Homer, he is already a despicable figure. When shamefully worsted in battle by Athena, the goddess of wisdom, he goes complaining to Zeus, king of the gods, who receives him with small sympathy:

> Do not sit beside me and whine, you double-faced liar.
> To me you are most hateful of all gods who hold Olympos.
> Forever quarreling is dear to your heart, wars and battles.
> (*Iliad* 5.889ff. [trans. Lattimore])

Armies sometimes sacrificed to Ares before battle, and the Thebans considered him their ancestor. But most Greeks were far more likely to call upon the civilized gods who protected the city both in peace and war. In Tyrtaeus's poem it is Zeus and Hercules who bring victory, while "lamentable

Ares" seems to personify everything horrid about warfare. Does the presence of such an unheroic war god in so militaristic a culture testify to some deep ambivalence in the Greek attitude toward war?

As with most things military, we are better informed about the war gods of Sparta than anyplace else. We know from contemporary sources that in the classical age, Spartans performed prebattle sacrifice to Artemis the Huntress (Xenophon, *Hellenica* 4.2.20), and later writers attributed to them some surprising military cults, complete with philosophical rationales. We are told that the Spartans, the Cretans, and the Sacred Band of Thebes sacrificed before battle to Eros, god of love, because of their well-known practices of military homosexuality (Athenaeus 13.561); that Spartans sacrificed to the Muses to remind them of the war songs and dances that played an important role in Spartan military training (Plutarch, *Life of Lycurgus* 21); that if Spartans won a victory by open battle they sacrificed a cock to Ares, but if the victory was the result of stratagem they sacrificed a bull, the latter method being a mark of superior generalship (Plutarch, *Ancient Customs of the Spartans* 25). These stories may reflect authentic traditions, but they also reflect the later philosophical tradition of Sparta as military utopia. The last item sounds particularly un-Spartan. As we will see, the Greeks in practice were no more averse to the use of stratagems in war than we would expect the people of Odysseus to be. But when they were painting idealized pictures of the hoplite ethic, they liked to pretend that they, or at least their ancestors, were above such trickery. (In fact, surprise attacks are rarely heard of in early Greek warfare, but this is surely because there could not have been much opportunity for them in hoplite tactics.)

Sea Power and Strategy, 480–431 B.C.[12]

The Greek tradition of limited land warfare just described continued into the early fifth century B.C. For generations, the Greek cities pursued their endemic little wars. We can dimly perceive a slow shift in the balance of power. At an early date, the contest threw up a clear winner. Sparta, whose unique military and social institutions gave that city-state a clear advantage in hoplite warfare, had become the dominant power in Greece by the sixth century. Spartan territory stretched across the southern Peloponnesus—a monstrous territory for a Greek city-state, as big as Rhode Island—and in addition, Sparta had built up a network of alliances, known as the Peloponnesian League, that covered most of central and southern Greece. But expansion had been slow and gradual, had made no obvious break with the traditional patterns of Greek border warfare, and had reached its limits early. Not until much later did other Greeks inquire into the reasons for Sparta's success or show any interest in the strange Spartan communistic institutions. The recalcitrant autonomy of Greek political and military values had prevented the struggle for power from resulting in unification. However, it had produced a stable hegemony, which left to itself might have remained stable.

But it did not remain so because the coming of the Persians rudely introduced the Greeks to a world of radically different war practices and vastly larger strategic concerns. In 480 B.C., an enormous combined fleet and army, possibly the largest military operation that had ever been organized, moved inexorably on Greece, impressing upon the Greek mind that a large fleet of warships could make war possible on a scale they had associated with gods rather than men.

The Greeks were awakened to the possibilities of strategy, especially the maritime variant. For a century to come, they would often assume that truly grand strategies aiming at conquest and empire had to be based on sea power. They tended to take for granted everything about land power and land warfare, even on a scale as stupendous as the Persian empire. But it was immediately obvious that there was something about sea power that was not in the natural order of things. It suggested new possibilities for human ingenuity and technology, for long-range planning, for sudden and dramatic accretions of power over immense distances.

However, the Greeks tended to overestimate the capacities of sea power. Genuine naval warfare in antiquity required fast rowing ships and was confined to the Mediterranean, an almost tideless inland sea ideally suited to such ships. Ancient Mediterranean navies did not "command the sea" in the sense that navies have aspired to since the sixteenth century A.D. When Greeks spoke of "command of the sea" (for which they had a word, *thalassocratia*), they meant "command of selected sea lanes," mostly coastal, and above all, the narrow passages. The opportunity for such control presents itself often in the maze of islands, straits, and inlets on the north Mediterranean coast, and that opportunity arose more often in antiquity because of the ancient mariners' aversion to losing sight of land.

The oared galleys, which have been aptly described as large racing sculls, were incapable of much else. They were too slow to catch sailing ships with a good wind in their favor. They could not carry much of anything except rowers. They carried too few marines to secure a landing on a hostile coast and too few provisions to stay at sea for long periods, so normally they were beached every night. They could not prevent a fleet from crossing the open sea, nor could they blockade any long stretch of coast or operate at all without a friendly shore that could be reached in a few hours' rowing.

But they were independent of the wind and, over a short distance, were faster and more maneuverable than any sailing ship. They could attack or defend the supply lines of a large army. The Persians used them for this when they invaded Greece in 480 B.C., for so huge an army had to be supplied by sea. In the year 415 the Athenians launched another huge amphibious force against Sicily, and again the real function of the galleys was to protect the supply lines of the army. Both invasions failed as soon as the fleet was lost. Likewise, galleys could attack or defend the supply routes of a large city. In the fifth century, a major function of the Athenian fleet was to guard the grain route from the Black Sea, which ran through the bottleneck of the Hellespont, a passage highly vulnerable to the galleys. The galleys were most effective against small islands or other exposed points easily cut off by sea; their ideal theater was the island-studded Aegean, the inmost arm of the inland sea.

Even in the Aegean, the galleys could command the sea only to a limited extent. During the Peloponnesian War, when the Athenians moved to take over the little island of Melos, they warned the Melians that they could expect no help from Sparta, as Athenian ships controlled the sea. The Melians replied that on the west they were separated from the mainland by a seventy-mile stretch of open water, where the Athenians could never be sure of intercepting ships (Thucydides 5.110). The Melians were grasping at straws: Spartan help never came, and if it had, the Athenians would have done their intercepting not on the open sea but at Melos harbor. Nevertheless, this exchange shows the common assumptions about the reach of the galleys. Their real function was not interception on the open sea but ambush in a narrows. In 480, Greek strategy consistently relied upon positioning their fleet in a narrow strait, first by Thermopylae and then by Salamis, knowing that the Persian fleet could not afford to ignore them and move on (as the fleet of Drake or Nelson could have done easily), because of the threat the Greek ships posed to the vulnerable Persian supply lines. The galleys might score occasional successes in bolder strategies. In 396 B.C., the Carthaginians launched a great fleet (said to contain 600 transports carrying 300,000 infantry) against Sicily, keeping its route a strict secret so as to prevent interception; but somehow the fleet of Dionysius, tyrant of Syracuse, managed to intercept the Carthaginians off the Sicilian coast and sent to the bottom 50 transports carrying 5,000 men and 200 chariots (Diodorus of Sicily 14.54–55). This sounds like a stroke of luck, and even then, most of the Carthaginian fleet was able to escape as soon as a favorable wind rose.

Galleys certainly had their uses. Still, in the fifth century B.C., there were few urban centers in the Mediterranean, and fewer armies, large enough to be dependent on sea transport; and the geopolitics of the Aegean were unique. To us today, the most striking fact about the ancient navy is its extremely limited utility. We wonder why the Greeks were so impressed.

Of course, we have that impression largely because the place most affected by sea power was Athens, the source of most of the extant classical Greek literature. But perhaps the sheer novelty of naval power also had something to do with it. The navy was the most important innovation of a purely technological nature that had ever appeared in the history of warfare. And it appeared very late in that history. In the seventh century B.C., some experiments were made to increase the rowing power of galleys and fit their prows with metal beaks for ramming. The innovators must have been either insular Greeks or their trade rivals, the Phoenicians. Sometime in the seventh or sixth century, some Greek or Phoenician invented the classical war galley, the trireme, a ship propelled by three superimposed banks of oars. It was a highly specialized craft useful only for war, with all the capabilities and limitations previously mentioned, and it made genuine naval tactics possible. Just what it was invented for is a mystery. In any case, the possibilities of thalassocracy, in the ancient sense, were soon realized.

In the sixth century, the first naval powers arose. The Phoenician colony of Carthage united all the other Phoenician cities around the coasts and islands of the western Mediterranean into the first maritime commercial empire. Their fleet dominated the western waters for the next three centuries, but their empire reached the limits of its expansion quickly and thereafter the Phoenicians pursued a defensive policy aimed at guarding the trade routes and keeping the Greeks out of the west.

Later in the sixth century B.C., the Persian empire reached the Mediterranean, absorbed the old Phoenician cities and their fleets, and became the first great naval power to the east—a far more dynamic and dangerous power than Carthage, for the Persians were interested from the start in using their navy as an ancillary to their land forces and in further Mediterranean conquests. The Great King Cambyses, who added Egypt to the empire in 525, sought allies among the Greek cities of the Aegean islands, and it was said he planned to send a joint army and fleet against Carthage (Herodotus 3.19), which might have created a trans-Mediterranean thalassocracy on the scale eventually realized by Rome. The Greeks thought Cambyses quite mad, but something about sea power encouraged such delusions of grandeur. The barriers of communication and transport that nature had placed to stunt the growth of empires seemed suddenly to fall away.

As it happened, the first major experiment in the use of sea power for conquest—the Persian invasion of the Aegean Basin in 480—was on a somewhat less ambitious but still unprecedented scale. The Persian forces certainly did not number in the millions, as was firmly believed by later Greeks, including Herodotus, but some modern scholars have thought they could have approached one hundred thousand, which may have been the largest army that had so far marched in human history. Why they bothered to assemble so huge an army, probably too cumbersome for any military advantage, is not clear—perhaps it was done for publicity, to advertise to the world the unity of the empire and the power of the Achaemenid. In any case, such an experiment would not have been possible without the new logistical capabilities of sea power.

The experiment ended, of course, in total disaster on both land and sea. On land, the hoplite forces of the allied Greek cities, led by Sparta, repeatedly smashed the lightly armed Orientals. The Greek phalanx was invulnerable in shock combat, but it should have been vulnerable to an army of cavalry and archers willing to avoid such combat. Thus, it would appear that the Persians repeatedly made the mistake of meeting the Greek on Greek terms and not their own, being handicapped by the terrain, the size of their army, and the constraints of time. As Herodotus said, the land and the sea fought against them. It was more surprising to find the sea on the side of the Greeks, yet the jerry-built fleet of Athens managed to defeat the lords of the Mediterranean on their own element.

Still, the Greeks were rightly impressed. The Great King had come one thousand miles, with what looked like half of Asia at his back, and he might come against them again. The problems of war, on land and sea, would never seem simple again; the habits of concerted long-range planning could not be given up. It was now clear that the Aegean Sea was the gate to Greece. To guard it against the Persians, some 150 maritime cities on the coasts and islands formed an alliance under the hegemony of Athens. Athenian control gradually tightened: The alliance grew into a confederation, the confederation into an empire. By mid-century, the Greek world was divided between a land power and a sea power: The old Peloponnesian League led by Sparta, a loose hegemony of hoplite cities, confronted the new centralized maritime empire of Athens. From 461 B.C. on, hostilities between the two alliances were endemic, and in 431, the general conflict known as the Peloponnesian War broke out, which changed the nature of Greek warfare forever.

Never again would wars be settled quickly by hoplite battles. Hoplites were to remain formidable, when properly used, for centuries to come, but the hoplite *system* was doomed. Now, even hoplites had to make more use of tactical maneuver, and they had to be supplemented by naval operations, sieges, raids, ambushes, the defense of passes, the hit-and-run warfare of light infantry, and the secret warfare of treason, assassination, and the fifth column. By the late fifth century, the Greek art of war was more complex than any kind of warfare ever known, and the dynamic political culture of the Greek Enlightenment, now entering its maturity, raised it to a new level of reflection. The rise of sea power brought a social and cultural as well as a military crisis: It put an end to landed timocracy and made it possible for any citizen to take on the defense of the city. For centuries, Greek warfare had remained almost immune to the slow but steady material progress of the *polis,* but that long insulation was now over, and the Greek genius was free to apply itself to problems of war without ethical or religious restraint. By around 431 B.C., the old Greek way of war was practically dead, and the serious history of military thought was beginning.

The Military Revolution

The great intellectual breakthrough in Greek warfare came toward the end of the fifth century B.C., but the Greek *practice* of warfare attained maturity during the century that followed. These later developments I will sketch briefly here; for the history of ideas, they were less decisive than the achievements of the fifth century, and the purpose of this chapter is not to provide a history of Greek warfare but rather to outline the political and social context of the Greek ideologies of war.

In the major set battles of the fourth century, it was still the hoplites who won or lost the day, but the experiments begun during the Peloponnesian War continued. There was more and more use of other arms and weapons, more need for complicated maneuver, combined-arms tactics, long-range planning, employment of professional mercenaries, specialized military training, and a specialized military literature. All this climaxed around the middle of the fourth century with the perfection of the Macedonian military machine. The armies of Philip and Alexander combined an improved and heavier phalanx with light infantry, light and heavy cavalry, and an elaborate siege train. Alexander added to all this the logistical and organizational capabilities of the Persian empire, and his fantastic expedition into the heart of Asia raised strategy and tactics to new levels. It is difficult to exaggerate the importance of these changes. The Greek city-states had practically no regular taxation and had neither the ability nor the desire to carry out sophisticated war making on the Macedonian scale. The perfection of siegecraft by the Macedonian army, especially the invention of the torsion catapult around 350 B.C., rendered obsolete the ideal of city-state autonomy. It seems correct to speak of a genuine military revolution in the Greek world between the time of Pericles and the time of Alexander, climaxing around the year 350 B.C.—a change comparable in many ways to the "military revolution" that historians often see in European history during the late sixteenth and early seventeenth centuries A.D.[13]

It is ironic that the major phase of this revolution took place in the middle and later fourth century B.C., yet the extant Greek literature on warfare (and much else) is far richer for the late fifth and early fourth centuries B.C. We may have lost much valuable literature from the fourth century and from Hellenistic times through accidents of textual transmission, but I will argue later that in ancient Greece, as in ancient China, military thought peaked early and probably never surpassed the level of sophistication achieved by the historians, orators, and philosophers who wrote during the Peloponnesian War and the decades immediately following. The next three chapters are devoted to an examination of this literature.

Notes

1. Herodotus probably wrote this circa 430 B.C. and Mardonius's critique of traditional hoplite warfare, which by that year was rapidly becoming obsolete, probably echoes criticisms made by contemporary Greek Sophists, who taught a "scientific" approach to the art of war. Criticism of the hoplite tradition would have been especially welcome to a democratic audience. See F. W. Walbank, *A Historical Commentary on Polybius,* vol. 2 (Oxford, 1967), on Polybius 13.3.4. But did Herodotus agree

with this critique? Herodotus's audience knew perfectly well, and Herodotus would shortly remind them, that in fact the simple assault tactics of the Greeks proved superior to the sophisticated Persian strategies. Herodotus seems to use the "Persian" speech to parody the advanced military thought of his own day and to suggest that the old-fashioned military virtues were better.

2. There has been much controversy over the extent to which early Greek warfare relied on shock combat of the sort described here, but there is a general consensus that in comparison with other ancient societies, it did so very heavily. See the reconstruction of hoplite warfare in V. D. Hanson, *The Western Way of War: Infantry Battle in Classical Greece* (New York, 1989), and his references to the earlier literature. G. L. Cawkwell, "Orthodoxy and Hoplites," *Classical Quarterly* n.s. 39 (1989), 375–389, argues that hoplites sometimes fought in open order, rather than using the concerted push (*othismos*) of the "orthodox" view. The issue is difficult, first, because our earliest detailed account of a hoplite battle is Thucydides's description of Delium in 424 B.C. (Thucydides 4.93–96) (Herodotus's battles are Greek against Persian), and therefore all our useful narratives come from a period when hoplites were capable of far more flexible tactics than in the age of pure hoplite battle, and, second, because Greek historians tend to fall into a disjunctive narrative mode that can make it hard to tell the exact sequence of events. A passage in Plato's *Laches* is highly relevant to this debate: Two Athenian generals are discussing the novel technique of *hoplomachia*, or fencing with hoplite weapons, a skill useful only for individual open-order fighting; they agree there might be some use for it in any battle, but it would be chiefly useful *after* the real battle, in the fluid retreat and pursuit after a phalanx broke and turned (*Laches* 181–182). This passage has been quoted in support of both sides, but surely it supports mainly the "orthodox" thesis: The generals know that many accidents can happen in battle and individual duels might occur, but these are not a typical or expected feature of regular hoplite battle. See J. K. Anderson, "Hoplites and Heresies: A Note," *Journal of Hellenic Studies* 104 (1984), 152. In any case, even "heretics" like Calkwell do not deny the existence and centrality of the *othismos*.

3. W. R. Connor, "Early Greek Land Warfare as Symbolic Expression," *Past and Present* 119 (1988), 3–29.

4. See Xenophon's *Anabasis* for testimony to the ability of hoplites to fight their way through mountain passes held only by light troops.

5. The theory that the Greek way of war was determined by economic constraints was developed by G. B. Grundy, *Thucydides and the History of His Age*, 2d ed., 2 vols. (Oxford, 1948), and was generally followed until the 1980s. For example, Yvon Garlan, *Guerre et économie en Grèce ancienne* [*Warfare and the Economy in Ancient Greece*] (Paris, 1989). The "symbolic" interpretation I have adopted here I owe to Hanson, *Western Way of War;* Connor, "Early Greek Land Warfare"; Keegan, *A History of Warfare* (New York, 1993).

6. Peter Krentz, "Casualties in Hoplite Battles," *Greek, Roman, and Byzantine Studies* 26 (1985), 13–20, estimates losses in an average hoplite battle at 5 percent for the victors and 14 percent for the defeated. These estimates are based on battles in the classical period, and it seems possible that smaller battles were less bloody.

7. W. G. Runciman, "Doomed to Extinction: The *Polis* as an Evolutionary Dead-End," in *The Greek City from Homer to Alexander,* ed. Oswyn Murray and Simon Price (Oxford, 1990), 364–366.

8. G.E.M. de Ste. Croix, *Origins of the Peloponnesian War* (London, 1972), 218–220, argues that disputed border territories were the "characteristic" cause of Greek wars. The sources he cites do not seem to me to support this view. Border disputes are mentioned as *one* cause of war in Thucydides 1.122, 4.92, 5.79; Diodorus 3.33.

9. On religious practices in Greek warfare, see essays in W. K. Pritchett, *The Greek State at War,* 5 vols. (Berkeley, 1971–1991), and *Hoplites: The Classical Greek Battle Experience,* ed. V. D. Hanson (New York, 1991); K. J. Dover, *Greek Popular Morality in the Time of Plato and Aristotle* (Berkeley, 1974); Yvon Garlan, *War in the Ancient World: A Social History,* trans. Janet Lloyd (Ithaca, 1975); A. J. Holladay and M. D. Goodman, "Religious Scruples in Ancient Warfare," *Classical Quarterly* n.s. 36 (1986), 151–171. Readers familiar with Italian may consult V. Ilari, *Guerra e diritto nel mondo antico, I: Guerra e diritto nel mondo greco-ellenistico fino al III secolo* [*The Laws of War in the Ancient World,* vol. 1: *The Laws of War in the Greek and Hellenistic World to the Third Century*] (Milan, 1980).

10. When I speak of the world of Homer, I should make it clear that I refer to his literary world, not his real world, the reconstruction of which is immensely controversial. Homer probably lived late enough to know something about phalanx warfare, and many scholars, including Pritchett, have discerned phalanxlike formations in the *Iliad.* But the foreground is occupied by a much more antique kind of fighting—individual duels between heroes using chariots, bronze weapons, and throwing spears—in part perhaps a deliberate anachronism to satisfy Homer's aristocratic audience.

11. For this idealizing tendency (a touch of which I have noted in Herodotus), see E. L. Wheeler, "Ephorus and the Prohibition of Missiles," *Transactions of the American Philological Association* 117 (1987), 157–182.

12. For an introduction, see C. G. Starr, *The Influence of Sea Power on Ancient History* (New York, 1989). F. E. Adcock, in his widely read *The Greek and Macedonian Art of War* (Berkeley, 1957), may underestimate the effectiveness of ancient navies when he expresses doubt that triremes could have rammed sturdy sailing ships (38). But if not, they would have been useful only for fighting other triremes, which is to say, for nothing. Triremes were expected to ram and board freighters (see Plato, *Laches* 183), and they had no difficulty in turning to piracy with profit (see Herodotus 6.17).

13. The concept was popularized by Geoffrey Parker, *The Military Revolution: Military Innovation and the Rise of the West, 1500–1800* (Cambridge, 1988), who pointed out the parallel between the military revolution of early modern Europe and that of ancient China, but rather surprisingly did not mention the ancient Greeks, though the phrase "military revolution" had already been applied to fourth-century Greece in Arther Ferrill's *The Origins of War* (London, 1985).

The effects of the new developments in siegecraft on the autonomy of the *polis* are emphasized by Josiah Ober, *Fortress Attica: Defense of the Athenian Land Frontier, 404–322 B. C.* (Leiden, 1985).

Chapter Four

The Ethics of Greek Warfare

Just Warfare

The semifictional orations in Thucydides leave the impression that in the fifth century B.C., Athenian political rhetoric was capable of a startling degree of Machiavellian realism, but we have no real political speeches from that period. Many survive from the fourth century, and they are decidedly more moralistic in tone than the Thucydidean speeches. Outside Athens, this was probably the dominant tone of Greek political rhetoric at any time. Orators did not hesitate to apply to states the same moral standards they applied to individuals. The worldwide primitive code of honorable vengeance was taken for granted: No war could be undertaken without a just (*dikaios*) cause, and justice (*dikaion*) was a key word in relations with other states; and a just cause meant simply that the enemy had wronged the state. As the speakers in the dialogue *Alcibiades* agreed, the job of the orator was to persuade his audience that they were victims of violence, deceit, or spoliation.

The Athenian funeral orations (*epitaphioi*) honoring those killed in war provide a unique record of the public self-image of a Greek citizen body.[1] They place great importance on foreign policy: They claim that Athens never started a war without good cause, and they especially emphasize the services Athens rendered to all the Greeks during the Persian Wars. The *Funeral Oration* attributed to Demosthenes asserts that the Athenians had never done wrong to either Greek or barbarian and in addition, intervened actively to prevent injustices elsewhere—stopping unjust wars between Greek cities and protecting all the Greeks from Persian conquest (*Epitaphios* 7–11).

Moralism reaches its height in the work of the great rhetorician Isocrates, who considered himself a sort of philosopher with a mission to raise political oratory to a new level of reflection and ethical purpose. His discourses are filled with praise for the deeds of the Athenians, and his great influence on

later Greek, and European, literature made his work a major influence on
the rhetoric of war and peace. He repeated the themes of the Funeral Orations even before non-Athenian audiences. In his *Panegyric,* delivered at the
Olympic Games around 380 B.C., he told the Panhellenic crowd that the
Athenians were the only Greeks to have always possessed the same land (a
favorite theme of the funeral orations), and therefore their polis was not
based on conquest like some others (a pointed reference to Sparta); the naval
empire that Athens acquired after the Persian Wars was granted willingly by
the other Greeks; the Athenians were regarded as saviors by their subject
cities, whom they protected from foreign invaders and domestic oligarchs
(*Panegyric* 24, 72, 80, 104–106). His advice to the Cypriot prince Nicocles—
the earliest specimen of the "mirror for princes" literature, which would go
on repeating this high-flown advice to princes until Machiavelli finally punc-
tured it—shows the generally accepted Greek views about the ethics of interstate relations: Make no unjust wars, honor all treaties, do not desire to
rule all men (*To Nicoles* 22–26). Be *polemikos,* "warlike," in always being
prepared for war, but *eirenikos,* "peaceable," in never going to war without a
just cause (*To Nicoles* 24; compare *On the Peace* 136). The foreign policy of
Athens is said to have followed the principle "It is not just for the strong to
rule the weak"(*On the Peace* 69). This maxim comes from a pamphlet written about 355 to persuade the Athenians to curb their imperial ambitions.
The advice was meant to refute those principles of *raison d'état,* taught by
certain Sophists and familiar to us from Thucydides's speeches, that claimed
it *is* just for the strong to rule the weak.

Just Hegemony

These moralistic statements about foreign policy are so common in Greek
literature that they have led some modern historians to assume that Greeks
were so dedicated to the principle of *polis* autonomy that they condemned
any attempt by any city to dominate other cities; and some have attributed
to this mindset the failure of the classical Greeks to create a unified political
framework.[2] This interpretation misses an important point about the Greek
idea of justice in interstate relations. Being just to one's neighbors did not
prevent one from dominating them. *Hegemonia* (leadership) was not a bad
word. Even *arche* (rule) was not always a bad word. Isocrates said that the
Athenians in their great days had been leaders (*hegemones*) of other Greeks,
not *despotai,* or slavemasters (*Panegyric* 80); rulers (*archein*), but not tyrants
(*tyrannizein*) (*On the Peace* 91). Greeks thought hegemony a noble goal and
assumed that any city that was able to would aim for it. No contradiction
was felt between the hunger for freedom and the desire for hegemony. In
fact, they were almost two sides of the same coin. Freedom was assumed to
entail a desire to rule others. It was said of Cyrus the Great that he found the
Persians slaves and made them free, found them subjects and made them

kings (Herodotus 1.210). Thucydides summarized the Athenian character by calling Athenians accustomed not only to being free but to ruling other cities (8.68). The implication of such language is that freedom is somehow incomplete without domination.[3]

The vindicativeness of the ancient just war concept made it easy for just warfare to become just hegemony. The principle that all wars were honorable if one sided with the injured party provided a ready excuse for intervention in the affairs of other states. The orators previously cited declared Athens a just city not only because Athens refrained from unjust wars but also because it took up the cause of other cities that were victims of unjust war; that is to say, Athens exercised a just hegemony. The mark of a just hegemony was that it was excercised for the benefit of weaker states, which submitted to it willingly and gratefully. Therefore just wars were often fought to acquire just hegemonies, without any sense of contradiction. Furthermore, all agreed that a city must fight for its honor and that honor and glory were supremely valuable for their own sake. Isocrates told the crowd at the Olympic Games that the gods must have brought about the Persian Wars deliberately so that the Athenians could win deathless fame (*Panegyric* 84). Finally, just wars brought gain as well as glory and safety, and there was nothing wrong with accepting it. Isocrates assured his Cypriot prince that a just ruler was one who left his kingdom enlarged (*Nicocles* 63)—perhaps not necessarily larger in *extent*, but surely not excluding this possibility. The final speech Thucydides attributed to Pericles contains a justification for the Athenian empire that is less moralistic than those cited earlier but still accords with the general Greek notions of international conduct:

> Even if now (since all things are born to decay) there should come a time when we were forced to yield: yet still it will be remembered that of all Hellenic powers we held the widest sway over the Hellenes, that we stood firm in the greatest wars against their combined forces and against individual states, that we lived in a city which had been perfectly equipped in every direction and which was the greatest in Hellas. (2.64 [trans. Rex Warner])

When Pericles speaks here of the greatness of Athens, he is not thinking of the Parthenon.

The productions of Isocrates may smell of the study, but real orations delivered in the open air of the Pnyx on questions of war and peace sound much the same. One of the earliest political speeches we have, Lysias's *Against the Subversion of the Ancestral Constitution* (*Oration* 34), delivered immediately after the end of the Peloponnesian War, justified the Athenian empire that had just been lost in the same moralistic terms. The series of speeches by Demosthenes against the rising power of Macedon reiterated the unswerving justice of Athenian foreign policy and praised the voluntary and beneficial nature of the old Athenian empire. The Peloponnesian War, according to him, had been fought by Athens to defend the rights of all the

Greeks against Sparta (*Second Olynthiac* 24; compare *Third Olynthiac* 24–26, *Fourth Philippic* 24–27).

Sometimes the orators so emphasized the aggressive and vindicative character of the just war as to imply that neutral states had a positive duty to intervene in a war on the side of the injured party even when it was no quarrel of their own. Demosthenes, in his *Third Philippic* (341 B.C.), urged the Greek cities to unite against Macedon, claiming that in the past Greeks had never hesitated to unite against any city that was perceived as practicing injustice against its neighbors, whether the culprit was Athens or Sparta (23–29). If taken literally, this theory would, of course, make neutrality immoral. Rhetoric of that sort may appear in any war that takes on the character of a moral crusade: Neutrals in World War II were accused of failing to fight Nazism; those during the Cold War were blamed for not fighting Communism. But the vindicative concept of the just war made every war seem a moral crusade and made it very easy to condemn neutrals.[4]

In fact, the rhetoric of just war could be used to defend not only hegemony but outright imperialism. One of the most influential texts about warfare produced in antiquity was Xenophon's *Education of Cyrus* (*Cyropaedia*), an enormous and fanciful quasi-historical work purporting to be a biography of Cyrus the Great, the founder of the Persian empire and the most successful conqueror who had ever lived up to that time (the mid-fourth century B.C.). In the text, the author makes the young Cyrus declare early in his career that he will fight only just wars, to protect himself and his friends (1.5.13). Most of the ensuing narrative is taken up by the indubitably just war that Cyrus wages against the great alliance formed against him by Croesus of Lydia. In the course of this war, Cyrus conquers all sorts of people, whom he immediately makes his friends, thereby winning their admiration and voluntary submission. "Friendship" (*philia*) in Greek diplomatic usage implied a relationship of nonhostility between two states, not necessarily including a military alliance, though the Greeks could also speak of "friends and allies." After he takes Babylon, Cyrus makes a long speech to his army praising the gods for his victory (7.5.72–86). He justifies his brand-new empire on the following three grounds: (1) It is a law of nature that all the possessions of the conquered become the property of the conqueror; (2) This was a just war because our enemies plotted against us; (3) We Persians have proven ourselves better than they, so we deserve to rule them.

This is an interesting summary of the Greek ethic of war. The Sophists and orators of the late fifth and fourth centuries often classified wars under three headings—gain, safety, and glory, as Hobbes called them. Cyrus's first point reflects sophistic rationalism and belongs to a tradition of thought entirely different from the one just surveyed; it will be discussed in the next chapter. The second point repeats the familiar just war doctrine; and the third presents an unusually blatant statement of the doctrine of just hegemony, reflecting the idealized picture of an Athenian empire governed through the voluntary cooperation of its subjects and justified by the benefits it brings them, which we have just traced in the Attic orators. Throughout Xenophon's history, Cyrus has fought just wars and built up this empire of virtue. But what follows comes as a surprise to the modern reader. Cyrus now proceeds cheerfully and effortlessly to conquer all the rest of the known world (8.6.20–23), without the slightest attempt at any further justification of his conquests. There is no suggestion that from now on any of Cyrus's victims will be so foolish as to provoke him. Apparently, once Cyrus has established the just empire and demonstrated his fitness to rule it, there is no objection to expanding it. His continued popularity among his subjects is emphasized, and probably there is an underlying assumption that all future wars of expansion have to be just wars, too; in other words, Cyrus cannot conquer anybody unless they have first done something to offend him, though Xenophon is certainly casual about the matter.[5]

The same assumptions, in a less imperialistic form, appear in Plato and Aristotle. The ideal city described in the *Laws* of Plato is to be isolated from foreign contact as much as possible, yet Plato assumes that even this city must be prepared to fight wars—not only to defend itself, but also to assist neighboring cities when they are being wronged (*Laws* 737).

The work of Aristotle offers the clearest theory of warfare. He takes for granted the necessity of the just war: A state must be self-sufficient or it cannot be a state, therefore one of the basic elements of any state is that which protects its freedom (*Politics* 4.4, 1291a). He criticizes excessively warlike states like Sparta and various barbarian states because they make war for its own sake and seek to dominate their neighbors without their consent (7.2, 1324b). In Aristotle's view, the just city will take peace, not war, as its aim and will fight wars only to get peace; only peace is seemly (*kalos*), war is merely necessary and useful; therefore "we should choose war for the sake of peace, work for the sake of leisure, necessary and useful things for the sake of the noble" (7.14, 1333a [trans. Sinclair and Saunders]).

According to Aristotle, in addition to wars fought for freedom and safety, wars may be fought "to win a position of leadership, exercised for the benefit of the ruled, not with a view to being the master of all" (7.14, 1333b, trans. Sinclair and Saunders). He assumed that any state, if it is to live the life of a state and not that of a hermit, must maintain a large military establishment and conduct regular military interventions into the affairs of other states, and he criticizes Plato's ideal state in the *Laws* for its isolationism (2.6, 1265a). Further, if the state is to be a hegemonic state it must also have a big navy (7.6, 1327a). It is taken for granted that hegemony is desirable.

Aristotle's views on just war and just hegemony are therefore entirely traditional. But this is not the case with a third type of warfare he distinguishes—the war against the barbarians.

The Panhellenic Crusade

"Panhellenism" is a modern coinage describing the spirit of cultural and national unity that arose among the Greeks during the Persian Wars. Greek unity against the barbarians was a major theme in the histories of Herodotus, to which we will turn shortly. During the Peloponnesian War, which tore that unity apart, the Sophist Gorgias made a speech at the Olympic Games urging all Greeks to bury their quarrels and unite against the Persians as their fathers had done. The orator Lysias made a speech on the same theme at the Olympic Games of 384 B.C. (*Oration* 33). It was a recurrent idea in the discourses of Isocrates. In his *Panegyric,* delivered at the Olympic Games of 380, he called upon Athens and Sparta to bring together all the other cities under their leadership for a war of revenge against the Persians, referring to this kind of war as the only type that is better than peace, more like a *theoria* (festival or sacred embassy) than a *strateia* (military campaign) (*Panegyric* 182). The identity of the barbarian enemy might change: Around 354, Demosthenes was still calling for Greek unity against Persia (*Oration* 14) but soon afterward tried to substitute Macedon for Persia. In his long series of anti-Macedonian orations he repeatedly portrayed the Macedonians (who in fact spoke a sort of Greek dialect but had never been much influenced by southern Greek culture) as total barbarians and called for a Panhellenic crusade against them. Isocrates, who belonged to the pro-Macedonian faction at Athens, naturally took the opposite line, baptizing Philip of Macedon as a full Greek and urging him to lead a Panhellenic war against the traditional Persian enemy (*To Philip,* 346 B.C.).

The novelty of Panhellenism can easily be exaggerated. In practice, the appeal to pan-Greek feeling was almost always an excuse for hegemony.[6] The literature of this era shows how commonly the Athenian hegemony was justified by references to the leadership Athens had provided against the Persians. The Spartan hegemony that succeeded it was justified in the same way. When Panhellenism meant something deeper, it seems to have appealed to a small circle of intellectuals, none of whom suggested that it meant the individual *polis* should sacrifice its autonomy. Even they used the traditional just war rhetoric, for the crusade was always justified as an act of vengeance for the Persian attack on the Greeks. According to Herodotus (5.49), Aristagoras of Miletus came to Sparta just before the Persian Wars to persuade the Spartans to liberate the Greeks of Asia from Persian rule, offering arguments based on safety, glory, and gain: Firstly, they would please the gods by defending the freedom of fellow Greeks (the traditional just war argument); secondly, the Spartans had a particular obligation to do this because they were the strongest power in Greece (the traditional just hegemony argument); thirdly, they could then seize all the wealth of Asia (which he next described in detail). The third argument was thought especially appropriate for a war against barbarians. It is true that Greeks saw nothing wrong in profiting from a just war even against other Greeks, but at that time, wars among Greeks offered little chance for large-scale spoliation.

Nevertheless, Isocrates seems to suggest that there is something qualitatively different about a war against barbarians. This idea was then being developed at the Academy of Plato. In Plato's *Republic,* probably written at about the same time as Isocrates's *Panegyric,* it takes the form of a utopian scheme; indeed, this is the first plan for the reform of international relations that deserves the adjective "utopian." In the new code of warfare Plato proposed, all wars between Greek cities would be regarded as civil wars, and no defeated Greek city would ever be occupied, enslaved, or dishonored. Wars against barbarians, however, would be fought to the limit, using every extreme of ruthlessness and deceit. It is hinted that the need to capture slaves from the barbarians (for under the new rules they could no longer be taken from Greeks) would provide an incentive for Greeks to unite in crusades, or slave raids, into barbarian territory and would help to reduce warfare among Greeks (*Republic* 469–471).

Plato's pupil Aristotle presented this idea systematically in a passage already quoted in part:

> As for military training, the object in practicing it regularly is not to bring into subjection those not worthy of such treatment, but to enable men (a) to save themselves from being subject to others [the just war], (b) to win a position of leadership, exercised for the benefit of the ruled, not with a view to being master of all [the just hegemony], and (c) to exercise the rule of a master over those who deserve to be slaves [the holy war]. (*Politics* 7.14, 1333b38–1334a2 [trans. Sinclair and Saunders])

Aristotle refers here to the notorious theory of natural slavery that he developed in the first book of the *Politics.* He argues there that some peoples (barbarians) are slaves by nature, so it is in accordance with nature to make war on them for the purpose of ruling and exploiting them, without regard for their welfare. Such warfare is one of the natural human economic systems: Some peoples live by farming, some by pastoralism, and some by predation, which may be directed against wild beasts, against fish, or against the sort of men who are slaves by nature. If we prey upon beasts, it is called hunting; if the prey is piscine, it is called fishing; and if we go after slavelike men, we call it either piracy or war, depending apparently on the scale of the effort (*Politics* 1.8, 1256ab; 7.2, 1324b).

This anthropological theory drew upon certain older Greek ideas about the origins of society.[7] Some Sophist, perhaps Protagoras (author of a lost work called *On the Original State*), had suggested that the original cause of warfare was greed for wealth. This theory seems implicit in the description of early mankind at the beginning of Thucydides's history, and it was assumed by Plato both in the *Republic* (373) and the *Laws* (678). To suggest that predation is in the course of nature is of course to suggest amoral realism in politics and the rejection of the traditional Greek ethic of warfare. Some Sophists had not hesitated to draw that conclusion, as will become clear in the next chapter. But that is not at all the conclusion that Plato and Aristotle wished to draw. Aristotle says that warfare is a basic and natural mode of economic life on the same moral level as the fishing industry but then immediately adds that it is natural only when used against such men as are natural slaves: "We must try to exercise master-like rule not over all people but only over those fit for such treatment—just as we should not pursue human beings for food or sacrifice, but only such wild animals as are edible and so suitable to be hunted for this purpose" (trans. Sinclair and Saunders) (*Politics* 7.2, 1324b).

This is the clearest statement in Greek literature of the view that a crusade against barbarians is quite distinct from the normal wars of justice and leadership and that one does not need a just cause to make war on inferior human races. We do not know how widely shared this concept was. Isocrates also says that warfare against barbarians is like hunting animals (*Panathenaic Oration* 163). When Aristotle's pupil Alexander invaded the Persian empire, we know that he justified the war in traditional ethical terms, as a war of vengeance for the Persian invasions of Greece; but the later Alexander legend also emphasizes how Alexander enriched himself with fantastic booty, asserting that all the possessions of the conquered belong to the conqueror, as his teacher would have approved in the case of conquered barbarians.[8] And later Greek and Latin literature was always ambivalent about the morality of Alexander's conquests, as will be discussed later on.

In conclusion, Greek morality placed few restrictions on warfare. Any wrong could provide a legitimate excuse for war. Wrongs might include insults as well as injuries; in *Alcibiades I*, for example, deceit is considered just as valid a cause for war as violence or spoliation. There was no statue of limitations for either insult or injury, so no one seemed to think it strange when Alexander claimed he would attack the Persians in just retaliation for the Persian Wars—which had taken place more than a century earlier. Ideas about justice in interstate relations were always compatible with the exercise of hegemony by a powerful state. The elasticity of these ideas made it relatively easy to justify almost anything. Nevertheless, by the later fourth century, warfare among Greek cities was increasingly regarded as an unmitigated evil, and there was a movement among philosophers and rhetoricians to terminate it and deflect its energies into a cultural holy war against the East.

The Moral Theory of History: Herodotus[9]

The ideas discussed here were widespread in the classical Greek world. All professed to believe in the justice of war for honor, all acquiesced when convenient in just leadership, and many had at least heard of the notion that there was something specially just about a war of all the Greeks against the non-Greek. But there was another way of looking at warfare, probably not yet widely known except to some intellectuals, that deserves attention here: The idea that history operates according to a moral and divine law that reveals itself in the rise and fall of states and empires. Warfare is the main instrument of this law, and therefore warfare has a meaning and a cause concealed from the human actors. This philosophy of history—and written history itself—was the invention of Herodotus, who developed the new genre for the purpose of commemorating and explaining warfare.

The concept of a prose epic about the Persian Wars issued from the mind of Herodotus with the unexpectedness of Athena springing from the brow of Zeus. Before he wrote, the Greeks were poor in records of the past. They had no royal or priestly documents like the king-lists, annals, and inscriptions of the East; this was well and good, for no genuine curiosity about the past could have arisen from that tradition of triumphal theocracy. For knowledge of the legendary past, Greeks depended upon a mass of mythological traditions, constantly reenacted by the poets; for recent events, popular storytellers probably recited, perhaps wrote down, praises of the deeds of famous men and cities. To weave this material into a connected Homeric narrative was, so far as we know, the inspiration of Herodotus.

In doing so, Herodotus established certain expectations about historical narrative that were to last as long as the classical tradition. These are summarized in Herodotus's opening sentence: "I, Herodotus of Halicarnassus, am here setting forth my history [*historie,* literally 'inquiry'], that time may not draw the color from what man has brought into being, nor those great and wonderful deeds, manifested by both Greeks and barbarians, fail of their report, and, together with all this, the reason why they fought one another" (trans. David Grene). The purpose is twofold, poetic and investigative. The new genre is a commemoration of great deeds of war in epic fashion but also an inquiry into the *aitiai,* the causes or reasons of the war.

Let us consider first the affinities between the historian and the poet. It was assumed in antiquity that the historian, like the epic poet, should deal not with the past as such but only with great and memorable deeds, especially wars; that the historian's narrative should be a unified and artful composition, given a natural unity by the theme of a great war, imposing its own explanation upon events, not through direct statements interjected by the author but through a creative process of selection and emphasis using narrative and dramatic devices borrowed from the poets. Herodotus created word pictures like Homer, giving his characters speeches and conversations to dramatize situations; he visualized sequences of episodes like the scenes of an Attic tragedy, scenes that often consisted of dialogues between a leader and his councillors or messengers. Dramatic construction and fictionalized speeches would always remain standard devices of classical historiography, imparting to it an immediacy like that of a historical novel: The historian puts us in the place of the historical figures and invites us to vicariously share their experience.

But the narrative strategies of Herodotus are closer to epic than those of any later historian. He creates a linear, strung-out, episodic narrative, moving from one topic to the next with a storyteller's logic, often ignoring chronological sequence, relying on the devices of oral style to bind the story together. There is much use of the epic framing device called ring composition: Herodotus reminds us at the beginning and again at the end about the significance of the Trojan War, prefigurement of all later East-West conflicts; the story begins with the enslavement of Ionia and ends with the liberation of Ionia; episodes and digressions are enclosed by framing sentences, rounded off by repetition at the end of the formula heard at the beginning. Within these concentric rings, the stories (*logoi*) are connected by links that take us sometimes forward, sometimes backward, and sometimes sideways, but the narrative progresses.

The main narrative link is the simple principle of *reciprocal action*. Herodotus presents us with a cast of about one thousand characters, gathered from the Greek collective memory that stretched back one hundred years, all of which information was stored and organized in his own astonishing memory. The characters are linked by exchanges of benefits that commonly take the form of gifts and exchanges of injuries that commonly turn into blood debts. Both alliances and enmities are hereditary and often span generations, connecting past and present through a tangled web of contracts. This network of inherited obligation forms the basic structure of Herodotean narrative—in effect a chain of stories linked together by the principle of action and reaction, of tit for tat.

Some exchanges have hidden hooks connected to events that lie in the future. For instance, the first alliance between Greeks and Orientals—a key link—was made when the Spartans sent to Croesus of Lydia the gift of a great bronze bowl, which somehow ended up on Samos (1.70). Long after, this bowl reappears. In recounting the Persian conquest of Egypt, Herodotus mentions that some Samians were involved in it, then goes back to fill us in on the recent history of Samos. We learn that Samos was attacked by the Spartans in revenge for the theft of Croesus's bowl (3.39ff.). The bowl, which earlier symbolized the first Spartan alliance in Asia, now causes the first Spartan military venture on the Asian coast. It suggests a growing network of exchanges, drawing Europe and Asia fatefully together. And it gives Herodotus an opportunity to insert a digression, the famous story of Polycrates's ring, which reminds us of one of his key themes—the gods' jealousy of prosperity.

The chain of action and reaction is not meaningless. It reveals a pattern in the world, which manifests itself at the *transgression of limits*. The central metaphor of Herodotus is that there are important spatial boundaries that men in pursuit of their multitudinous contracts cross only at their peril. The natural boundary between Europe and Asia is mentioned at the beginning, and the Persian temptation to cross it is a recurrent theme, repeated on a progressively larger scale in the reigns of Cambyses, Darius, and Xerxes. The epic story ends with the magical revenge of the hero Protesilaus, the first Greek to land at Troy, reminding us of the mythic theme of East-West conflict with which the tale began.

These boundaries are set by the gods. Sometimes we are told that the gods take vengeance for human crimes. Herodotus explains the fall of Troy in that way (2.120) and, likewise, the fall of Lydia (1.13), but this belief seems to weaken as we approach the present, for he does not try to explain the fall of Persia in those terms. More often we are told that the gods are simply jealous of human prosperity. At the council where Xerxes orders the invasion of Greece, Artabanus, a folkloric wise counselor, warns him that the gods' lightning strikes the tallest trees (7.10; compare 1.32, 1.207, 3.40). Sometimes there is a sense of a vague necessity behind the gods. The Delphic oracle tells Croesus of Lydia that even Apollo could not prevent his defeat, though the god had managed to delay the course of fate for Croesus for three years (1.91). There seems to be an overarching plan or providence in the world, a plan that keeps down the numbers of lions but multiplies hares (3.108). The gods' just retribution, the gods' jealous lightning, the beneficial providence of the gods or fates—all are different ways of describing the same thing. Herodotus and his people assume there is an order in the cosmos, which takes on different masks at different times, and are not interested in a more precise theology.

Herodotus was unique among pagan historians in the importance he assigns to divine forces, and such summaries as the one made here may leave the impression that his characters are mere puppets controlled by divine forces, but that is hardly the impression left by *reading* Herodotus. His main actions have two parallel sets of causation, the divine and the human, which constantly interact. Such multiple causation is a habit of the primitive mind. It is everywhere in the Homeric poems, in which gods continually interfere in human actions; yet humans are assumed to be completely responsible for their actions, and divine causation is never pleaded as an excuse. Herodotus writes for an audience that perceived no tension between the two levels of causation: Everything that is fated must be worked out by human agency, everything of importance done by human agency must be fated, and human events may be viewed from either perspective.[10]

In practice, the plans of the gods are effected through the chain of retributive action that forms the basic structure of Herodotean narrative and the Herodotean world. This is not only a narrative device but a historical explanation. If it reflects an old-fashioned view of the world, it is for that reason appropriate to the times Herodotus describes. As we have seen, the traditional Greek concept of war is essentially revenge war. Communities are connected in time by a process of vengeance and countervengeance that has an inherent tendency to transgress limits. Men have to avenge wrongs, with the help of the gods; but they will always be tempted to overreact and over-reach, to exceed natural boundaries, to disturb the balance of the world, thus inviting the gods' jealousy, which, from another point of view, is the gods' retribution and, from yet another, the gods' wise providence.

These great metaphors or myths—the chain of retributive action, the proper realm and the danger of crossing its boundaries—are the ultimate "causes" of events in Herodotus's story. These myths are, among other things, *political* explanations. Herodotus's boundary crossing is a political idea as well as a literary motif; he had perceived a main problem of interstate relations and warfare, the tendency of power to overextend itself. But Herodotus's political explanations are never separated from their mythical nexus, and political actions are always described in terms of personal inten-tion and moral evaluation. The poetic conventions of Herodotus's culture did not call for further analysis. His main literary models, the Greek epic and tragedy, are about the willed acts of heroic individuals and, behind them, the inscrutable will of the gods; and the willed act remains a final mystery. At the core of Herodotus's narrative is a theme out of tragedy—the tale of the wrath of Xerxes, who tried to pass limits set by gods and men.

But there are other kinds of "causes." Sometimes Herodotus can see cer-tain patterns in history. The dominant motif is a vision of human life as a *kyklos,* a revolving wheel, which allows no one to remain long in prosperity (1.207). He sees the uniqueness of human events, but under the glass of eter-nity the main lesson is their essential sameness. His opening declaration that certain great deeds are uniquely worthy of remembrance is soon followed by a reminder that there is nothing new under the sun: "I will go forward in my account, covering alike the small and great cities of mankind. For of those that were great in earlier times most have now become small, and those that were great in my time were small in the time before. Since, then, I know that man's good fortune never abides in the same place, I will make mention of both alike" (1.5 [trans. Grene]).

The other pattern is that of the succession of empires—an idea that does not seem wholly compatible with that of the revolving wheel, as it implies that not all events are the same.[11] In the background of Herodotus's story lies the assumption that there had been a series of major empires in Asia: first, the Assyrian, then the Median, and finally the Persian (1.95, 130). He suggests that the sequence was not accidental: Poor peoples are tough and warlike and rich peoples soft and unwarlike, so the poor tend to attack the rich and the rich tend to make easy marks (1.71, 1.126, 5.49, 7.102, 9.122). Implicit in this scheme is an idea that there is something natural and fated in the succession, because a nation that becomes imperial becomes soft and vul-nerable almost immediately. The theme of the succession of empires later be-came popular, for it provided not only an explanation for the rise of empires but a means of predicting their fall. It may have caught on at the end of the fourth century, when the Persian empire fell to Alexander, and Greeks immediately cast Macedon as the fourth world empire. The philosopher Demetrius of Phalerum, as reported by Polybius (29.21), made this connection in Alexander's lifetime and drew the conclusion that it was only a matter of time until the empire of the Macedonians went the same way. It will be explained later what happened when Rome became the fifth and last of the world empires.

Notes

1. Nicole Loraux, *The Invention of Athens: The Funeral Oration in the Classical City,* English trans. (Cambridge, Mass., 1986), thinks the *epitaphios logos,* which was unique to Athens, was invented in the mid-fifth century to celebrate democracy. Examples attributed to Lysias and Demosthenes, and fragments of funeral orations by other orators, have survived, along with fictional specimens like the Funeral Oration of Pericles in Thucydides (which is untypical in that it says nothing about the past history of the city) and the oration attributed to Aspasia in Plato's *Menexenus,* which some think was meant as a parody of the genre but which was taken seriously in later antiquity.

2. W. S. Ferguson, *Greek Imperialism* (New York, 1941), said the political thought of Aristotle was blinded by "the aversion instinctively felt by his age for imperialism," which made it impossible for the Greeks to contemplate any political organization larger than the city-state (111ff.).

3. J.A.O. Larsen, "Freedom and Its Obstacles in Ancient Greece," *Classical Philology* 57 (1962), 230–234.

4. A recent book, *The Concept of Neutrality in Classical Greece* by R. A. Bauslaugh (Berkeley, 1991), asks, I think, the wrong question. The Greeks did not really have a concept of neutrality in the sense Bauslaugh means. They knew, of course, that the option of "keeping the peace" (their usual expression for "neutrality") was often open. But for them, neutrality was not an important goal of foreign policy. Their central concept in such debates was not neutrality but rather the just war; the main question was not Should we remain neutral? but Must we go to war? Neutrality becomes a positive goal in itself only in a modern diplomatic world where war is seen as an avoidable evil that should be practiced only in self-defense.

5. I must disagree with Bodil Due, *The Cyropaedia: Xenophon's Aims and Methods* (Aarhus, Denmark 1989), who finds in Cyrus's policies a modern and sophisticated distinction between offensive and defensive warfare (158–163).

6. S. Perlman, "Isokrates' Advice on Philip's Attitudes Toward Barbarians (V, 154)," *Historia* 16 (1967), 338–343; "Isocrates' *Philippus* and Panhellenism," *Historia* 18 (1969), 370–374; and "Panhellenism, the Polis and Imperialism," *Historia* 25 (1976), 1–30.

7. Thomas Cole, *Democritus and the Sources of Greek Anthropology* (Cleveland, 1967).

8. Michael Austin, "Alexander and the Macedonian Invasion of Asia: Aspects of the Historiography of War and Empire in Antiquity," in *War and Society in the Greek World,* ed. John Rich and Graham Shipley (London, 1993), 197–223.

9. There has been a notable revival of interest in Herodotus in recent decades. For a short introduction to the subject I recommend John Gould, *Herodotus* (New York, 1989). The interpretation offered here also owes much to H. R. Immerwahr, *Form and Thought in Herodotus* (Cleveland, 1966); M. L. Lang, *Herodotean Narrative and Discourse* (Cambridge, Mass., 1984); Donald Lateiner, *The Historical Method of Herodotus* (Toronto, 1989). Herodotus's reliability as a reporter has been much attacked, but he is ably defended by W. K. Pritchett, *The Liar School of Herodotus* (Amsterdam, 1993).

10. E. R. Dodds, *The Greeks and the Irrational* (Berkeley, 1951), is a classic study of this syndrome.

11. Some have attributed the succession-of-empires theory to Oriental sources because the three empires in the original scheme were all Asian, but it seems more likely an invention of Greek historiography. The only large empires known to the Greeks then *were* Asian. See J. W. Swain, "The Theory of the Four Monarchies: Opposition History Under the Roman Empire," *Classical Philology* 35 (1940), 1–21; Jacqueline de Romilly, *The Rise and Fall of States According to Greek Authors,* trans. Philip Thody (Ann Arbor, Mich., 1977); D. Mendels, "The Five Empires: A Note on a Propagandistic *Topos,*" *American Journal of Philology* 102 (1981), 330–337; E. J. Gruen, *The Hellenistic World and the Coming of Rome* (Berkeley, 1984), 329, 339; Austin, "Alexander and the Macedonian Invasion of Asia."

Chapter Five

The Greeks and Raison d'Etat

The Sophists of War

The most original contribution of the Greeks to military thought was their self-conscious development of the concept of *raison d'état:* They perceived warfare as a rational and utilitarian instrument of politics and thought of interstate relations (at times) as a structure of power politics independent of moral questions. This approach to interstate affairs was pioneered by the Sophists of the fifth century B.C. and became common in political oratory, especially at Athens. The history of Thucydides is the great monument to this tradition. Thucydides actually wrote earlier than most of the extant orators, but we will consider the orators first, as they gave Thucydides his inspiration.

In the late fifth century, the art of war, like every other aspect of Greek political culture, came under the influence of the itinerant lecturers known as Sophists, with their generalizing, systematizing, classifying habits of thought. Sophists claimed that all political affairs, including war, could be controlled by dialectical reasoning, reduced to a skilled art or craft, and taught—for a suitable fee. Before the Sophists appeared there had been no such thing as formal military training in the Greek cities, except for Sparta and perhaps elite units like the Sacred Band of Thebes. In the Funeral Oration of Pericles, it is mentioned as a point of Athenian pride that Athens did not prepare its sons for war, in contrast to the strenuous training of the Spartans (Thucydides 2.39). But under the stresses of the long exhausting war of 431–404 B.C., the traditional cult of hoplite amateurism gave way to a new demand both for military professionalism and for experts to teach these skills, and they soon presented themselves.

During the war, several types of military training became fashionable.[1] The most elementary was called *hoplomachia,* the art of fencing with hoplite weapons, which was taught by many itinerant drillmasters. Plato's *Laches,* a dialogue set around 420, contains a discussion of this discipline, representing a sort of argument that must have been heard often in the Athens of Plato's youth. The fencing master eventually became one of the fixtures of the Greek gymnasium. His art was valued mostly as a gentlemanly accomplishment and exercise but was also a stepping-stone to certain more important military studies: *taktika,* the art of arranging troops, and *strategika,* the art of generalship.

In the early years of the war, there appeared at Athens two Sophists from Chios, Dionysodorus and his brother Euthydemus, who claimed they could teach anyone how to succeed in the office of general (*strategos*), which was filled by annual election. They offered training in all three techniques—*hoplomachia, taktika,* and *strategika.* They had the misfortune to be noticed both by Plato and by Xenophon, both of whom ridiculed them. In Plato's *Euthydemus* (271–273), Socrates exposes the pair as pompous frauds. In Xenophon's *Memorabilia* (3.1), one of Socrates's young friends, ambitious to be elected general, takes the course given by Dionysodorus, but is disappointed to find that Dionysodorus teaches nothing but *taktika,* the technique of drawing up soldiers in the phalanx, and does not instruct on how to use them in battle. There is more about this in Xenophon's *Education of Cyrus* (1.6.12–14), where the young Cyrus is forced to waste his time with another incompetent teacher who promises to teach the art of generalship but in fact knows nothing but *taktika.*

If Xenophon is to be believed, Dionysodorus of Chios was a mere drillmaster whose instruction could have little use outside the parade ground. But the Dionysodorus described by Plato claimed at least to be much more than a drillmaster. Perhaps Xenophon uses Dionysodorus as a straw man to represent a type of military Sophist he distrusted; or perhaps Dionysodorus, like some later military consultants, made large promises to justify his large fees.

By the end of the fifth century, these experts were well known throughout the Greek world, and some were entering the service of the Persian empire. In 401 B.C., Xenophon encountered a Greek mercenary in Anatolia named Phalinus, an expert in *hoplomachia* and *taktika,* who was advising a Persian satrap (*Anabasis* 2.1.7). Whether he was the one who gave Xenophon his contemptuous opinion of the type we do not know. Nor do we know what the higher military art of the Sophists was like. No treatises survive from before the middle of the fourth century. Still, it seems that the major breakthrough in systematic military thought came in the late fifth century. At that time, warfare came to be perceived as a rational art (*techne*) comparable to the arts of medicine, architecture, and rhetoric, to be analyzed logically and in purely human terms, leaving the gods out of it. The rhetorical education the Sophists imparted taught men how to argue through a situation, considering all the alternatives and making judgments based on principles of human behavior. They taught, that is, what we usually mean by "strategy."

The semifictional speeches in Thucydides suggest that they taught strategy on a high level. If the Sophists claimed to teach everything a general should know, this must have included the ability to make convincing speeches on foreign policy to the assembly. In Xenophon's view (attributed to Socrates), the art of generalship should include knowledge of finances, treaties, and alliances, as well as all other subjects that figure in political oratory (*Memorabilia* 3.1–6).

No examples of political oratory are extant before the end of the fifth century, but some early forensic (judicial) and epideictic (display) orations have survived that give us some notion of what political speeches before the assembly must have been like. The famous Sophist Gorgias has left us two pieces, called the *Helen* and the *Palamedes,* both of which are fictitious legal defenses of figures from the Trojan War. The *Palamedes* (13ff.) attempts to exonerate Palamedes, whom Odysseus accused of treachery to the Greeks, by listing all the possible motives for treachery—power, wealth, honor, safety, and so on—and showing that Palamedes could not have been tempted by any of them. This reminds us of the techniques used by some of Thucydides's orators: the analysis of a situation by listing all possible hypotheses, the attempt to give the impression that every possibility has been included, and the judgment of likelihood based on allegations about normal and expected human behavior. Thucydides's Athenian orators defend Athenian imperialism in the same way, by listing all possible motives for empire (all three of which—wealth, honor and safety—appear in Gorgias's list), based on generalizations about human nature (Thucydides 1.76).[2]

The Just and the Advantageous

One of the leading insights of the sophistic revolution was to make a clear distinction between the just (*dikaion*) and the advantageous (*sympheron*), which permitted rational debate about war and diplomacy. This seems to have been more common in fifth-century political rhetoric, as will be apparent when we turn to Thucydides; but even in the fourth century, the generally high-minded ethical tone of the orators was not thought inconsistent with a blunt recognition that there exists a code of reality or nature that is indifferent to human notions of justice.

The ambivalence of Isocrates on this question in his *Panathenaic Oration* is remarkable. He tells his audience that relations with other states can be carried out either in accordance with law, which means that states do not go to war without just cause, or according to reality (*aletheia*), which means that only power matters (46). He condemns the Spartans for their "realistic" foreign policy and praises Athens for following justice, which was one of his favorite themes. But later in this discourse, he admits the Athenian empire was unjust and excuses it on the grounds that Athens had no choice, saying it is better to do wrong to other states than to suffer wrong oneself (117).

Therefore, there are some circumstances in which realism must be preferred to justice, at least where freedom is at stake. Isocrates seems troubled by this admission and later returns to the problem: Why does justice not always pay in dealing with other states? The answer he gives is this: It is because the gods are careless and their vast negligence often permits the just to lose and the unjust to win. He then comments that to be sure, men *should* esteem a just defeat over an unjust victory, and sometimes they can, for men praise the Spartan defeat at Thermopylae as grander than any victory; but alas, this is not the common attitude (185–187).

Demosthenes is sometimes blunter. In his *First Philippic,* he warns the Athenians that according to nature (*physis*) all the possessions of the weak belong to the strong and that Philip of Macedon is merely acting on this principle (5). His point here is that Athenian democracy is just in its foreign policy and amoral naturalism is something expected of monarchy, but there is also the implication that if the Athenians have to deal with a leader like Philip of Macedon, then justice is better forgotten. This is said more explicitly in his *For the Liberty of the Rhodians,* delivered in 351 B.C.:

> In my opinion it is right to restore the Rhodian democracy; yet even if it were not right, I should feel justified in urging you to restore it, when I observe what these people [the Rhodian oligarchs] are doing. Why so? Because, men of Athens, if every state were bent on doing right, it would be disgraceful if we alone refused; but when the others, without exception, are preparing the means to do wrong, for us alone to make profession of right, without engaging in any enterprise, seems to me not love of right but want of courage. For I notice that all men have their rights conceded to them in proportion to the power at their disposal . . . Of private rights [*dikaioi idioi*] within a state, the laws of that state grant an equal and impartial share to all, weak and strong alike; but the international rights of Greek states [literally, "the rights of the Greeks," *Hellenikoi dikaioi*] are defined by the strong for the weak. (28–29 [trans. J. H. Vince])

Demosthenes seems to say here that justice does not exist in relations between states—and this before the whole Assembly. But he is referring to an emergency situation. Earlier in the speech, he reminded the citizens that conflicts between democracies and oligarchies are characterized by a special ruthlessness, because freedom itself is at stake (17–18). He means that justice is to be followed whenever possible; but if a democracy must fight for its survival and independence against oligarchies or monarchies, then some relaxation of this standard is permissible.

In spite of these ambiguous statements, it is the usual strategy of the orators to claim that the just and the advantageous coincide. The orator is explicitly advised to take this line in the rhetorical handbook called the *Rhetoric to Alexander,* written about 300 B.C. and erroneously included in the works of Aristotle. The speaker is counseled that if he wishes to exhort his audience to war, he should present as many arguments as possible: He should show that the city or its allies are being wronged by the other side or have been wronged by them at some time in the past (notice the absence of any statute of limitations on the Greek notion of injustice in war), so that they will have the favor of gods and men: But in addition, the orator should prove that the war will be advantageous, first, because it will bring one of the usual objectives, like wealth or glory or power, and second, because the city is stronger than its adversary in resources, allies, location, or planning. An orator who wants to argue for peace must, of course, show the exact opposite: He must convince his countrymen that the war would either be hopeless or unjust, preferably both, with much emphasis on the unpredictability of the fortunes of war (1425).

It was rarely difficult for orators to find connections between the just and the advantageous. One such argument was that unjust powers collect enemies, which is disadvantageous, and a hegemonic power that fails to treat its allies justly is doomed to fall shortly, which is also disadvantageous. When the orators do separate the just from the advantageous, it is often a rhetorical trick. Demosthenes assured the Athenians that he would advise them to go to war for the freedom of the Greeks even if that was not in their own interest (*On the Chersonese* 48–51; *Fourth Philippic* 24–27); but of course he really meant to persuade them that it was *both* just and advantageous.

The audiences of fourth-century oratory were clearly familiar with the distinction between the just and the advantageous, but the speakers rarely, if ever, attained the level of sophistication of the debates in Thucydides. And in philosophical literature of the fourth century, there is little discussion of the subject at all. The approach of Plato and Aristotle, as we have seen, was to limit wars among Greeks to just warfare and to admit the legitimacy of warfare for naked power only against barbarians. But there are also interesting passages in the usually sententious and moralistic *Education of Cyrus* of Xenophon. King Cambyses tells the young Cyrus that a ruler must be two different men, one a righteous man and the other a thief and robber (1.6.27–43). The point Xenophon makes is that in war one must sometimes fight in open battle and sometimes use tricks and devices, especially those that allow one to take the enemy by surprise; a general must be adept at both ethics. Elsewhere, Xenophon had Socrates himself declare that a general must be both a good protector and a good thief (*Memorabilia* 3.1.6). In the *Cyrus,* Xenophon repeatedly compares warfare to hunting and makes Cambyses declare that enemies in war are like wild beasts, against which every kind of deceit is legitimate. Contemporary philosophers were capable of comparing warfare against barbarians to the hunting of wild animals, but always with the implication that wars among Greeks were on a different level. Xenophon implies that *all* warfare is as amoral as a beast hunt. To be sure, he immediately backtracks: At the end of the speech in which Cambyses gives this Machiavellian advice, the king adds that nevertheless all wars must be fought for just causes and after consulting oracles and omens to make sure of the favor of the gods. *Raison d'état,* apparently, applies to the *jus in bello* but not to the *jus ad bellum.* Xenophon did not follow his insight through. But he left an explicit justification for deceit and immorality in warfare, at least at certain levels, embedded in a work that greatly influenced later military thought, particularly that of Machiavelli.

Oratory and History

The sophistic type of political oratory was invented about the same time as historical writing, in the late fifth century B.C., and soon established a close connection with it. In the fourth century, it was widely assumed that one of the primary purposes of historical writing was to provide information for orators on matters of war and peace. The influential rhetorical school of Isocrates regarded historiography as one of the essential elements in the education of a gentleman. Isocrates called it "writings about the deeds of war" or "the old deeds and wars of the Greeks" and spoke of it as one of the established genres of prose composition (*Antidosis* 45; *Panathenaic* 1). About 370, he wrote to prince Nicocles, "Reflect on the fortunes and accidents which befall both common men and kings, for if you are mindful of the past you will plan better for the future" (*To Nicocles* 35, trans. George Norlin).

Aristotle was more explicit about the uses of history. In his *Rhetoric,* he says war and peace constitute one of the major subjects of political oratory and insists that orators must be knowledgeable about such matters. The successful political orator must know

> the power of the city, both how great it is already and how great it is capable of becoming, and what form the existing power takes and what else might be added, and, further, what wars it has waged and how (it is necessary to know these things not only about one's native city but about neighboring cities) and with whom there is probability of war, in order that there may be a policy of peace toward the stronger and that the decision of war with the weaker may be one's own. [It is necessary to know] their forces also, whether they are like or unlike [those of one's own city]; for it is possible in this respect as well to be superior or inferior. Additionally, it is necessary to have observed not only the wars of one's own city but those of others, in terms of their results; for like results naturally follow from like causes. (*Rhetoric* 1.4, 1359–1360 [trans. George Kennedy; his interpolations])

Aristotle speaks as though the orator must have a comprehensive knowledge of all wars of the past, their conduct, and their results. Where does the orator go for such knowledge? "It is clear that in constitutional revision the reports of travelers are useful (for there one can learn the laws of foreign nations) and [that] for debates about going to war the research of those writing about history [is useful]. But all these subjects belong to politics, not rhetoric" (*Rhetoric* 1.4, 1360 [trans. Kennedy]). The phrase translated by Kennedy as "debates about going to war" appears in the manuscripts of the *Rhetoric* as *politikas symboulas,* or "political debates"; but the most recent edition of the *Rhetoric,* by Rudolf Kassel, emended this to *polemikas symboulas,* or "debates about going to war," on the basis of the medieval Latin translation of the *Rhetoric* by Herman the German.[3] For information about warfare and foreign affairs, we must turn to "the inquiries of those who write about deeds" (a more literal rendering of the phrase translated by George Kennedy as "the research of those writing about history").

By the mid-fourth century, there existed a large and well-known body of Greek literature that had as yet no convenient name—it was not yet called *historia*—but was generally described as the "writings of the deeds of war" or "inquiries about the deeds of war": It included Herodotus, Thucydides, the several continuations of Thucydides, which went under the title *Hellenica (Affairs of Greece)* (only Xenophon's survives), and the accounts of the western Greeks by the lost Syracusan writers Antiochus and Philistus, which went under the title *Sicelica (Affairs of Sicily).* It was taken for granted that this literature was the source of knowledge for anything about war, diplomacy, or interstate relations. It is interesting that Aristotle explained the purpose of these writings in terms similar to those of Thucydides: "Like results naturally follow from like causes" (compare Thucydides 1.22, 3.82). It is also worth noting the frequency with which Thucydides's orators drew on historical examples. For instance, the Mitylenians justified their revolt against Athens by citing examples of Athenian misconduct (Thucydides 3.11); and Cleon said, "The fate of those of their neighbors who had already rebelled and been subdued, was no lesson to them [the Mitylenians]," implying that it should have been (Thucydides 3.39, trans. Crawley). The symbiotic relationship between oratory and history soon produced a new type of realistic historiography intended to serve as a storehouse of examples for political orators.

The Realist Theory of History: Thucydides[4]

Thucydides of Athens took from Herodotus the ambition to tell the story of a great war, the confident assumption that great deeds deserve commemoration, the literary devices of epic and drama, and the urge to seek the *aitiai* that lie behind the rise and fall of states. At the same time, he self-consciously portrayed himself as an innovator. His basic innovation was the invention of a new style of prose narrative for describing warfare, the most adequate term for which is realism. The new style was defended pugnaciously in Thucydides's preamble: He distanced himself from Herodotus by emphasizing his concern for *akribeia* (precision or carefulness), claiming to write only about what he had seen himself or had learned from eyewitness accounts (1.22); he said that he had recorded events as they occurred winter and summer (2.1), which seems to imply the inclusion of *all* events in strict chronological order, in contrast to Herodotus's epic selectiveness and discursiveness. Thucydides wished to give the impression that he was not concerned with entertainment but rather with an austere presentation of things as they were, implicitly stressing blame and criticism more than praise, disaster more than expansion, the fall of states more than their rise.

The eschewal of rhetorical embellishment is, of course, a rhetorical device itself. Thucydides was as concerned as Herodotus to tell a good story, though a different kind of story, and beyond his preamble, he showed no more concern than Herodotus with problems of conflicting evidence. There has been much controversy over whether Thucydides and other classical historians should be read as historians in the modern sense or as literary artists.[5] But the real difference between classical and contempory historians is that the classical historian thought, with no sense of contradiction, that history was both a highly wrought literary presentation using traditional poetic techniques and an empirical and dialectical instrument for getting at the truth about important human affairs—even if their perception of "truth" was not quite ours. Rhetoric cannot be separated from content. The literary effort to give the appearance of painstaking accuracy and comprehensiveness must produce a more accurate and comprehensive account. The Thucydidean style implies at least an awareness of the problem of evidence, the gap between the semifictionalized presentation of narrative and its underlying factual base—a problem that would be unavoidable for Thucydides because he dealt with current events, not Herodotean events already half-receded into legend. But in the final analysis, the priorities of Thucydides and his audience are not ours. As Kenneth Dover remarked, they lived in a culture where techniques of literary art were very highly developed, and those of scientific investigation, hardly at all. We tend to assume Thucydides adopted the rhetoric of realism out of concern for the problem of evidence, when it is more likely the reverse—he had to show some concern for evidence because he had adopted the rhetoric of realism.

Accepting the rhetoric of realism as a rhetoric, let us begin to identify its main features. The prose of Herodotus was flowing and expansive, a series of tales or arguments linked by the principle of action and reaction. The narrative of Thucydides is antithetical rather than linear. He constantly balances one thing against another, sometimes symmetrically, as in the famous sentence in the Funeral Oration of Pericles—"We cultivate refinement without extravagance and knowledge without effeminacy" (2.40, trans. Crawley). But more typically, Thucydides uses broken symmetries and unexpected variations, especially contrasting words that express speech or intent (*logos, gnome,* and so on) with words expressing facts, deeds, or power (*ergon, dynamis,* and so forth). Adam Parry counted 420 examples of such word-deed antithesis. This antithetical style, developed by the Sophist Gorgias, was popular then in Athenian oratory. Thucydides adapted it to the purposes of historical narrative because it conveyed a certain realistic view of the world, a blunt tough-minded appraisal of a reality filled with surprise and struggle, where rational planning had a tendency not to work out as expected. This style was imitated later by the Latin historians Sallust and Tacitus and thereafter had a long history in European literature; and it was often associated with political realism and the doctrine later called *raison d'état.*

Not only the sentences but the narrative structure is antithetical. The basic unit of composition is the *logos-ergon* combination, a juxtaposition of the word and the deed, of the speech and the action. In Herodotus, the speeches and the dialogues are narrative devices that move the story along; in Thucydides, they are analytical devices. Herodotean narrative is a series of actions; Thucydidean narrative becomes a series of debates followed by actions. At crucial points in Thucydides's story, someone usually makes a speech before an assembly or council, predicting success or failure as the result of a certain action; or Thucydides may present the reader with arguments for both sides of the question, giving a complete picture of the situation. This is the *logos.* And then the *ergon:* The action the assembly decides upon is described, and we see the outcome, confirming or refuting what the speakers have said. The speeches are the hinges of history.

Not all Thucydidean narrative fits the dramatic *logos-ergon* pattern. Thucydides also uses a day-to-day type of narrative, composed of long stretches of close-packed detail, often highly compressed and difficult to follow. There is a certain degree of incompatibility between the *logos-ergon* narrative, which is an adaptation of Herodotus's methods, and the day-to-day narrative, which is peculiar to Thucydides and arises from his need for accuracy and comprehensiveness. At times the story seems to almost separate into two histories: One of these is highly selective and schematic, consisting of the dramatic elaboration of a handful of important episodes, highlighted by much fictional speech making; the other type of narrative is highly comprehensive and often devoid of interpretation, apparently aimed at including as many events as possible for their own sake. What readers remember best about Thucydides is the first type, the dramatic set pieces: the Funeral Oration of Pericles, the great debate in the Athenian assembly over the fate of Mitylene, the chilling dialogue on Melos where the envoys of Athens explain the meaning of empire to a small state that happened to be in their way. These set pieces sometimes seem so unrelated to the detailed day-to-day narrative that some commentators have seen a conflict between Thucydides as selective artist and Thucydides as comprehensive fact gatherer. But more often, there is a creative tension between the two, producing a narrative unlike any other historical work ever written, a unique combination of intellectual detachment and emotional power. The big dramatic moments would lose effectiveness if we had not lived through the war with the participants; the events on Melos and Corcyra would lose their fascination and fearfulness if we had not followed the grim routine of the war summer by winter in slogging detail, so that when we finally come to Corcyra we can understand what such things can do to a social fabric and how easily they can happen again.

The purpose of narrative realism is to impart a new perspective on the past. The main impression we receive from reading Herodotus is the essential sameness of things within the cosmic order; but Thucydides emphasizes the uniqueness of events and the efforts of men to impose a human order on them. Herodotus sees mostly the similarity of the revolutions of the wheel of history; Thucydides is more interested in the variations. He makes the point—a simple one, but the essential key to an empirical approach to history—that the future is never an exact reflection of the past: "If [this work] be judged useful by those inquirers who desire an exact knowledge of the past as an aid to the interpretation of the future, which in the course of human things must resemble if it does not reflect it, I shall be content" (1.22 [trans. Crawley]). There are repeated patterns in the past, for otherwise Thucydides would not be able to make sense of the past at all, but they are the patterns of air and water. Under the glass of eternity, all things may look alike, but under the glass of politics, all things are unique. The whole point of his preamble is to show the unique scale and significance of the Peloponnesian War.

There is no sense of cosmic order in Thucydides. The ultimate *aitia* of Herodotus, the will of the gods or fates, is quietly moved upstairs and out of sight. Instead of Herodotus's two levels of causation, the divine and the human, Thucydides has only "human things" (*to anthropinon*). It is this *anthropinon*, the constancy of human nature, that makes events repeat themselves in fluid patterns that can be compared, contrasted, and organized into a connected narrative; this is the purpose of the new style of political realism. The central metaphor of Herodotus is a chain of retribution that tends always to run against mysterious limits, and his central theme is the helplessness of man before fate. In contrast, the central metaphor Thucydides uses is the antithesis of words and action, and his theme is the effort of men to control fortune through the exercise of intelligence and planning, art and skill. As Herodotus's retributive cycle corresponds to the social and political realities of the archaic world he portrayed, so Thucydides's narrative strategies reflect realistically the way political decisions were made during the Peloponnesian War—by open debate carried out in the spirit of dialectical rationalism taught by the Sophists.

The realistic style implies a candid acceptance of *raison d'état*. Causation is only a "human thing" and, furthermore, not all human things are the result of deliberate intention, nor are all open to moral evaluation. Thucydides made an effort unique in ancient historiography to describe the causes of war and empire in terms of long-developing institutional factors that the actors are not wholly conscious of and that are not wholly chosen by them. He tried to find the locus of power in states and resources rather than in individual wills. Moreover, he attempted to understand interstate relations in terms of the strategic logic of power relationships operating in an anarchic and amoral world.

Thucydides's opening section, called the "Archaeology," introduces a group of themes that play important roles throughout his narrative: the hegemonic tendency of the strong to dominate the weak, the deciding factors of resources (*chremata*) and preparedness (*paraskeue*) in determining that balance of power, and the value of sea power as a source of these qualities. Herodotus had been well aware of the importance of sea power. He probably gave Thucydides the idea developed in the "Archaeology" that there had been a succession of thalassocracies in the Aegean going back to the legendary Minos and culminating in the Athenian empire (Herodotus 3.122). Herodotus knew that the naval power of Athens had been the deciding factor in the Persian Wars (Herodotus 7.139), an observation that actually implies everything Thucydides has to say about causation, but to Herodotus these are casual asides that are not allowed to interrupt the grand flow of his story. Thucydides saw in them the key to history. Only sea power, he thought, tends to expand beyond clear limits, and only sea power permits preparedness and empire on the Athenian scale. Naval policy—so obviously a *techne,* so clearly dependent upon elaborate technology, money, planning, and preparedness—had imparted a peculiar precocity to Athenian political discourse, the most lasting monument to which was Thucydidean realism.

If these are the causes of wars, they are outside human blame. No one was responsible for the Peloponnesian War, "without parallel for the misfortunes that it brought upon Hellas." The war was made inevitable by the "growth of the power of Athens, and the alarm which this inspired in Lacedaemon" (1.23, trans. Crawley). The point of this sentence is not to place the responsibility for the war upon either Athenian policy or Spartan policy—though modern commentators have argued for one or the other—but upon both. The real cause was a problem situation, compounded of rising power and reacting power, that combined to *anangkasi* the war—they "made war inevitable," in Crawley's translation. The impersonal institutional factors that bring about these long-term shifts in the balance of power are the *anangkai,* the necessities of war.

Was the new style intended to impart any lessons, other than those intended by Herodotus? The lessons of Herodotus are those of the poets. Herodotus's repeated warnings not to overstep boundaries teach no practical political lessons because we never know where those boundaries are. The revolutions of the wheel are erratic. Croesus, had he taken to the sea, would have overstepped limits (Herodotus 1.27); but somehow it was all right for the Athenians to take to the sea, and Herodotus does not tell us what the difference between the two situations may have been. At the height of his power, Xerxes makes a genuine effort to resist the temptation to cross the Hellespont into Europe, but he is tricked and manipulated by divine forces (Herodotus 7.12ff.).

Thucydides pretended to a bleak and exact realism that was supposed to make his story more "useful" (*ophelimos*) than that of Herodotus, and many have supposed he wanted to teach practical lessons in statecraft and warfare to a select audience of generals and politicians like himself. But it is as difficult to extract lessons of immediate practicality from Thucydides as from Herodotus, because Thucydides emphasizes the unpredictability of events even more than Herodotus. Therefore, some have concluded that Thucydides's history is essentially another commemorative epic whose usefulness, like that of Herodotus, lies in its contribution to human knowledge and moral sensibility.

His work is certainly that, but the concern with realistic detail and the focus on the decisionmaking process suggest that Thucydides did mean the new style to be useful in a political and strategic sense. It is not accidental that the same issues rise again and again in Thucydides' narrative, creating running arguments that bind the story together. One central theme is *raison d'état,* the conflict between the just and the advantageous in human affairs. The earliest clear formulation of this idea in all literature is to be found in the defenses put forward by Athenian orators to justify the Athenian empire. The Athenian envoys at Sparta in 431 B.C. declare

> that it was not a very wonderful action, or contrary to the common practice of mankind, if we did accept an empire that was offered to us, and refused to give it up under pressure of three of the strongest motives, fear, honour, and interest. And it was not we who set the example, for it has always been the law that the weaker should be subject to the stronger. (1.76 [trans. Crawley])

Some Sophist must have popularized this tripartite scheme of the causes of war, as versions of it turn up in several authors; I have already quoted similar passages from Xenophon and Aristotle. It was used by Thucydides's translator Hobbes, who reformulated the scheme thusly: "In the nature of man, we find three principal causes of quarrel. First, competition; second, diffidence; thirdly, glory. The first maketh men invade for gain; the second, for safety; and the third, for reputation."[6] The Athenians do not deny the existence of the sphere of justice; they do not claim that might makes right, a position attributed to certain Sophists of that time in the dialogues of Plato. Rather, they claim that the mechanics of power in interstate relations limit the scope of justice, for men and states are uniformly egotistical and naturally at odds with one another. Even in interstate relations, justice ought to be observed as far as possible, and they claim Athens had in fact done this: "Praise is due to all who, if not so superior to human nature as to refuse dominion, yet respect justice more than their position compels them to do." This thesis is repeated by Athenian orators whenever they have to defend their empire to outsiders. The scope of justice, very limited even in the speech at Sparta, is further diminished in the later defenses—the other two major speeches are those on Melos (5.85ff.) and on Sicily (6.82ff.). This style of *raison d'état* is particularly associated with Athenian oratory, though we also hear it in the speech of Hermocrates at Syracuse (4.61). It is surely no accident that Syracuse is also a naval democracy.

The principles of *raison d'état* seem to be taken for granted by Thucydides himself in his account of the events leading up to the war. They are taken for granted by Pericles, the Athenian general whom Thucydides admired more than any other living politician. The author attributes to Pericles several major speeches (especially those at 1.140 and 2.60) on strategy—the first strategy, in the sense of a rational long-term plan for foreign policy, described in all literature. Pericles brushes aside traditional notions of just warfare: "For what you hold [the empire] is, to speak somewhat plainly, a tyranny; to take it perhaps was wrong, but to let it go is unsafe. And men of these retiring views, making converts of others, would quickly ruin a state . . . such qualities are useless to an imperial city, though they may help a dependency to an unmolested servitude" (2.64, trans. Crawley). The strategy he proposes amounts to a drastic break with traditional agonal notions of warfare. He persuades the Athenians to refuse battle on land and to allow their ancestral fields to be laid waste—the ultimate dishonor according to traditional views—and to exploit the enemy's lack of sea power, fighting a long war of attrition without decisive battles. These arguments demonstrate the brilliant political culture developed by the Sophists. They may be almost wholly Thucydides's inventions except for the main points, but they show the level of argument that must have been common in the Athenian assembly.

Is *raison d'état* therefore the "useful" lesson Thucydides wants his history to teach? Does he mean to show how intelligence (*gnome*) can control fortune (*tyche*)? Does he want his readers to emulate Themistocles, founder of Athenian sea power (who could "excellently divine the good and evil which lay hid in the unseen future," 1.139), and Pericles, its first great strategist? The text may easily be read that way. Yet the lessons are never clear. *Gnome* turns out to be a fragile weapon. Just after this encomium to Themistocles, we are told of his death in exile, perhaps by suicide. The Funeral Oration of Pericles is followed immediately by the great plague. Intelligence is constantly frustrated by fortune, the more so the deeper we get into the war. The long series of *logoi* alternating with *erga* give the effect of cumulative experience, but often they demonstrate a failure to learn from experience. By the time we reach the Corcyraean revolution the repetitiousness of human situations seems no longer an opportunity, but a trap. The will to power seems inescapable, yet power will always raise up other powers to check its growth: The inevitable expansion of a city like Athens will run up against the inevitable resistance of a city like Sparta; our most careful exercises in preparedness will encounter somebody better prepared. These warnings are reiterated in the speeches and confirmed by the narrative, wherein we see one well-laid plan after another foiled by the chaos of war. The only general lesson would appear to be the one stated at the start of the war by the Athenians at Sparta: "Consider the vast influence of accident in war, before you are engaged in it. As it continues, it generally becomes an affair of chances, chances from which neither of us is exempt, and whose event we must risk in the dark" (1.78, trans. Crawley).

It is difficult to say what general conclusions the author drew, because the few comments he makes in his own person are obiter dicta and are not to be taken as his definitive interpretation of his history. His history was supposed to be its own definitive interpretation. Still, one of these obiter dicta is unusually revealing. In his account of the civil strife (*stasis*) on Corcyra, Thucydides intrudes himself into his narrative to point out a general lesson in a tone of unaccustomed passion:

> The sufferings which revolution entailed upon the cities were many and terrible, such as have occurred and always will occur, as long as the nature of mankind remains the same; though in a severer or milder form, and varying in the symptoms, according to the variety of the particular cases. In peace and prosperity states and individuals have better sentiments, because they do not find themselves suddenly confronted with imperious necessities; but war takes away the easy supply of daily wants, and so proves a rough master, that brings most men's characters to a level with their fortunes ... Thus every form of iniquity took root in the Hellenic countries by reason of the troubles. The ancient simplicity into which honour so largely entered was laughed down and disappeared. (3.82–83 [trans. Crawley])

This is one of those patterns that recur in the course of "human things," the contemplation of which makes their retelling "useful." The author of this passage could not have entirely shared the amoral sophistic doctrines of *raison d'état* recited by many of his statesmen. The motives that lead to war may get out of hand, turn on the city, and tear it apart. War, as Thucydides says here, is a rough master, a harsh teacher (*biaios didaskolos*)—a statement that A. W. Gomme, in his commentary on Thucydides, called the nearest thing to a moral the historian had to offer. Certainly this warning is *one* of the lessons Thucydides wanted his audience to take away: The demands of justice are not forever ignored with impunity, even under the necessities of war.

The most thorough discussion of the conflict between the just and the advantageous is the debate over Mitylene, an Athenian ally that had revolted in wartime and was to be punished by the execution of all Mitylenean adult citizens (3.37–48).[7] Cleon defends the proposed massacre in the name of justice; Diodotus argues for mercy in the name of expediency. The opposing principles seem at first clearly cut, but they start to blur as soon as the reader tries to analyze the complex arguments. Cleon's arguments are really based upon expediency as much as justice. He argues that ruthless punishment is just but also advantageous, as it will deter other dependencies from rebellion; in fact, he admits that even if it were unjust, they would still have to carry out the punishment.

To sum up shortly, I say that if you follow my advice you will do what is just toward the Mitylenians, and at the same time expedient; while by a different decision you will not so much oblige them as pass sentence on yourselves. For if they were right in rebelling, you must be wrong in ruling. However, if, right or wrong, you determine to rule, you must carry out your principle and punish the Mitylenians as your interest requires; or else you must give up your empire and cultivate honesty without danger. (3.40)

Diodotus's counterargument purports to be based upon expediency alone: "The question before us as sensible men is not their guilt, but our interests. Though I prove them ever so guilty, I shall not, therefore, advise their death, unless it be expedient . . . we are not in a court of justice, but in a political assembly; and the question is not justice, but how to make the Mitylenians useful to Athens" (3.44 [trans. Crawley]). Often this passage is quoted as a classic statement of Machiavellian realism, and often it is assumed that the otherwise unknown Diodotus is Thucydides's mouthpiece. Both assumptions are questionable. Diodotus actually ends up arguing on grounds of justice as well as expediency, observing that it is neither just nor expedient to punish the Mitylenian common folk along with the oligarchs, for the oligarchs were responsible for the revolt, and the common people in Mitylene and in other cities are well disposed toward the Athenian democracy. It seems unlikely that Thucydides shared this view. He disagreed with Diodotus's assessment of the imperial situation, believing that the Athenian empire was generally disliked by its subjects, no matter what their class.[8] His comments on the Corcyraean turmoil, which come soon after the debate over Mitylene, show that the most hateful and destructive aspect of the war to him was the way both sides followed the strategy of Diodotus—using ideological pretexts to meddle in the internal constitutions of cities and stir up civil strife.

In this debate, Thucydides seems to be exploring the consequences of *raison d'état*. This is the first explicit discussion in literature of the relationship between the two vocabularies of war, the moral and the strategic; and the main point appears to be the difficulty of separating them, for neither Cleon nor Diodotus manages to disentangle expediency from justice, and neither policy could have saved the Athenian empire. In its tantalizing inconclusiveness, the debate resembles the teaching methods of Socrates, Thucydides's contemporary.

Thus, the special "usefulness" of realistic history was to provide examples of political discourse like this. For all his irony and skepticism, Thucydides seems to believe in the value of rational political discussion. He very often uses might-have-been arguments: If the Greek expedition in the Trojan War had been properly financed, the Greeks might have taken Troy at once (1.11); if Nicias had attacked Syracuse at once, the Sicilian expedition might have succeeded (7.42); if the Persians had intervened after that, they might have ended the war, but they preferred to keep the balance of power (8.87); if the Spartans had followed up their victory at Eretria in 411 B.C., they could have ended the war then (8.96). Thucydides wants to educate his readers to think things through in this way, exploring all possible alternatives and contingencies, shifting all arguments, subjecting all *erga* to *logos*. He must have entertained to some degree the hope that intelligence could master and ride the course of fortune. His actors, in the dark, must risk the chances of war, but as they grope, they try to light the way with intelligence and experience as best they can. For all his pessimism, Thucydides hoped to provide his readers with vicarious experience in the making of such decisions, so that they might divine a bit more clearly the good and evil hidden in the future. In such a realistic appraisal of events, there is a kind of usefulness that derives neither from the practicality of the orator nor from the contemplation of the philosopher. This is the utility of history. The purpose of historical examples is not to furnish simple precepts but to extend and stimulate the political intelligence. By studying how people behaved in a large number of actual cases, we can deduce some criteria of possibility and probability and use these as guides to action. The study of history may help us to avoid some mistakes: to stop the growth of empire before the point of overextension; to be mindful of the need for restraint and calculation; to know that the just and the advantageous, whatever clever Sophists might say, are strangely linked; and if we cannot avoid our fate, to adjust to it. The most adequate summary of Thucydides's intentions seems to me to be that of Colin Macleod, "a passionate, though often gloomy, enquiry into the possibility of rational behaviour in politics and war."[9]

The Legacy of Thucydides

One of the problems about Greek military thought is to explain why the brilliant strategic philosophy of the fifth century faded so quickly. Doubtless this was partly because the art of war in the fourth century became terribly complicated. The main issue of the fifth century, the conflict between the traditional hoplite strategy of pitched battle and the Periclean naval strategy of avoiding battle, became irrelevant, for the Peloponnesian War showed that as a pure strategy neither would work. Old-fashioned hoplite warfare makes its last appearance in Plato's *Republic,* where it exists in a heavenly city that will never be realized on earth. The purely naval strategy attempted by Pericles had been equally discredited and the limitations of sea power were becoming obvious. There was great fear of enemy invasion, for the threat to the land was no longer symbolic; the well-organized and well-supplied armies of the fourth century were capable of inflicting real devastation on agriculture. Therefore, it was deeply desirable to keep warfare away from one's own territory, and the preventive strike became a favorite strategy. Timolaus of Corinth, urging an immediate attack on Sparta in 394 B.C., pointed out that the best way to deal with wasps is to burn them in their nest (Xenophon,

Hellenica 4.2.12). The anti-Macedonian speeches of Demosthenes repeatedly urged the Athenians to attack the Macedonian wasps in their nest or at least to fight them as far from Attic soil as possible (*Third Philippic* 52). If the enemy could not be stopped by a preventive strike, then he must be stopped at the borders, and much planning and money were now spent on border fortifications, a pet subject for Xenophon (*Memorabilia* 3.5.25–27, 3.6.10–11). If the border could not be held, the enemy must be met in pitched battle outside the walls in the old-fashioned way, though with more complicated tactics. The last resort was to endure a siege, because siege tactics were increasingly formidable and, after about 350, deadly.[10] Demosthenes told the Athenians in 341 that in his lifetime no art or craft had undergone such revolutionary improvement as the military art (*Third Philippic* 47).

There was intense discussion of all this in the fourth century, but it rarely rose above the practical and technical. As we have seen, orators rarely handled strategic problems, the causes and consequences of warfare, or the ethical problems of justice versus advantage with the philosophical fearlessness and sophistication of the fifth century—though we should remember that Thucydides may have made fifth-century oratory sound more philosophical than it really was.

Another sign of the increasingly practical and technical quality of military thought is the appearance of a professional military literature. Around 350 B.C., a soldier called Aeneas the Tactician wrote a series of handbooks on the art of war, perhaps known collectively as the *Strategica* (Art of generalship), which assumed the status of a standard reference work in the Greek and, later, in the Latin world.[11] In the following century, this work was epitomized by a general named Cineas, who was in the service of King Pyrrhus of Epirus; this epitome was still being used by Cicero in the first century B.C. Only the section dealing with sieges (*The Defense of Cities*) has come down to us; perhaps if we had more of it, we would be more impressed, but the extant books are narrowly technical. One aspect of this work that makes it worth mentioning here is Aeneas's interest in collecting tricks and surprises for the deception of the enemy, illustrated by historical anecdotes. These devices, later called *stratagemata,* became a principal subject of later Greek and Latin military literature and one of the channels whereby the classical realist approach to warfare was transmitted to medieval and Renaissance Europe. That will be considered further in a later chapter.

But what of the historians? The fifth century had bequeathed two major narrative styles, the linear epic style of Herodotus and the antithetical realistic style of Thucydides, which were associated with two different views of the world—the encomiastic Herodotean world of moral achievement and cosmic law, versus Thucydidean pessimism and irony. At the beginning of the fourth century, the influence of Thucydides was strong; several authors wrote continuations of his unfinished history, of which only the *Hellenica* (*Affairs of Greece*) of Xenophon survives. But later in the century, the

Herodotean style and manner seems to have won out. Even in Xenophon, it is the main literary influence, and since Xenophon imitated Herodotus in a fashion much easier for later historians to read and to imitate, this style remained the main tradition of historical writing to the end of antiquity. Herodotus doubtless owed much of his popularity to the fact that he had set the upheavals of war and empire within a universal moral order. But by the fourth century, Herodotus's faith in cosmic order was largely replaced by the cult of Tyche (Fortune, or Chance), worshiped as a goddess. Even Xenophon had lost interest in the causes of wars: The central theme of his *Hellenica* is the unpredictability of history, and the lessons he wants to convey are mostly practical lessons for commanders, which he collected in his *Education of Cyrus* at greater length and with more freedom from the encumbrances of historical fact. Polybius's acerbic comments on his predecessors leave the impression that most Hellenistic historians were fascinated by dramatic and unexpected turns of fortune, which they often exploited for sensationalistic effect in a fashion Polybius thought more appropriate for a tragic poet than a historian (the sort of tragedy he has in mind in this passage [15.36] sounds more like Seneca than Sophocles). The example of Alexander the Great and the influence of the many lost Alexander historians could only have strengthened the tendency to focus on meteoric individuals and sensational effects. The emphasis on unpredictability led to a widespread belief that the function of history was to teach moral lessons, especially on how to bear the changes of Fortune.[12]

But there were some who continued the Thucydidean tradition. Perhaps our greatest loss is Hieronymus of Cardia, courtier of the Antigonid kings, whose history of the wars of Alexander's successors covered the years 322–273 B.C. Some of it survives in the form of an epitome written by Diodorus of Sicily in the first century B.C.: These books (18 through 20) are unlike anything else in Diodorus in their clear descriptions of strategy, realistic battle narratives, and use of speeches and debates to clarify issues.

But our understanding of this tradition is dependent mostly upon Polybius of Megalopolis, its only representative and, indeed, the only Hellenistic historian whose work has survived unless we count the late epitomizer Diodorus.

Polybius self-consciously tried to revive Thucydidean history, which he thought had been neglected by recent historians. His methodological observations are of interest because he stated the purposes of this type of history more explicitly than Thucydides ever did (Thucydides left it to his narrative to say this). He calls this tradition *pragmatike historia,* for which "realistic history" seems the most adequate translation—the adjective *pragmatike* implies the serious, the businesslike, the systematic, the practically useful. Polybius means by it a narrative devoted exclusively to political and military affairs, stripped of all rhetorical embellishment and entertainments, meant for an audience of active statesmen and soldiers (Polybius 9.1–2).

I have recorded these events [of the First Punic War] in the hope that readers of this history may profit from them, for there are two ways by which all men may reform themselves, either by learning from their own errors or from those of others ... From this I conclude that the best education for the situations of actual life consists of the experience we acquire from the study of serious history. For it is history alone which without causing us harm enables us to judge what is the best course in any situation or circumstance. (1.35 [trans. Ian Scott-Kilvert])

Realistic history provides an enhanced awareness of recurrent situations and possibilities, always informed by appreciation of the uncertainties of war. It focuses on the decisionmaking process: "The special function of history, particularly in relation to speeches, is first of all to discover the words actually used, whatever they were, and next to establish the reason why a particular action or argument failed or succeeded" (12.25b). Polybius is much more aware than Thucydides of the difficulties created by fictive speechwriting in a history that purports to be realistic. And causal analysis, Polybius claims, is essential: "Neither writers nor readers of history should confine their attention to the narrative of events, but must also take account of what preceded, accompanied, and followed them" (3.31 [trans. Scott-Kilvert]).

Polybius's most original contribution is his view that causes are most adequately explored in a "universal" (*koina*) history. He thought that this kind of history became possible after the Second Punic War, because only then did the whole Mediterranean world become unified under Rome.

Now my history possesses a certain distinctive quality which is related to the extraordinary spirit of the times in which we live, and it is this. Just as Fortune [Tyche] has steered almost all the affairs of the world in one direction and forced them to converge upon one and the same goal, so it is the task of the historian to present to his readers under one synoptical view the process by which she [Fortune] has accomplished this general design ... while various historians deal with isolated wars and certain of the subjects connected with them, nobody, so far as I am aware, has made any effort to examine the general and comprehensive scheme of events. (1.4 [trans. Scott-Kilvert])

This concept of history as a unified organic structure, which becomes intelligible only when we see the entire pattern, was a profound insight. Unfortunately, Polybius could not clearly explain why this is so. His discussions of causation often suggest that he thought of the causes of wars in terms of conscious strategies. But in the passage that follows, he shows an awareness that there are impersonal, institutional, Thucydidean forces working in history:

Thus I regard the war with Antiochus as having originated from that with Philip, the war with Philip from that with Hannibal, and the Hannibalic War from that fought for the possession of Sicily [First Punic War], while the intermediate events, however many and diverse they may be, all converge upon the same issue. All these tendencies can be recognized and understood from a general (*koina*) history, but this is not the case with histories of separate wars. (3.32 [trans. Scott-Kilvert])

Polybius never quite decides whether Rome had a conscious plan for world dominion. Sometimes he describes the Hannibalic War as the first step in a Roman strategy of world conquest and sometimes as the event that first led the Romans to conceive the idea of world conquest (1.3, 1.63, 6.50). He is certain there is a grand design, though he is not sure whether it is the plan of Rome or Tyche; but he is sure that the traditional war monograph is inadequate to reveal it. He may not explain clearly just why it is useful to see the big picture, but he did not really have to. His history had demonstrated it.

The realism of Polybius was less bleak and uncompromising than that of Thucydides. He knew perfectly well that states tended to follow their own interests. He commended the Syracusans for switching their support from Rome to Carthage in the First Punic War, though Rome had been their loyal friend, on the grounds that it is always prudent for small states to maintain the balance of power (1.83—this is the earliest passage known to me in which the concept of the balance of power is stated as a general principle). He knew that the just and the advantageous rarely coincide, but he had high praise for statesmen who could combine them (21.32); he admitted no excuse for breaches of faith, and one of the reasons he admired the Romans was that they preserved better than the contemporary Greeks the ancient hoplite traditions of honest battle (13.3). Unlike Thucydides, he introduces many historical examples simply for moral imitation, in the Hellenistic fashion.[13] Nor did he try to imitate the harsh antithetical style that won Thucydides his austere immortality. In the eyes of posterity, his sound morals did not compensate for his lack of stylistic brilliance. One hundred years after Polybius died, the critic Dionysius of Halicarnassus listed him, along with many other prolix and dull Hellenistic historians, as one of the authors no one ever read through. Only a fragment of his huge narrative survived to the Renaissance, when Polybius finally won recognition, but even then, not so much for the Thucydidean qualities described here as for his constitutional theories, which are treated in the next chapter.

Notes

1. E. L. Wheeler, "*Hoplomachia* and Greek Dances in Arms," *Greek, Roman, and Byzantine Studies* 23 (1982), 223–233; "The *Hoplomachoi* and Vegetius' Spartan Drillmasters," *Chiron* 13 (1983), 1–20.

2. I owe this comparison to Jacqueline de Romilly, *The Great Sophists in Periclean Athens*, trans. Janet Lloyd (Oxford, 1992), 61–63. The speeches are translated in *The Older Sophists*, ed. Rosemary Sprague (Columbia, S.C., 1972).

3. *Aristotelis Ars Rhetorica*, ed. Rudolf Kassel (Berlin, 1976), 23; see also *Aristotle, On Rhetoric: A Theory of Civic Discourse*, ed. George Kennedy (New York, 1991).

4. The literature on Thucydides is vast. For a short introduction to the subject, see Simon Hornblower, *Thucydides* (Baltimore, 1987). Other recent works to which I am indebted include Virginia Hunter, *Thucydides: The Artful Reporter* (Toronto, 1973); Lowell Edmunds, *Chance and Intelligence in Thucydides* (Cambridge, Mass.,

1975); P. R. Pouncy, *The Necessities of War: A Study of Thucydides' Pessimism* (New York, 1980); H. H. Rawlings III, *The Structure of Thucydides' History* (Princeton, 1981); W. R. Connor, *Thucydides* (Princeton, 1984); Colin Macleod, *Collected Essays* (Oxford, 1983); Adam Parry, *The Language of Achilles and Other Papers* (Oxford, 1989).

5. For guides to this controversy, see W. R. Connor, "A Post Modernist Thucydides?" *Classical Journal* 72 (1977), 289–298; K. J. Dover, "Thucydides 'as History' and 'as Literature,'" *History and Theory* 22 (1983), 54–63. A. J. Woodman, *Rhetoric in Classical Historiography* (London, 1988), argues the "literature" interpretation.

6. Hobbes, *Leviathan*, 1.13. See Gabriella Slomp, "Hobbes, Thucydides, and the Three Greatest Things," *History of Political Thought* 11 (1990), 565–586; L. M. Johnson, *Thucydides, Hobbes, and the Interpretation of Realism* (De Kalb, Ill., 1993).

7. The Mitylenian debate is discussed in nearly every major study of Thucydides. I have been influenced by Colin Macleod's essay in *Collected Essays,* "Reason and Necessity: Thucydides III 9-14, 37-48," 88–102, and by Clifford Orwin, "The Just and the Advantageous in Thucydides: The Case of the Mitylenian Debate," *American Political Science Review* 78 (1984), 485–494.

8. An attempt to defend the Athenian empire from Thucydides's critique by G.E.M. de Ste. Croix, "The Character of the Athenian Empire," *Historia* 3 (1954–1955), 1–41, has had considerable influence, but I do not find it persuasive. Ste. Croix argues that Thucydides's speeches are largely fictions apart from the main point, so when Thucydides makes Pericles and other Athenian orators say the empire is hated by its subjects, we should take this as Thucydidean editorializing. I share this view of Thucydides's speeches, but that does not mean he was free to make his characters say anything he wanted. Literary realism requires dramatic plausibility, and I find it impossible to believe the historian could make politicians like Pericles and Cleon declare in the open assembly that the Athenian empire was a tyranny detested by its subjects unless this was a well-known fact. Thucydides did not gain his reputation for veracity that way. If he also shows us cases where the loyalties of faction overrode loyalty to the city, there is no contradiction: He describes this phenomenon in detail in his account of the Corcyraean revolutions, and there he emphasizes that such factional and ideological conflict is a *new* thing, largely brought on by the war itself.

9. Macleod, *Collected Essays,* 70.

10. On fourth-century military thought, see J. K. Anderson, *Military Theory and Practice in the Age of Xenophon* (Berkeley, 1970); Josiah Ober, *Fortress Attica: Defense of the Athenian Land Frontier, 404–322* B.C. (Leiden, 1985); E. L. Wheeler, *Stratagem and the Vocabulary of Military Trickery* (Leiden, 1988).

11. *Aeneas the Tactician: How to Survive Under Siege,* ed. David Whitehead (Oxford, 1990); and Wheeler, *Stratagem.*

12. The following treatment of later Greek historiography is indebted particularly to Charles Fornara, *The Nature of History in Ancient Greece and Rome* (Berkeley, 1983); K. S. Sacks, *Polybius and the Writing of History* (Berkeley, 1981), and *Diodorus Siculus and the First Century* (Princeton, 1990); and Jane Hornblower, *Hieronymus of Cardia* (Oxford, 1981).

13. The moralistic side of Polybius is brought out by A. M. Eckstein, *Moral Vision in "The Histories" of Polybius* (Berkeley, 1995).

Chapter Six

Warfare and the Greek Constitution

Which Constitution Is Best at War?

The hoplite organization was supposed to produce both the best type of army and the best type of state. Its dramatic success over the Persian superpower early in the fifth century helped to inspire the precocious development of Greek political speculation, in which the relationship between the constitution and warfare was a central theme. Herodotus is our earliest source for this. Although his poetic conventions required him to explain events mostly in terms of personal intention, he also registers glimpses of impersonal and collective factors, for which the only general concept he had was *nomos* (law or custom), a term much discussed by the Sophists. A half-hidden constitutional theory can be discerned in Herodotus, less articulated than the more archaic levels of explanation in terms of personal motivation and moral values. He includes a long and implausible debate (3.80ff.) among three Persian nobles on whether Persia should adopt monarchy, oligarchy, or *isonomia* (government by free and equal citizens of the Greek type). As the faults attributed to monarchy in this debate are the faults later exemplified by Xerxes, Herodotus seems to hint that the mistakes committed by Xerxes in his invasion of Greece sprang from weaknesses inherent in absolute government. He leaves no doubt at all that the Greek victory was a result of their isonomic constitutions, which enabled them to fight as free men against slaves. The king of Sparta tells the king of Persia that the Spartans "are free—but not altogether so. They have as the despot over them Law, and they fear him much more than your men fear you. At least whatever he bids them do, they do, and he bids them always the same thing: not to flee from the fight before any multitude of men whatever, but to stand firm in their ranks and either conquer or die" (7.104 [trans. Grene]).

This is as close as Herodotus comes to historical explanation in institutional terms, and the earliest literary expression of the ideal I have described as civic militarism. He implies that monarchies of the Oriental type are prone to overexpansion, whereas a Greek city of free citizens is best at fighting just wars. Some have suggested that Herodotus meant to imply that the Greeks would now conquer the Persians and become the next in the succession of world empires, but I doubt that. The constitutional theory, which comes to the fore in the European sections of Herodotus, does not fit well into the succession-of-empires theory, which provides the scaffolding for the earlier Asiatic narrative. In Herodotus's view, revolutions of the cosmic wheel cause monarchies to overextend themselves and start unjust wars that destroy them; but free cities only fight just wars and so should be free from that temptation. In the speech Herodotus gives to the Spartan king, the purpose of Greek military prowess is to protect Greek freedom, not to dominate others. In fact, the hoplite ideology was essentially defensive and capable only of limited wars, hence to some extent it probably acted as a brake on the natural aggressiveness and vindictiveness of the Greek just war code.

Herodotus wrote about the traditional Greek way of war, which assumed a constitution dominated by the hoplite class, essentially a broad oligarchy. But after the Persian Wars there appeared an alternative constitutional model: the naval democracy of Athens. The hoplite model was associated with old-fashioned chivalrous and ritualistic warfare, but the naval model was linked with imperialistic expansion, a capacity for long-range strategic planning, and a degree of ruthless acquiescence in *raison d'état*. The treatise on *The Constitution of Athens* written probably around 425 B.C. by the unknown author often called the "Old Oligarch"—the earliest surviving prose treatise on political thought in Greek—makes explicit the connections between military organization and constitutional form: Hoplite powers like Sparta are oligarchic and good, sea powers like Athens are democratic and unjust, but regrettably more successful at warfare and hegemony. The writer has an exaggerated view of the effectiveness of sea power: He assumes land powers have a very limited reach, whereas a navy is free to sail anywhere and land anywhere, blockade any city it wants, and conduct raids against the land with impunity.[1] The capacity of ancient fleets to do any of these things was in fact strictly limited, and this is one of the reasons for dating this tract early in the Peloponnesian War, before the limitations of sea power had been demonstrated.

In Thucydides, the idea that the Peloponnesian War was a conflict between two constitutional-military systems is a leitmotiv, and at least in his early books, he seems to share the illusions of the Old Oligarch about the superiority of sea power. His concept of *nomos* is more sharply defined than Herodotus's. To Herodotus, *nomoi* (laws or customs) might mean almost anything, but Thucydides thinks of the *nomoi* of a city as a cultural complex inculcated by education, as a distinctive national character. Much more than

Herodotus, he recognizes a kind of motivation that is collective and civic rather than personal. He had to, of course, since Herodotus's story was largely about kings, and Thucydides's is largely about citizen bodies. Even in Thucydides, there is much narrative of the Herodotean type, especially in campaign narratives, which focus on the plans and actions of individual commanders. But Thucydides also uses a collective or civic type of narrative that personifies cities: Instead of individuals, he writes of the plans and actions of "the Athenians" or "the Corinthians." Each of these constitutions has its distinctive *nomoi.* Thucydides's orators repeatedly contrast the volatile, ambitious, curious Athenian character with the stolid, stable, disciplined character of the Spartans, making the implicit assumption that the first is typical of naval democracies and the second, of hoplite oligarchies. And Thucydides sometimes implies that the naval state is prone to imperialism (see the speech of the Corinthians at Sparta, Thucydides 1.68ff.).

The debates in Thucydides suggest that in the late fifth century, Sophists and orators spent much time comparing constitutions, with their military aspects in the foreground. Whenever we encounter this theme, there is an obvious question: Which system is better at war? In the fifth century, the future seemed to lie with naval power, which awed not only democrats but enemies of democracy like the Old Oligarch. But after the Athenian debacle in 404 B.C., Sparta became the model for imitation, and the traditional hoplite ideal was revived. There appeared a number of writers who praised the Spartan system on the grounds that it was best suited for war and conquest. Aristotle argues against them in *Politics* 7.14. The only surviving example of this pro-Spartan literature, Xenophon's *Constitution of the Lacedaemonians,* declares at the start what was doubtless the common thesis of this school: Spartan military success proves the superiority of the peculiar Spartan institutions. We often forget that the communistic and militaristic ideal state depicted in Plato's *Republic* is based ultimately upon a simple military argument— Sparta is better at war than any other city, and therefore the best city must have a professional warrior elite of the Spartan type. But these assumptions were soon undermined. The Spartan hegemony proved even more fragile than the Athenian. Sparta was too dedicated to the egalitarian hoplite ideal to produce an imperial elite. Soon after Plato wrote the *Republic,* the Thebans destroyed Spartan armies at Leuctra (371) and Mantinea (362) and with them the myth of Spartan invincibility on land. A decade after that, the rising power of Macedon threw its lengthening shadow over all the city-state armies.

Authors with conservative views long continued to pay lip service to the hoplite tradition. Isocrates blamed the fifth-century Athenian empire for its unjust wars and mistreatment of allies and attributed these crimes to the corrupting effects of sea power, which he thought always tempted men to excessive ambition; upon inheriting the Athenian sea empire after the Peloponnesian War, Sparta became equally corrupted: Dominion over the sea is dominion over misfortune (*On the Peace* 101). The cowardly policy of the Periclean democracy, which allowed the land of Attica to be ravaged repeatedly, is contrasted with the valiant hoplite ethic of the old Athenians, who always went out to meet the enemy in pitched battle (*On the Peace* 77, 84). Isocrates accuses the democrats of being careless of their own possessions and covetous of the possessions of others. It is more surprising to find the same attitudes in Xenophon, who was deeply knowledgeable about the new military art of the fourth century and wrote a treatise on cavalry in addition to his military histories. Yet in his *Oeconomicus* (*On Estate Management* 6.6–6.7), this seasoned commander made Socrates argue for the superiority of the agricultural life on the grounds that when an enemy invades, the artisans and merchants would want to stay behind the city walls, while the hoplite farmers would vote to march out to battle—as he puts it, those who tilled the soil could be trusted to defend it. (Fourth-century democratic orators did not, of course, share these views. Demosthenes even turned the traditional argument upside down, claiming that democracies are always peaceful and just, in contrast with land-grabbing monarchies like Macedon [*On the Chersonese* 40–43].)

But even traditionalists had to face reality. The traditional civic militarist ideal simply no longer worked. In Plato's *Laws,* written about 350 B.C., the ideal state is still a hoplite oligarchy, albeit more realistic than in the *Republic,* but no longer is it claimed that it will invariably be successful in war. Instead, the solution is to isolate the ideal city from outside contact as much as possible. The proposed city must not be on the seacoast, so that it might avoid the corrupting effects of navies and democrats. It must be unwalled like Sparta, so that the citizens will not be tempted to cower behind their walls like the Athenian democrats in the Peloponnesian War, and its defenders will march out to meet invaders in traditional hoplite fashion (*Laws* 778). The speakers in the *Laws* still feel that the hoplite way of war is good for the city morally, but they have lost confidence that it will be successful militarily.

In Plato's *Laws,* we can discern the beginnings of a divorce between the internal and external affairs of the city-state. Greek political thought has begun to concentrate almost exclusively on the internal constitution; foreign affairs is no longer considered a fit subject for philosophy because it is too unpredictable and unmanageable. In the works of Aristotle, this divorce becomes pronounced.[2] Aristotle thought Plato's solution inadequate because a city cannot live in isolation—it must live the life of a city, not that of a hermit—and even if it does not pursue an active foreign policy, it must have sufficient military force to repel and deter invaders (*Politics* 2.6). Aristotle was aware, in other words, that a stable constitution required a successful foreign policy. He was as aware as his predecessors that the form of the constitution is largely determined by warfare and military organization. His own ideal constitution is essentially a hoplite city of the traditional sort (*Politics* 3.7,

4.8–9, 4.11–13). He knew Plato's ideal of an unwalled city was totally obsolete, yet he retained vestiges himself of the traditional chivalrous code: "Doubtless there is something dishonourable in seeking safety behind strong walls, at any rate against an enemy equal in number or only very slightly superior" (*Politics* 7.11, 1330, trans. Sinclair and Saunders). But Aristotle never pretends that this type of constitution will be more successful at war than any other. He was aware of how complicated warfare had become in the late fourth century. He knew that an army consisting of nothing but a hoplite phalanx was hopelessly outmoded: A modern military establishment must also have light infantry, cavalry, a fleet, and a siege train (*Politics* 6.7, 7.6, 7.11). He seems to be aware that the traditional hoplite army was becoming obsolete militarily, and as a result, his prized hoplite constitution was becoming politically obsolete. But he suggests no way to adapt the hoplite ideal to new conditions. In the *Rhetoric,* Aristotle had called the study of warfare and interstate relations an important branch of political science and had recommended the reading of historical works for information about these matters. But in the *Politics,* the most systematic and sophisticated treatment of political life in ancient literature, warfare and interstate relations go practically untreated. Aristotle summarizes traditional views about the ethical and constitutional implications of warfare, but he has no solutions to the problems of war. He thinks that wars between Greeks are bad, but he suggests no way to end them. He says that certain military factors produce good constitutions, but he suggests no way to bring them about. He did not believe that history could explain anything of philosophical value by the time he wrote the *Poetics:* "Poetry is more akin to philosophy and is a better thing than history; poetry deals with general truths, history with specific events. The latter are, for example, what Alcibiades did and suffered, while general truths are the kind of thing which a certain type of person would probably or inevitably do or say" (*Poetics* 9, 1451b, trans. G.M.A. Grube).

In the late fourth century, Greek political discourse was taking on a marked "introspective" quality, as Sheldon Wolin puts it.[3] From that time on, it would essentially be a study of the internal affairs of the state, with little attention to its external affairs in war or peace. Just at the time when Greek philosophy was rising to its climax in the work of Plato and Aristotle, war dropped out of philosophy, and the promising start made in the fifth century in the exploration of warfare and empire was not followed through. If the Greeks were losing faith in their ability to control warfare by the time of Aristotle, the best explanation would appear to be that warfare was in fact becoming uncontrollable. The decisive change came around the middle of the fourth century, when the new siegecraft, added to the already formidable armies of Macedon, put an end to the self-sufficiency of the city-state and removed the forum that had cultivated the unique political culture of classical Greece.

The Constitutional Theory of History: Polybius

Historians, as well as philosophers, seem to have lost interest in the study of constitutions in the fourth century. The subject hardly appears in the historical works of Xenophon. In the second century B.C., the discussion was revived by Polybius, but the nature of the question had changed. No one asked any more what constitution was best at war in the short run, for the Greek wars had shown that no constitution could be consistently successful. But then came the Roman conquests, which seemed to impose once again a certain order, pattern, and direction on the meaningless flux of history. The rise of Rome suggested to Polybius that there was something after all to the old notion that only one type of constitution could be supremely successful at war; but it also suggested that this would become obvious only in the very long run. Polybius was the first and only historian to make constitutional theory the main key to history and the ultimate cause of the rise and fall of states, rather than an occasional factor among many others.

Polybius said his main purpose was to show "by what means, and by virtue of what political institutions" Rome had become lord of the world, for "it is from this source [the constitution], as if from a fountainhead, that all designs and plans of action not only originate but reach their fulfillment" (6.2, trans. Scott-Kilvert; compare 1.1). He speaks as though the internal constitution *determines* external events. He sometimes seems to believe that these events are controlled *either* by constitutional factors or by pure chance, and if by pure chance, then he concludes that such events are not a fit subject for a serious and realistic historian. On these grounds, Polybius dismisses the histories of Athens and Thebes: The short-lived hegemonies won by those cities were mere gifts of Fortune, nothing else being possible in a democracy owing to the fickleness of the masses (6.43–44). In his view, the Spartan constitution was admirable for its domestic stability but was incapable of ruling other states (6.48–50); his own Achaean League had a much superior constitution, capable of both domestic and foreign success (2.37–42); but the most successful of all constitutions in both foreign and domestic affairs was the Roman.

We may pass briefly over Polybius's analysis of the Roman constitution. He mistook it for an Aristotelian "mixed constitution," a combination of several different constitutional types—the usual ideal of Greek conservative thinkers. Rome, as will be explained, was nothing of the sort but rather an oligarchy of peculiarly militaristic and expansionist character. The misconception was of great importance for the later history of Western political thought, which never really emerged from this mirage of the mixed constitution, but that need not concern us here. Polybius tries to give this abstraction some explanatory power by proposing the odd theory (which he wrongly attributes to Plato) that all constitutions have to pass through the same cycle, beginning in monarchy and ending in extreme democracy. How Rome could fit into such a cycle is not clear, because Polybius's treatment of early Roman history is lost. He probably claimed that the cycle could be arrested at some point by adopting a mixed constitution and that Rome had managed this at some point in its early history.

Why was so sensible a man captive to such a theory? It is likely that the clue lies in his remark that every state "is liable to decline from two sources, the one being external, and the other due to its own internal evolution. For the first we cannot lay down any fixed principle, but the second pursues a regular sequence" (6.57, trans. Scott-Kilvert). Polybius could not escape from the philosophers' teaching that no meaning could be found in the flow of events unless these could be reduced to a fixed predictable pattern. Interstate relations were not considered philosophical because they were not predictable. The notion that a constitution must follow a predetermined cycle is a reductio ad absurdum of this notion, probably borrowed from some earlier Hellenistic writer equally determined to show that history could be philosophical. When he could escape from the influence of his philosophy lectures, Polybius had no difficulty in making sense of the flow of events. But by his time, history and philosophy tended to get in one another's way; and both were passing into the hands of the Romans, whose political culture was never so open to rationalism as that of the Greeks.

Notes

1. *Constitution of the Athenians 2*, trans. in *The Greek Historians*, vol. 2, ed. F.R.B. Godolphin (New York, 1942).

2. The lack of attention to interstate affairs in Greek thought has often been noticed. Different interpretations of it have been offered by Arnaldo Momigliano, "Some Observations on the Causes of War in Ancient Historiography," in his *Studies in Historiography* (New York, 1966), 112–126; Peter Manicas, "War, Stasis, and Greek Political Thought," *Comparative Studies in Society and History* 24 (1982), 673–688; M. I. Finley, "War and Empire," in *Ancient History: Evidence and Models* (Trowbridge, England, 1985), 67–87. The interpretation I offer here is defended at length in my forthcoming article "Aristotle on War and History."

3. Sheldon Wolin, *Politics and Vision: Continuity and Innovation in Western Political Thought* (Berkeley, 1960), 73.

Part Three

Roman Warfare

Now in general the Romans rely upon force in all their undertakings.
—Polybius (trans. Ian Scott-Kilvert)

Chapter Seven

The Roman Way of War

Early Roman Practices of War

Early in the second century B.C., the eastern Greeks felt the full weight of Roman expansion, beginning the long exchange between the two peoples that eventually produced the dual culture of classical antiquity. In warfare as in much else, the Greek element in this amalgam was the more original, but the Roman contribution was the more decisive influence on later Western civilizations.

Roman warfare was an adaptation of Greek hoplite warfare and the hoplite ideology of decisive battle, but with peculiar features, the most striking of which was its sheer success. This was especially striking to the defeated and humbled Greeks of the second century. At the beginning of his histories, Polybius posed the question that was troubling his compatriots and has never ceased to fascinate the world:

> There can surely be nobody so petty or so apathetic in his outlook that he has no desire to discover by what means and under what system of government the Romans succeeded in less than fifty-three years [220–167 B.C.] in bringing under their rule almost the whole of the inhabited world, an achievement which is without parallel in human history. Or from the opposite point of view, can there be anyone so completely absorbed in other subjects of contemplation or study that he could find any task more important than to acquire this knowledge? (1.1 [trans. Scott-Kilvert])

Polybius could not produce an entirely satisfactory answer to this question, but he saw one important key to it. He realized that the rise of Rome owed little to Fortune, the fickle goddess of the Greeks. The triumph of Rome was not the triumph of a meteoric individual like Alexander but the triumph of a system; and the Roman system had come to stay. The Roman republic was a society superbly organized for war. Its capacity for sustained, long-distance, aggressive war making had no earlier parallel and was to have none again until the rise of the modern European nation-states.

The capacity was obvious to the Greeks, but the explanation for it was not, and it has eluded many modern scholars as well. The Romans never interpreted themselves as the Greeks did, and such interpretations as we find in Latin authors were written at a time when the old Roman military system scarcely existed any longer and the Roman aristocracy had acquired a veneer of Greek philosophical culture that made it difficult for the members of this elite to honestly confront their ancestors. Hence, the Roman legacy is largely a legacy of myths and mirages.

The military system itself is well known to us and needs only the briefest description here.[1] The study of Roman military institutions in the age of Roman expansion, before the "Marian" reorganization of the first century B.C., raises no problems comparable to those encountered in the study of archaic Greek warfare. The Roman legion was essentially an adaptation of the Greek phalanx, which the Romans broke up into several lines, with each line in turn broken up into small units capable of independent maneuver. Most soldiers were armed with swords and javelins, though the rear line retained the Greek thrusting spears. The Romans sacrificed the depth and cohesion of the phalanx for mobility, sending in their units in waves to attack and retreat in turn, in a fashion that in Greek warfare was associated more with cavalry than with infantry. The system could function smoothly in the heat of battle because the legionaries were subjected to intense drilling and were led by a semiprofessional officer corps, the centurions; neither institution had any parallel in the Greek world outside Sparta.

The legion was obviously a more flexible formation than the phalanx, but in some ways it was less tactically effective. The Roman insistence upon uniformity caused them to neglect cavalry and light infantry, and they therefore never developed the combined-arms tactics perfected by Alexander and his successors. They paid for this when they met a general as brilliant at those tactics as Pyrrhus or Hannibal. But again, the most important feature of the Roman military system was simply the fact that it *was* a system. Rome did not need brilliant generals and rarely produced them. Romans knew that in the long run nothing could defeat their well-drilled military machine (Roman warfare always evokes the metaphor of a machine, and traditional Greek warfare, that of a duel). Romans knew that all wars with Rome would have a long run because Rome never gave up. Only a society that regarded almost constant warfare and its attendant discipline as normal expectations could have operated such a system. The key to it lies not in the military institutions themselves but in the militaristic culture behind them.

Causes of Early Roman Warfare

When the Greeks thought about societies organized for war, they thought first of Sparta. But Sparta was a hoplite oligarchy whose war aims were essentially defensive, even isolationist at times, and the egalitarianism of the hoplite class, which Sparta carried to communistic extremes, kept its members in line. The contrast between the defensive militarism of Sparta and the expansionary militarism of Rome was perceived by Polybius, but he was too enmeshed in the constitutional theories of Greek philosophy to see the reason for it. And modern scholars have often been misled by Roman historiography, which leaves the impression that none of Rome's wars were offensive.

Until recently, most historians have followed the interpretation of Roman imperialism laid down in the late nineteenth century by the great scholar Theodor Mommsen. Most have denied that Rome had a conscious policy of imperialism. Some have spoken of a "defensive" imperialism. Cicero said that Rome conquered the world merely by defending its allies. Others have emphasized the element of accident in the Roman conquests, often with reference to the example of the British Empire, which, as the saying went, was acquired in a fit of absence of mind. But if "imperialism" means a policy of expansion—the usual meaning of the word since the late nineteenth century—then "defensive imperialism" seems oxymoronic. Those who think the Roman republic did not consistently seek conquest have never provided a coherent explanation of how it managed nevertheless to conquer so much. The parallel with nineteenth-century Britain should remind us that empires are not really acquired absent-mindedly; there is a wide area between grand strategy and absence of mind. This is another case where we tend to confuse the ancient concept of a just war and the modern concept of defensive war. Just wars could be aggressive, and the just wars of Rome were particularly so.

Recent studies have suggested a new approach to the problem.[2] In brief, the Roman public ideology can be described as a highly elitist form of civic militarism. Rome was dominated by a fiercely competitive warrior oligarchy, which at the same time shared the benefits of conquest with the masses, perhaps more fully than any other conquest state had ever done; the dynamism of the system sprang from the interaction between elitist and civic elements.

Unlike most ancient Mediterranean oligarchies, membership in the Roman ruling class was not guaranteed by birth or wealth. This was an oligarchy of officeholders. Admission to the Senate, the ruling council of Rome, was achieved only through election to magistracies, and the functions of magistracies were essentially military. In the early republic, a young noble had to spend years in military service before he was even eligible for office. Admission to the inner circle of the Senate came through election to the consulship, the supreme magistracy, whose supreme function was leadership in war. There were only two consuls, elected annually, and since in the early republic the nobility insisted on sharing office, election to the consulate was usually a once-in-a-lifetime opportunity. Therefore, a noble who won the consulate had a single year to demonstrate his *virtus* and win *laus* and *gloria* for himself and his house. The original meaning of "virtue" was military valor, and "praise" and "glory" originally meant military glory. The highest achievement of a consul was to be awarded a "triumph," a victory procession through Rome displaying his captives and booty, which could not be awarded unless the consul had killed at least five thousand of the enemy. Much of this seems atavistic, reminding us of the shamanistic killing quotas and head-hunting raids of tribal warfare. The roots of it were primitive, indeed, but here they had been adapted to a highly evolved political system whose net effect was to place enormous pressure on the male members of its elite to compete with one another for military success. Greek cities did not train such elites. The supreme Greek symbol of military glory was the communal dedication of captured arms and armor in a temple, not the general's triumph. In the Athenian funeral orations no individuals were ever mentioned by name. The Greeks suppressed the element of individual glory in the martial-values complex as systematically as the Romans encouraged it.

This was a very elitist form of militarism, but it never lost its civic foundation. Not only the leadership but the whole society was geared for expansion. Romans expected war to be profitable as well as glorious, profitable for the noble above all, but also offering substantial material rewards to the entire citizen body—in the form of plunder, slaves, distributions of land in the new Roman colonies that soon dotted Italy, and opportunities for social advancement through a centurion's career. Until the late second century B.C., when the great age of expansion was over, there was little sign that any citizens objected to the constant campaigning that distinguished Rome from all other ancient city-states. The Roman republic went to war almost yearly, and even before the war with Hannibal, it normally had four legions under arms each year, constituting about one-fifth of the eligible citizens. It has been said that this was the highest rate of military participation known in any preindustrial society except those of Prussia under Frederick the Great and Napoleonic France, which matched it only for short periods.[3]

Warfare in Early Roman Religion

Connections between war and religion, strong in all ancient societies, were nowhere stronger than at Rome; and Roman religion, in warfare as in all else, was characterized by an intense legalism. Rome and the other Latin-speaking cities of central Italy had special colleges of priests called *fetiales*, whose sole function was to preside over interstate relations.[4] A Latin city could not go to war until the fetials had proclaimed the cause to be just, calling upon Jupiter and all the gods, and had demanded reparations from the offending city. No other ancient cities ever seem to have had a special priesthood for war and diplomacy. The rites included elements suggestive of Neolithic antiquity—a pig had to be sacrificed with a stone knife to solemnize a treaty, a spear with a fire-hardened point had to be hurled into enemy territory to declare war—but in spite of these archaic trappings, the likeliest explanation for this strange institution is that it was an artificial creation of the Latin peoples intended to prevent or at least regularize warfare among themselves.

The full ceremony required both cities to have fetials, and since fetials were unknown outside central Italy, the custom was gradually dropped as Roman expansion got underway. The functions of the fetials were taken over by secular ambassadors such as other cities employed, and only vestiges of the fetial law survived to the late first century B.C., when Augustus Caesar attempted to revive it along with other antique religious customs.

Nevertheless, the fetial law exercised a permanent effect upon the Roman mind. In later centuries, it was remembered that only the Latins had had such an institution, and Roman success in war was widely attributed to the fact that the Romans had always taken such care to ensure that all their wars were pious and righteous. The fetial code included *jus in bello* as well as *jus ad bellum,* for the fetials presided over all treaties and oaths with foreign cities and protected ambassadors. All these matters constituted the *fides Romana,* or the good faith of Rome. The basic concept was not new: Rituals to ensure the justice of war and regulate the conduct of war were universal in ancient societies, and Greeks were also proud of the good faith (*pistis*) of their city in its dealings with outsiders. But the elaborate legalistic form that these rites acquired in early Rome would make it difficult for the later Romans to separate religion from policy.

In addition to the fetial ceremonies at the start of a war, all campaigns and battles were accompanied by the usual sacrifices, prayers, and auguries. There was an unusually large pantheon of war gods. The principal god of war, Mars, was a far more majestic figure than his Greek counterpart, Ares. Many other deities had military functions. Fides, the good faith of Rome, was herself an ancient goddess associated with Jupiter, and both were responsible for oaths and treaties. In the third century B.C., the pivotal century of Roman expansion, a uniquely Roman cult of the goddess Victoria (Victory) was introduced. The Roman religious calendar was studded with military festivals, from the exercising of the cavalry horses at the Equirria in March to the purification of arms at the Armilustrium in October, which marked the end of the campaigning season.

One aspect of the state cult is of special interest here. William Harris has presented considerable evidence that Rome, alone among ancient city-states, made *expansion* a public and religiously sanctioned aim. In the reign of Tiberius, a rhetorician named Valerius Maximus compiled an anthology of historical anecdotes for the use of orators that contains some interesting bits of historical information, among them the fact that the duties of the important magistrates called censors had in early times included the recital of a prayer calling upon the gods to make the Roman state prosper *and grow:* "Quo di immortales ut populi Romani res meliores amplioresque facerent rogabantur" (Valerius Maximus 4.1.10). A. N. Sherwin-White has pointed out (in "Rome the Aggressor?") that the censors were responsible for taking the census and therefore were concerned with population and fertility, so the prayer just cited, "May the immortal gods make the things of the Roman people better and bigger," does not necessarily refer to *territorial* expansion.

We have observed that Greeks could use similar expressions, with similar ambiguities. But to my knowledge, Greeks did not say such things in such an official religious forum, and when Greeks and Romans prayed for the expansion of the state, I doubt that they meant to *exclude* the possibility of territorial expansion. In the case of the Romans, there is reason to think that they had that possibility explicitly in mind. The historical traditions relayed by Livy recalled that in the eastern wars of the second century B.C., the *haruspices,* the official soothsayers who read the future in the flight of birds and the entrails of sheep, repeatedly prophesied that these wars would extend the frontiers of the Roman people (Livy 31.5, 36.1, 42.30), and there seems to be no question here but that territorial expansion was meant.

There was also a tradition that Rome's victorious wars always ended with a *deditio* or unconditional surrender. According to Livy, this practice went back to the period of the kings. King Tarquin in the seventh century B.C. was supposed to have addressed the following formula to the spokesmen of a conquered Sabine city: "Do you surrender yourselves and the People of Collatia, city, lands, water, boundary marks, shrines, utensils, all appurtenances, divine and human, into my power and that of the Roman People?" (Livy 1.38 [trans. B. O. Foster]). Some traditions make a distinction between surrender into the power (*potestas* or *dicio*) of Rome and surrender into the good faith (*fides*) of Rome, implying that a submission to the good faith of Rome guaranteed mild treatment, whereas surrender into the power of Rome put one into a more uncertain status (Livy 36.27, 39.54; Valerius Maximus 6.5.1); but we do not know whether this distinction was more than rhetorical. In any case, it was believed that the Romans had always fought for unconditional surrender. And that was rare in the Greek world until a very late date.

It is possible that all these traditions had been strongly colored by the attitudes of the post-Polybian Roman elite, which took it for granted that the gods had conferred world empire upon Rome and read this worldview back into earlier times. But at least this is how the Romans of the late republic interpreted the *mos maiorum,* the way of their ancestors: They believed the expansion of Rome had been sanctioned by the gods from the beginning, that Roman wars had always been fought with a dedication to total victory highly unusual among ancient city-states, and that Rome had always had a sense of moral and religious responsibility for those who accepted Rome's leadership.

The Roman Conquests

The Roman system developed in three stages: the conquest of Italy, circa 400–270 B.C.; the conquest of the western Mediterranean, circa 270–200 B.C.; and the conquest of the Greek world, circa 200–146 B.C.

The first phase was formative. It was during the fourth century B.C., in the course of continual warfare with its neighbors, that Rome, originally not very different from other city-states of central Italy, developed its peculiar military culture. Once the pattern was established, it fed on itself. As soon as a large part of the Italian peninsula had been brought into the Roman alliance, the drive to expand became irreversible because the Roman alliance, like everything else about Rome, was geared for war. The allies of Rome rendered to Rome only military service, not tribute. The contrast with the Athenian empire of the fifth century is striking: Athens had preferred to take tribute, not military service, from its allies. The fact that Rome could demand only military service provided an additional incentive to war, for the only way Rome could profit from its alliances was to make use of them in war, and if a year went by without a successful war, the resources of the hegemony were being wasted. By around 300 B.C., the Romans had brought almost the whole of the peninsula into a Roman confederation with the largest manpower reserves in the western Mediterranean, and the habits of more or less constant warfare had become ingrained.

The second stage, much better documented, brought the two great Punic Wars against Carthage (264–241 and 218–202 B.C.) and the Roman conquest of the western Mediterranean coasts and islands. There has been much dispute over the causes of the First Punic War in 264, but in the long view, it does not seem to matter much what made the Romans cross the straits into Sicily. That venture represented the first departure from traditional Roman policy, which had never looked beyond the Italian mainland, and it may have been a simple miscalculation. The important fact, however, was that once the Romans found themselves in Sicily, they stayed there. Rome managed to convert itself into a naval power, withstood appalling losses, and fought for Sicily for more than twenty years until Carthage conceded. The real secret of Rome's success was the Roman willingness to persist in warfare year after year. When the war was over, Rome absorbed the Carthaginian thalassocracy and became a Mediterranean power. The second round, the Hannibalic War of 218–202 B.C., the most titanic conflict ever seen in the west, did nothing more than confirm this conclusion and provide an even more impressive demonstration of the invincible tenacity of the Roman war machine.

By 202 B.C., Rome may have been ready to stop. The Senate seems to have been genuinely reluctant to enter the alien and complicated Greek-speaking world to the east. It is doubtful that any Romans at that time had any ambition for, or concept of, world empire. All its traditions rooted Rome in Italy; to hold down a fringe of coastland and island in the western seas did not detract from the Italocentric nature of Roman policy, and these territories provided consuls with opportunities for easy triumph hunting among ill-armed barbarians; but the Hellenistic world was another matter. Also, the Roman capacity to expand may have temporarily outrun the capacity to organize and exploit the conquests. For half a century, Roman policy toward the

Greeks alternated between sudden destructive intrusions and long periods of withdrawal. But the mechanisms of expansion in Roman society were still running and would not allow Rome to withdraw completely. During these intrusions, the Roman military system, hardened in the war against Hannibal, won decisive victories over the Greek kingdoms at Cynoscephalae (197) and Magnesia (189); a later intrusion destroyed the Macedonian monarchy at Pydna (168) and left Rome with no rivals. Thereafter, Rome was hegemon of the known world, and the Greek states, by expecting Rome to act like a hegemonic power, drew the Romans ever deeper into their affairs. By the middle of the second century, Romans were becoming accustomed to the idea of empire in the east and felt no more inhibitions about annexing territory there. The process was completed by 146 B.C., when both Carthage and Corinth were destroyed. All the Mediterranean Basin was now within the *imperium* of Rome, some of it organized into provinces governed by Roman magistrates, the rest reduced to client states.[5]

By this time, Romans were acquiring a sense that they possessed a world empire. (The phrase *imperium orbis terrae* first occurs circa 85 B.C. in the oratorical treatise called the *Rhetoric to Herrenius*.) They began to produce a Latin literature based on Greek models that adapted Greek ideas of war and conquest and sought to explain the Roman empire in those terms.

The emergent Latin literary tradition was also decisively influenced by the fact that it took shape at a time when the great period of Roman expansion had ceased. The machinery of expansion was still running, but now its energies were largely directed inward. The last century of the republic brought a series of devastating civil struggles among the great warlords of the Senate. Expansion continued intermittently, but the direction and nature of it had changed: Instead of being led by the Senate as a whole, expansion was directed by the warlords themselves, who acquired new provinces, like Caesar in Gaul, to strengthen their positions in the civil wars; instead of by the citizens as a whole, wars were fought by increasingly professionalized armies. Hence, the Latin tradition became permeated by a sense of decline and nostalgia for an earlier republic of domestic tranquility and glorious foreign conquest.

The Roman Frontiers

The dependence on Greek models and the ideology of nostalgia for the republican past caused the Latin literary tradition to become generally divorced from current political and military realities, in comparison to Greek literature. The principate never produced a realistic interpretation of itself and bequeathed no theories to posterity. In the eyes of posterity, the Latin writers who mattered most were those of the late republic and the Augustan Age, whose values were republican. Nevertheless the historical *fact* of the principate had an enormous effect on posterity. It was the major historical example of a great continental state faced with the problem of protecting a long land frontier, and we have ample evidence, mostly of a nonliterary nature, for the evolution of its frontier system over a period of several centuries. The subject deserves attention here because many modern scholars have thought that there must have been more systematic planning and thinking behind this system than appears in the literary record.

Three main stages in this evolution can be distinguished. The first stage was the hegemonial empire established in the late republic. The core Roman territories were surrounded with a cordon of client states, the friends and allies (*socii et amici*) of Rome. This system remained largely intact well into the first century A.D., but it generally ceased to grow after the Augustan Age, for reasons both internal and external. Although the ideology of expansion continued, the social engine that drove it practically stopped running under the principate, which put a halt to competition for office among the elite. In addition, the Roman war machine, which relied on heavy infantry and siege tactics, was best suited for high-intensity warfare against a dense agricultural population with fixed and vulnerable assets; it was less well suited for mobile warfare against cavalry or light infantry. The further the legions marched from the shores of the Mediterranean, the slower and harder conquest became. The Romans of the principate made repeated attempts to take over northern Europe and the Middle East, but the Germans had no cities to sack and the Parthians had few. The Romans of the republic might have persisted and taken both, but the energies had gone out of the system. Eventually the principate gave up.

By the later part of the first century, the second stage was emerging. The Romans gradually assumed direct control over their client states, and when they were all absorbed, a territorial empire took shape. The legions were now settled in permanent camps behind fortified frontiers, and behind these frontiers all the native elites were gradually incorporated into a single ruling class, united by a uniform Greco-Roman literary culture resembling the mandarin elite of China. The transition to "perimeter defense" (Edward Luttwak's phrase) was virtually completed by the reign of Hadrian (A.D. 117–138).

But perimeter defense is effective only against weak external enemies, and the enemies of the empire grew steadily stronger. After the defenses collapsed during the crisis of the third century, a third stage emerged: The frontier forces were weakened in favor of mobile central armies. The transition to this mixed security system was complete by the reign of Constantine (A.D. 308–337).

In the 1970s, when William Harris was offering a new approach to the military history of the Roman republic, the military analyst Edward Luttwak made a similar impact upon the study of the principate by applying the concepts of contemporary strategic thought.[6] Luttwak's analysis is illuminating and the sketch given above is indebted to it, but the use of modern strategic language implies a coherent system with an inner logic and the existence of conscious long-range planning such as we expect from the general staff of a modern army. In fact, the evidence for the Roman security system is mostly archaeological, and the existence of deliberate planning behind it is generally a matter of inference. We know there were debates among the elite as to whether the empire should expand here or there, and these have left traces in Roman historiography. But it not obvious whether there was anything that should be called a grand strategy. This question will be taken up in Chapter 9, in dealing with *raison d'état* among the Romans. But first we must deal with Roman traditions about the morality of warfare.

Notes

1. For an introduction to the Roman army, see the chapters by G. R. Watson, A. S. Anderson, and R.S.O. Tomlin in *The Roman World,* ed. John Wacher (London, 1987), vol. 1, 75–135. For the army of the early and middle republic, see L.J.F. Keppie, *The Making of the Roman Army* (Totowa, N.J., 1984). F. E. Adcock's *The Roman Art of War Under the Republic* (Cambridge, 1960) is still useful.

2. In the late 1970s, a number of important monographs changed the terms of this debate: Keith Hopkins, *Conquerors and Slaves* (Cambridge, 1978); C. Nicolet, *The World of the Citizen in Republican Rome,* trans. P. S. Falla (Berkeley, 1980); and above all, W. V. Harris, *War and Imperialism in Republican Rome, 327–70 B.C.* (Oxford, 1979). I share the view of J. A. North ("The Development of Roman Imperialism," *Journal of Roman Studies* 71 (1981), 1–9) that Harris's reinterpretation has rendered the theory of "defensive imperialism" untenable, at least in its traditional form. In brief, Harris has argued that republican Rome was persistently aggressive because the ethos of the whole culture was geared to war making, particularly the senatorial elite, and that Rome was unusual among ancient city-states in making expansion a publicly declared aim. Whether Rome had a conscious long-range strategy is a question Harris finds meaningless, because ancient states did not have such strategies. But he does think that Rome had a "continuing drive to expand" (Harris, 107). One weakness in Harris's argument is that he never fully explains what he means by a "continuing drive." In practice, he seems to have been thinking of a series of conscious decisions by the elite, for much of his book is taken up by an attempt to prove that virtually all the wars of the Roman republic during the period he studied had aggressive aims. One of his critics, A. N. Sherwin-White, has argued convincingly against this view in "Rome the Aggressor?" *Journal of Roman Studies* 70 (1980), 177–181, and *Roman Foreign Policy in the East, 168 B.C.to A.D. 1* (Norman, Okla., 1983). It seems to me that Harris's argument as originally formulated suffers from the Clausewitzian bias of modern military history, which assumes all warfare to be a rational political activity. I suggest the Harris thesis will be strengthened if we adopt a more anthropological perspective: Warfare is everywhere a matter of continuing drives, which are expressions of culture and values more than of politics and policy, and this is especially true of a traditional society. To show that Rome had a continuing drive to expand it is not necessary to prove that most of its leaders had a conscious policy of that kind most of the time, nor need one deny that Rome sometimes

acted defensively—as in the long and bloody wars fought in the third century B.C. to defend Italy from Greek and Carthaginian invaders.

3. The estimate of Hopkins, *Conquerors and Slaves,* 25ff., 102ff. He properly does not count primitive societies, which may have higher rates of military participation than any complex society but which are hardly comparable.

4. The fetial law is described by Livy 1.24, 32; Dionysius of Halicarnassus, *Roman Antiquities* 2.72; Plutarch, *Life of Numa Pompilius* 12. See Yvon Garlan, *War in the Ancient World: A Social History,* trans. Janet Lloyd (Ithaca, 1975), and M. D. Goodman and A. J. Holladay, "Religious Scruples in Ancient Warfare," *Classical Quarterly* n.s. 36 (1986), 151–171. The explanation for the origins of the fetial cult that I follow here was suggested by Alan Watson, *International Law in Ancient Rome: War and Religion* (Baltimore, 1993). I have not followed Watson's suggestion that early Rome was unique in regarding warfare as a trial before the gods; it seems to me that attitude is very general in primitive and ancient religion.

5. The political and cultural interactions between Romans and Greeks at this period are discussed in detail by Peter Gruen, *The Hellenistic World and the Coming of Rome* (Berkeley, 1984).

6. *The Grand Strategy of the Roman Empire from the First Century A.D. to the Third* (Baltimore, 1976). Similar approaches have been adopted by G.B.D. Jones, "Concept and Development in Roman Frontiers," *Bulletin of the John Rylands Library* 61 (1978), 115–144; Arther Ferrill, *The Fall of the Roman Empire: The Military Explanation* (London, 1986).

Chapter Eight

The Ethics of Roman Warfare

Just War in the Late Republic

The great orator Cicero, a leading figure in Roman political life during the middle decades of the last century B.C., is the first Roman author from whose works we can extract something like a comprehensive theory of warfare. It is essentially a Greek theory, but with some significant Roman contributions. The most complete version of it appears in the *On Duties* (*De officiis*), a summary of moral philosophy written at the end of Cicero's life (circa 44 B.C.), based upon a similar treatise by Panaetius of Rhodes, the Greek neo-Stoic who had introduced Stoicism to the Roman aristocracy one hundred years before. Because of the great influence of this treatise on later Western ethical thought, the statements on warfare in *On Duties* merit full quotation.

> The first office of justice is to keep one man from doing harm to another, unless provoked by wrong; and the next is to lead men to use common possessions for their common interests, private property for their own. There is, however, no such thing as private ownership established by nature, but property becomes private either through long occupancy (as in the case of those who long ago settled in unoccupied territory) or through conquest (as in the case of those who took it in war) or by due process of law, bargain, or purchase, or by allotment. (*Duties* 1.7.20–21 [trans. Walter Miller])

This passage summarizes a neo-Stoic theory of warfare that became influential at Rome. The judicial and vindicative purpose of warfare is taken for granted, as in all Greek philosophy. Also implicit is a theory about the origins of war that was particularly associated with neo-Stoics. This was a "euhemerized" version of the Hesiodic myth of the golden age: The golden age was thought to have been a real historical period when all men lived in peace and plenty, until the rise of civilization brought private property, inequality, and warfare. Conquest is said here to be a perfectly legitimate method of acquiring property, but in view of the first sentence, that must mean through victory in a just war, into which the conquerors had been provoked by wrongdoers. The basic assumptions resemble those of Plato and Aristotle, except for the emphasis on the pacifism of primitive man (the implications of this idea will be examined shortly) and the absence of any notion of a special kind of holy war against barbarians or natural slaves: These are the contributions of Stoic egalitarianism to Roman thought.[1]

This is followed by an unusually clear statement of the principle that vengeance is a common duty, implying that a powerful state is morally obligated, under the right circumstances, to intervene in the affairs of its neighbors:

> There are, on the other hand, two kinds of injustice—the one, on the part of those who inflict wrong, the other on the part of those who, when they can, do not shield from wrong those upon whom it is being inflicted. For he who, under the influence of anger or some other passion, wrongfully assaults another seems, as it were, to be laying violent hands on a comrade; but he who does not prevent or oppose wrong, if he can, is just as guilty of wrong as if he deserted his parents or his friends or his country. (1.7.23 [trans. Miller])

In addition to the *jus ad bellum,* natural law requires the *jus in bello:* Vengeance must be taken in accordance with humanity (*humanitas*) and balance (*aequitas*), with the significant qualification that follows:

> In the case of a state in its external relations, the rights of war [*iura belli*] must be strictly observed . . . The only excuse, therefore, for going to war is that we may live in peace unharmed; and when the victory is won, we should spare those who have not been blood-thirsty and barbarous in their warfare. (1.11.34–35 [trans. Miller])

> [Justice demands that we] avenge ourselves upon those who have attempted to injure us, and visit them with such retribution as justice and humanity will permit. (2.5.18 [trans. Miller])

Thus far, there is nothing here that is particularly Roman, for Cicero was far more Hellenized than most Roman senators of his time and at his most Hellenic in *On Duties.* But even there, and much more so in some of Cicero's other works, distinctively Latin aspects of his thought can be distinguished. Roman religiosity crops up even in *On Duties.* The rules of war are rooted in universal laws of nature, but the fetial law of Rome is their perfect expression. This is obviously Cicero, not Panaetius: "As for war, humane laws touching it are drawn up in the fetial code of the Roman people under all the guarantees of religion; and from this it may be gathered that no war is just, unless it is entered upon after an official demand for satisfaction has been submitted or warning has been given and a formal declaration made"

(1.11.36 ([trans. Miller]). The third book of Cicero's *On the Republic* (*De re- publica*), now lost except for fragments, apparently contained an argument that the practical Romans had made more contributions toward the develop- ment of an ideal state than the theoretical Greeks, mentioning the fetial rites as evidence of the Roman concern for strict morality in interstate relations. Two of these fragments were to have great influence on medieval and later European thought about warfare because they were quoted in the *Etymolo- gies* of Isidore of Seville, an encyclopedia of classical learning compiled in the seventh century A.D.: "Wars undertaken without cause are unjust. For no just war can be waged without a cause, either to take revenge or to repel an enemy. . . . No war is held to be just unless it has been declared, unless it has been proclaimed, unless reparation has been demanded" (*Etymologies* 18.1 [author's trans.]). These passages established the legalistic terms in which the problem of the morality of war has been discussed to the present day. We do not know how the two statements were connected in the original text, but they appear to be complementary. Taken together they lay down three con- ditions for a just war: There must be a formal declaration by proper authori- ties; this must include a charge, which must be one of two things, either an attempt to resist injuries or an attempt to avenge them; there must first be a demand for reparations, and the guilty party must be given a chance to sat- isfy this. The Roman contribution is the insistence on formal procedure, un- known to the Greeks because they had no institution comparable to the fe- tial priesthood.

There is little about religious matters in these treatises in which Cicero tries to sound like a Greek philosopher. More revealing are his speeches be- fore Roman audiences, especially a passing remark in a speech he delivered before the Senate shortly before he wrote the *Republic.* He asks the rhetori- cal question "Who is there so mad as to believe in the gods and yet not be- lieve that it is through the will of the gods that this great empire has arisen, has expanded, and has been preserved?" (*On the Responses of the Haruspices* 9.19, author's trans.). No senator would have admitted in public his disbelief in the gods, and it would have been as difficult to find a senator expressing any doubts about the divine mission of the Roman empire.

Even philosophically trained Greeks were impressed by Roman piety. Not long afterward, Dionysius of Halicarnassus wrote his history of early Rome for the express purpose of justifying Roman rule to his fellow Greeks, and in that work he made much of the fetial rites as the secret of Roman mil- itary success: No other people, he said, had taken such pains to make sure that all their wars were approved by the gods (*Roman Antiquities* 2.72).

Just Empire in the Late Republic

Greek orators could associate just warfare with just hegemony, speaking of the second as a sort of reward for the first. But they do not make this association with the same regularity as the Romans. The speech just quoted shows that Cicero and his colleagues assumed the gods had favored not only the preservation of the *imperium*—the usual Latin equivalent of the Greek *hegemonia*—but also its enlargement. In *On Duties,* Cicero called it the duty of every statesman to make the state expand in *imperium,* in lands, and in revenues (2.24.85). The Roman concept of the just war was, in the modern sense of this word, imperialistic.

The Romans thought the just *imperium,* like the just war, was just because it righted wrongs. The idea that a just hegemony should benefit its subjects was a commonplace in Greek thought, and Cicero doubtless found it in the Stoic treatise that was his source for *On Duties,* but there it appears in Roman dress. In discussing the laws of war, Cicero—clearly this is Cicero, not Panaetius—remarks that it was the Roman *mos maiorum,* the way of the ancestors, not only to spare the Italian peoples they defeated but to grant them Roman citizenship, and Roman generals often became the patrons (*patroni*) of the very cities and nations they had conquered (1.11.35). Elsewhere (2.8.27), Cicero describes the Roman *imperium* as not so much an *imperium* as a *patrocinium orbis terrae,* a patronage of all the world—at least it was such for as long as the old Roman ways lasted, until the corruption of the constitution began in the time of Sulla the dictator, around 80 B.C. This nostalgia for the past is a leitmotiv in Latin literature, which will be examined more closely in the next chapter. The point to be emphasized here is that Cicero has interpreted the Greek theory of hegemony as a patron-client relationship. Patronage was an important feature of all ancient societies, but at Rome was extraordinarily pervasive and formalized. Roman society was a network of ties between patron (*patronus*) and client (*cliens*), between rich citizen and poor citizen, the former offering financial aid and the latter a political following. Roman senatorial families built up similar networks of clients among the provincials and allies, though Cicero's claim that Roman generals normally became the patrons of the peoples they conquered is mythical. Cicero makes patronage a metaphor for the international system, casting the city of Rome as patron of the world, and all the peoples of the world as her grateful and loyal clients. The metaphor implies voluntary submission on the part of the clients, protection and support on the part of the patron. Greek theories of hegemony usually assumed that the lesser states within a hegemonic sphere would remain independent, but Cicero's metaphors imply a dependent relationship, often entailing the bestowal of Roman citizenship. It should be emphasized that this high-flown language has little or no connection with Roman practices or concepts of empire during the period of the conquests: It is an idealized theory of the late republic, when the *imperium* was a long-established fact, and may be wholly the invention of Cicero.[2]

But the conviction behind it was widely shared. We find much the same notions repeated in Cicero's speeches before Senate, law courts, and assemblies. A passing remark in the speech *In Defense of Sextus Roscius* is particularly interesting: The old Romans cultivated their own lands and were not covetous of the lands of other people, and therefore they added "lands and cities and nations" to the republic and "expanded the empire and the fame of the Roman people" (18.50). This seems to be based on a Greek rhetorical commonplace, examples of which I have cited from the works of Isocrates. But what Isocrates said was that the just city defends its land and never covets the land of others, and the unjust city does the opposite—this is the defensive hoplite ethic. The twist Cicero puts on the saying is Roman: The just city defends its land and acquires an empire. A fragment of his *Republic* contains the line "our people by defending their allies became masters of the whole world" (3.23.35).

We have seen that the Greeks perceived no contradiction between the desire for freedom and the desire to dominate. Thucydides summarized the Athenian character by saying Athenians were accustomed not only to being free but to ruling others. Cicero borrows this line in one of his last speeches, when he tried to arouse the Senate to resist Mark Antony by reminding the senators that their ancestors had gone to war not merely that they might be free but that they might rule ("non modo ut liberi essent, sed etiam ut imperarent," *Eighth Philippic* 4.12), and he contrasted this attitude with the degeneracy of the modern Senate, which would not even fight for freedom. The Romans knew that the Greeks shared their hunger for hegemonic power, and much Roman rhetoric about it was of Greek origin. But the Romans believed they did it better. In his speeches in the Senate, Cicero repeatedly brags that Romans are unique in pursuit of *laus* and *gloria*, congratulates Romans on their generous sharing of citizenship with client nations, and speaks of it as a normal expectation that Roman governors should be expanding the boundaries of their provinces.

In several of these passages, Cicero says the empire covers the whole *orbis terrae*, the circuit of the earth. In his treatise *On the Orator*, we are told that oratory is one of the many benefits that Roman rule has brought to the entire world (1.4.14). When he wishes to praise a commander, Cicero assures the Senate that the general in question has extended or is in the process of extending the Roman empire to the ends of the earth.[3] In Cicero's time, Romans took it for granted that their *imperium* covered the whole world and often cited this fact as proof of divine mission.

Cicero's early speech *On the Manilian Law* (66 B.C.) is of special interest because it was delivered before the Assembly and not the Senate, and therefore it provides evidence that even ordinary citizens shared the assumptions described earlier: The empire of the Romans, he says, is expansive and universal, and equally, it is righteous and divine. He tells the citizens that hunger for military glory is the special tradition of the Romans and the quality in which they surpass all other nations (2.6); it is a point of pride that Rome always took the most drastic vengeance for even the smallest slights, and the terrible sack of Corinth in 146 B.C. that resulted merely from an insult to a Roman ambassador is brought up as a glorious episode in Roman history (5.11); Rome always fought far from home, carrying the offensive to its enemies (12.32); but Rome is a just conqueror, so much so that other nations would rather be ruled by Romans than rule themselves (14.41).

The point about fighting far from home deserves attention, because it helps to explain how Romans could so easily conflate just warfare and just imperialism. The Romans were obsessed with the idea of the preventive strike, which was not a new idea. The Greeks, for instance, were familiar with it from the time Greek strategic thought began. The reasoning behind it was simple: Burn the wasps in their nest and keep the fighting far away from here, an obvious extension of the defensive hoplite ethic. But when the Romans use this rhetoric, the reader is frequently struck by their sharp eyes for wasps' nests.

The best testimony to the Roman fascination with preventive strategies are the war commentaries of Julius Caesar, the only ancient historical works written by a major military leader and the only accounts any such commander has left of his own campaigns.[4] A few years after Cicero reminded the citizens that Romans always fight far from Rome, Caesar, the proconsul of Gaul (the Roman province of Gallia Narbonensis, then confined to the extreme south of modern France), launched the series of brilliant campaigns that suddenly extended the *imperium* to the Rhine River and the English Channel. He wrote his war commentaries to justify these conquests, for his conduct was being closely scrutinized by his enemies in the Senate, and the justifications he offers in these commentaries throw a harsh light on the common assumptions of the Roman elite about justice in war.

Caesar's initial campaign against the migrating Helvetians in 58 B.C. is justified on the grounds that the Helvetians were approaching the borders of the Roman province and therefore constituted a potential threat; also, their intended destination was "not far" (*non longe*) from the province (it was in fact 130 miles away); moreover, he wished to avenge a defeat the Helvetians had inflicted upon Romans half a century earlier (*Gallic Wars* 1.7, 10, 14). Next, he marched to head off a German migration, after receiving an appeal for help from Gauls who were allies of Rome—he leaves the impression that all Gaul now looked to Rome for protection. He claims that if the Germans were allowed to settle in Gaul in large numbers, they might eventually threaten the Roman province in the south, and even Italy itself; this last suggestion is made to seem less implausible by reminding his readers of the invasions of the Cimbri and Teutones half a century earlier (1.30–33). Caesar informs the German king that he is merely defending Roman allies; but he adds that the Romans were in Gaul before the Germans and thus have a better right to rule the land (1.45). During the next year, 57 B.C., he carried war into the far north of Gaul on the grounds that the Belgic tribes were forming a conspiracy to attack the Roman sphere in the south (2.1–3). In 56, he invaded western Gaul on the mere suspicion that the Aquitanian tribes might join the alleged anti-Roman conspiracy, though he mentions, too, that these people had inflicted a defeat upon the Romans long ago (3.11, 20). He thought it no contradiction to say that these precautions were necessary because the Gauls, like all men, love freedom and hate servitude, and therefore would always be ready to resist the Romans at every opportunity (3.10). In 55, he invaded both Germany and Britain under the usual pretexts—particularly implausible in the case of the Britons—that these moves were necessary to forestall offenses against Roman provincials or allies (4.13, 16, 20).

It is also noticeable that Caesar describes his savage treatment of the enemy, including the massacre and enslavement of whole tribes, in the bluntest terms and clearly thinks this will make a good impression at Rome.

> Setting out once more to harass the Eburones, Caesar sent out in all directions a large force of cavalry that he had collected from the neighboring tribes. Every village and every building they saw was set on fire; all over the country the cattle were either slaughtered or driven off as booty; and the crops, a part of which had already been laid flat by the autumnal rains, were consumed by the great numbers of horses and men. It seemed certain, therefore, that even if some of the inhabitants had escaped for the moment by hiding, they must die of starvation after the retirement of the troops. (6.43 [trans. S. A. Handford])

At the sack of Avaricum, he reports with pride that his soldiers butchered more than thirty thousand people, sparing neither age nor sex (7.28, 47). These acts, of course, are represented as reprisals for atrocities previously committed by the Gauls. On one occasion—the treacherous seizure of a group of German chiefs who had entered Caesar's camp to parley—we know that there were protests in the Senate and that Cato, the Stoic, demanded that Caesar be handed over to the Germans for violating the laws of war. Treachery, not brutality, was generally thought the most heinous offense against the laws of war in antiquity, and Romans were supposed to display a special concern for the good faith of Rome. Cato the Censor, greatgrandfather of this Cato, had instigated a famous prosecution of the praetor Galba in 149 B.C. for a similar act of treachery Galba had perpetrated in Spain. But the inquiry into Caesar's conduct, which was of course politically motivated, came to nothing, and the manner in which Caesar describes this episode shows that he knew it would not be difficult to satisfy public opinion. He admits candidly that this was an act of premeditated duplicity; to save his *fides* he thinks it sufficient to simply assert that the German offer to negotiate must have been a trick, and as usual, he insists upon the need for prompt preventive action (4.13–14).

In that same year, 55 B.C., Cicero defended Caesar in the Senate in terms that show that Caesar had correctly gauged the mood of that body. The barbarous Gauls, the orator declared, have always been the greatest threat to Rome, yet until now Roman generals could do nothing but repel their attacks, even the great Marius who had defeated the Cimbri and Teutones. Only Caesar has carried the war to the Gauls, understanding that the only solution is to break and tame them (*frangi domarique*). Further, Caesar must be allowed to finish this work and extend the *imperium* over all Gaul or these enemies will attack again (*On the Consular Provinces* 30–35).

The Senate was familiar with the rhetoric of the preventive strike. According to Livy, the decision to invade the Hellenistic world in 200 B.C.—the most decisive break with traditional Roman foreign policy ever made—was supported by the argument that if Rome did not invade Macedon, the Macedonians would soon be in Italy (Livy 31.7).

Roman imperialism is best described as a "preventive," not "defensive," form of imperialism. There was nothing in either Roman or Greek military traditions to deny that just wars might be preventive, nor was there anything to even place any practical limitations on this assumption: There was much in Roman tradition to encourage it. P. A. Brunt has said, "Roman reactions to the possibility of a threat resembled those of a nervous tiger, disturbed when feeding."[5] The metaphor is arresting but not quite right, for tigers are not really that aggressive.

It was very important to Romans at all times, even in the cynical late republican age, to claim that all Rome's wars were fought to repel or avenge injuries and to think of the *imperium* as a shield held over Rome's grateful clients. But the past injuries might be very distant in time, the present threats very distant in space; the grateful clients might have been acquired yesterday for the purpose of providing pretexts for new wars and extending Roman influence into new areas. Thus the moralistic rhetoric can slide, without any evident sense of contradiction, into what seem to us open expressions of aggrandizement. Doubtless there was some conscious hypocrisy in all this. But I suggest that for the most part, we are dealing here with a unique pattern of values in which aggressive militarism and aggressive religiosity were inseparably tangled, buried so deeply in Roman aristocratic culture that it was difficult for the Romans to perceive any contradiction between just warfare and just imperialism.

Just War and Just Empire in the Principate[6]

Historians have tended to make a sharp distinction between the Roman republic and the Roman principate (a term modern historians use for the thinly disguised monarchy established by Augustus Caesar, circa 30 B.C.) and to think of the republic as a period of expansion and of the quasi-monarchy as a period when the frontiers were stabilized. Some of the literary sources from the latter period support this illusion. But in fact, expansion continued into the principate, as did the republican ideology of imperialism.

The propaganda of Augustus laid more emphasis on his image as world conqueror than any republican general had ever dared. In his *Res gestae*, a memoir composed by Augustus at the end of his life and inscribed on public monuments all over the empire, he declared in the opening sentence that he had "subjected the world to the power of the Roman people." He had, in fact, added more territory to the empire than any single individual before him. The glorification of Rome as world empire is a recurrent theme in the Augustan poets, receiving its greatest literary expression in the *Aeneid* of Virgil, in which Rome is fated by the gods to rule the world from the beginning (*Aeneid* 1.278–279, 286–290; 3.714–718; 6.791–800; 7.601–615). In the histories of Livy, the concept of the just universal empire was anachronistically read back into the remote past. Even Hannibal is made to call Rome the *caput orbis terrarum,* capital of the world (Livy 21.30). The Roman generals who invaded the Hellenistic world in the early second century B.C., and likewise the Greeks they defeated, are given speeches in which all say that Rome is lord of the world, fights no unjust wars, and is revered by the human race next to the gods (Livy 36.17, 37.45, 37.54). In Livy, the practice of granting citizenship to conquered peoples is a "way of the ancestors" that goes back to the early republic (8.13). Dionysius of Halicarnassus contrasted Roman magnamity with the harsh treatment the Athenians and Spartans had dealt out to their subjects and attributed to this difference the failure of the Greek empires and the success of the Roman empire (*Roman Antiquities* 14.6).

The Augustan Age was the last great burst of Roman expansion, but much of the elite continued to expect military glory from the *principes.* The historian Tacitus, writing circa A.D. 100, blames both Augustus and Tiberius for failing to expand the empire (*Annals* 1.3, 4.32). He reports a probably apocryphal story that the dying Augustus added a clause to his will forbidding future emperors to expand the empire any further, and he comments that Augustus must have been motivated either by cowardice or by jealousy (*Annals* 1.11). No other possible motives even occur to Tacitus, and he clearly expects none to occur to his readers. He reports that when the emperor Claudius ordered his general Corbulo to withdraw from Germany, Corbulo, who feared the ridicule of the provincials, remarked sardonically that earlier Roman commanders had been more fortunate ("beati quondam duces Romani," *Annals* 11.20), a statement implying that withdrawal was against all Roman tradition and that the Caesars had betrayed the military glory of the republic. Tacitus's biography of his father-in-law, Agricola, who conquered much of Britain, contains one of the most extraordinary examples of Roman preventive imperialism: He says that Agricola planned to invade Ireland, not out of any present fear but rather in anticipation of future threats ("in spem magis quam ob formidinem"), for Agricola thought the Irish might someday invade the Roman empire—meaning, apparently, not only the British province but also the provinces on the continent (*Agricola* 24). Through the fourth century A.D., some of the Caesars continued to style themselves "extenders of the empire" (*propagatores imperii*) on their coins, though the claim was usually false, and all must have known it.

To us, it seems odd that Romans from the late republic on believed so consistently that Rome ruled all the world, because, of course, this was not literally true at any time. But they had borrowed the concept of world empire from the Greeks, and *imperium* translated "hegemony." None of the previous world empires had literally ruled the entire world, either. In the second century B.C., Polybius called Rome the master of the entire *oikoumene,* the inhabited world, including the Hellenistic kingdoms, over which Rome at that time exercised only a loose hegemony. When Romans began to think of themselves as holding the lordship of the world, they interpreted these phrases in the same loose fashion. The *imperium* was always understood to include the allies of Rome, and the Roman concept of "our allies and friends" (*socii et amici*) could be conveniently vague. The *Res gestae* of Augustus managed to suggest that Augustus had achieved some sort of leadership over the Germans and Dacians to the north and over the Parthians and Indians (!) to the east. If these shaky pretensions, which sometimes rested upon nothing but the existence of a previous diplomatic exchange with the alleged "client," were taken at face value, then it would be possible to believe that Rome had a hegemonic position, or was at the point of achieving one, over practically the entire inhabited earth, which the Romans, of course, thought was far smaller than it is. (Roman geographers commonly believed that the *oikoumene* or *orbis terrarum* extended about ten thousand miles from east to west and four thousand miles from north to south.[7]) So long as the empire continued to expand intermittently, the claim to world hegemony seemed realistic enough, and though few additions were made after Augustus, the pretension had become too habitual to be dropped.

The continuance of the tradition of expansion is more difficult to understand than is that of universality. Although expansion had practically stopped, a good part of the elite still expected the Caesars to expand the frontiers, and Caesars who did not were widely blamed. We are confronted with the paradox of a continuing glorification of conquest in an empire that in practice had ceased to conquer long ago, a situation that produced tensions. By the second century A.D., when the reality of the stable frontier could no longer be denied, a body of influential opinion consciously opposed to further expansion can be discerned within the Roman elite.

Anti-Imperialist Currents

The Complaint of Peace

The literature of the Roman Empire is filled with criticisms of war and empire, especially from Stoics and Cynics, some of which is so extreme it has been called a "flirtation with pacifism."[8] But this rhetoric is not as radical as it may sound to us, for we tend to forget the grim bellicist assumptions that lie behind all ancient literature. When Latin and Greek poets compose elegant lyrics on the theme that making love is better than making war, they are displaying their wit, not making a political point of any kind.[9] We find in the philosophers and orators many denunciations of greed and selfish ambition, which do have a political point, but the point is not to condemn the just war, only to condemn selfish ambition and greed. The ancient doctrine of the just war invariably condemned wars fought for such motives, as these were unjust wars by definition, and a more general critique of warfare was not normally implied.

Cicero's warnings against glory in *On Duties* are perfectly typical:

> The great majority of people, however, when they fall a prey to ambition for either military or civil authority, are carried away by it so completely that they quite lose sight of the claims of justice . . . For whenever a situation is of such a nature that not more than one can hold preeminence in it, competition for it usually becomes so keen that it is an extremely difficult matter to hold a "fellowship inviolate" [*sancta societas,* a quotation from the old Latin poet Ennius]. We saw this proved but now in the effrontery of Gaius [Julius] Caesar, who, to gain that sovereign power which by a depraved imagination he had conceived in his fancy, trod underfoot all laws of gods and men. But the trouble about this matter is that it is in the greatest souls and the most brilliant geniuses that we usually find ambitions for civil and military authority, for power, and for glory, springing up; and therefore we must be the more heedful not to go wrong in that direction. (*On Duties* 1.8.26)

> Most people think that the achievements of war are more important than those of peace; but this opinion needs to be corrected. For many men have sought occasions for war from the mere ambition for fame. (1.22.74 [trans. Miller])

The latter passage is followed by a list of statesmen who achieved more in peace than in war; but the "achievements of peace" Cicero has in mind include planning for war, and one of his examples is Cato the Censor, whose relentless policies led to the destruction of Carthage in 146 B.C. To be absolved of the taint of ambition for fame (*gloriae cupiditas*), it is sufficient not to want a triumph for oneself. Nor is there any hint that this ambition is not in itself a desirable quality, for only the perversions of it are censured. The examples are Roman, and the warlike emphasis may be also, but it is unlikely Cicero found anything essentially different in his Greek Stoic sources.

There are, however, some other Stoic or Stoicizing texts suggestive of a more profound critique of warfare. The neo-Stoic theory of a peaceable golden age has already been mentioned. The Stoic philosopher and historian Posidonius, disciple of Panaetius, wrote an account of this primeval and pacific period, which has been transmitted by Seneca (*Epistle* 90). It is a familiar motif in the Latin poets. The best-known version in later centuries was that in Ovid's *Metamorphoses* (1.76–215):

> The first millennium was the age of gold;
> Then living creatures trusted one another. . .
> No cities climbed behind high walls and bridges;
> No brass-lipped trumpets called, nor clanging swords,

Nor helmets marched the streets, country and town
Had never heard of war: and seasons traveled
Through the years of peace.

The age of gold was succeeded by the increasingly violent ages of silver, bronze, and finally iron, when

men invaded
Entrails of earth down deeper than the river
Where Death's shades weave in darkness underground;
Where hidden from the sight of men Jove's treasures
Were locked in night. There, in his sacred mines,
All that drives men to avarice and murder
Shone in the dark: the loot was dragged to light
And War, inspired by curse of iron and gold,
Lifted blood-clotted hands and marched the earth.
(trans. Horace Gregory)

But like all golden-age myths this is a negative and pessimistic pacifism, for there is never any notion of reviving the lost golden age, and despite their nostalgia for lost innocence, these authors do not regard the rise of civilization as by any means a misfortune. Mostly, the golden age is a handy metaphor used to castigate immorality and greed; for example, Seneca's *Epistle* 94 contains another turn on the well-worn conceit that Nature put metals deep underground so that men would not be tempted by greed and warfare:

> Gold and silver, with the iron, which, because of the gold and silver, never brings peace, she has hidden away, as if they were dangerous things to trust to our keeping. It is we ourselves who have dragged them into the light of day to the end that we might fight over them; it is we ourselves who, tearing away the superincumbent earth, have dug out the causes and tools of our own destruction. (94.57 [trans. R. M. Gummere])

These metaphors reflect the Greek philosophical doctrine that the original cause of warfare was greed for land and wealth. But this teaching implied that greed for land and wealth is an *unjust* cause of war. The Greek philosophers did not think wars should be fought for booty, except against barbarians; the Romans denied that they ever fought wars for such motives against anybody. The point of the golden-age motif is always to condemn unjust wars and unjust empires, never just ones.

It is true that sometimes these critiques are so generalized as to leave the suggestion that all, or almost all, wars are fought for these improper motives. In the same *Epistle* 94, Seneca condemns Alexander the Great, Marius, Pompey, and Julius Caesar for their greed and ambition. He is fond of the rhetorical commonplace that the so-called conquerors conquered the earth but could not conquer themselves: "Marius led the army, but ambition Marius" (Marius exercitus, Marium ambitio ducebat) (94.66); "Alexander wanted to control everything except his passions" (Id enim egerat, ut omnia potius haberet in potestate quam adfectus) (113.29 [author's trans.]). Seneca can describe warfare as the *gloriosum scelus,* the crime of glory—a deliberate devaluation of the word *gloria*—and can affect shock that we hang men for murdering individuals and reward them for the murder of nations (*Epistle* 95.30–32). The Stoic preachers Epictetus (*Discourse* 1.22) and Dio Chrysostom (*Orations* 13.35, 17.10, 34.51) sometimes speak as though *all* warfare, from the Trojan War to their own time, has been motivated by greed and all other motives have been false pretexts. Alexander the Great is usually a monster in Stoic writings, often contrasted with Diogenes the Dog, founder of Cynicism, a great hero to both Stoic and Cynic. Tales about the meeting between Alexander and Diogenes are legion, and Diogenes always gets the better of these exchanges, the point of which is always the folly of conquest.[10]

Another popular historical scheme derived from Greek philosophy was the succession of world empires. Like the golden age, this idea contained an anti-imperialist bias. The belief that world empires are fated to fall could easily suggest that they deserved to fall, even that their very rise was evil. In Dio Chrysostom's oration *On Wealth,* the rise and fall of the Assyrian, Median, Persian, and Macedonian empires are simply examples of the wretched consequences of greed (79.6). He does not mention the last world empire, but perhaps he did not need to, the implications for Rome being clear enough.

Both the golden age and the succession-of-empires theories are prominent motifs in the world history written in the Augustan Age by Pompeius Trogus. A Roman citizen of Gallic origin, he did not belong to the circles that produced most Roman historiography (for which see the next chapter). A universal history was something new in Latin, so Trogus's *Philippic Histories* were necessarily based on Greek models, as his title acknowledged; and since this work survived in the form of a Latin epitome written by Justin in the second or third century A.D., it became an important source for historical theory in later times. Trogus portrayed the earliest period of human history as peaceable, using terms that suggested the idea of defensive warfare: "It was their custom to guard the boundaries of their empires, not to advance them" (Fines imperii tueri magis quam proferre mos erat). He maintained that the practice of going to war for greed was introduced by the evil King Ninus of Assyria (Justin 1.1). Trogus made much of the Scythians as a people practicing perfect peace and justice, owning no gold or silver, coveting nothing, never harming their neighbors (Justin 2.2–5, 9.1–3, 12.2). He used the Scythians as a foil to the aggressive world empires of the Persians and Macedonians and as an implicit foil to Rome. That conquerors come to grief when they invade poor nations was a stock item in the succession-of-empires tradition, going back to Herodotus; but usually, it is the warlikeness of the poor nations that is emphasized, not their peacefulness. Trogus may have influenced the Latin history of Alexander the Great written in the first century

A.D. by Quintus Curtius Rufus. Curtius brings Alexander onto the Scythian steppes so that his ambition can be rebuked by the just Scythians, who play the role usually assigned to Diogenes the Dog or to various Indian Brahmans in the Alexander legend (Curtius 7.8).

We should remind ourselves again that all these texts, even when they sound like blanket condemnations of warfare, are speaking of *unjust* wars. We should not read into them any criticism of just wars fought to preserve freedom, such as the Scythians practiced. But there are some Stoic passages that seem to criticize even wars for freedom. In his *Oration* 38, Dio Chrysostom lists the reasons men go to war—rulership, freedom, territory, dominion over the sea—to make the point that all wars are bad, with no suggestion that wars for freedom belong in any different category (38.16–19). His oration *On Freedom* plays with the irony that men fight wars for a false "freedom," when the only true freedom lies within (80.3–4). And here is Epictetus on freedom:

> Fix your eyes on these examples [Socrates and Diogenes], if you wish to be free, if you set your desires on freedom as it deserves ... Men hang themselves, or cast themselves down headlong, nay sometimes whole cities perish for the sake of what the world calls "freedom," and will you not repay to God what he has given, when he asks it, for the sake of true freedom, the freedom which stands secure against all attack? (*Discourse* 4.1.171 [transl. P. E. Matheson])

But when we read such passages we tend to forget the idealizing tendencies of classical moral and political philosophy, which made possible very elevated standards precisely because these were not expected to have much practical effect in the real world. Stoics carried this to extremes. Stoic ethics was meant for an ideal wise man, a morally perfect human being; when Stoics contrast true freedom and false freedom they mean the true freedom of the wise man. But Stoics believed there were probably no wise men living and perhaps had been none since Socrates and Diogenes; therefore to hold up this ideal standard was not to suggest that men who live in the world as it is should *not* fight and die for freedom. Stoics, especially the neo-Stoics who followed Panaetius, accepted the existence of a sphere of second-best ethics for those who were not wise but were "progressing" toward wisdom, which is to say, for people in the real world. And they accepted that at this level, external values like freedom, though not to be compared with the inner virtue of the wise man, possessed a certain worth of their own. Even the false freedom was worth fighting for.

Stoics repeatedly contrasted the king and the tyrant and thought one of the main differences between them was that the good king goes to war for the right reasons and the tyrant for frivolous reasons, like greed and false ambition. (Dio Chrysostom has Diogenes the Dog make this comparison in his *Oration* 6.50.) The true king is compared to a brave bull who protects his herd from lions (Dio, *Oration* 2.69; Epictetus, *Discourse* 3.22). Epictetus says that the emperor Trajan brought peace to the world so that people could travel anywhere without fear of war or brigandage; but he also says this is not the same as the inner peace that only comes from philosophy (*Discourse* 3.13). His point is to demonstrate the superiority of the higher sphere of values, in the usual Stoic fashion; no one in his audience would have taken him to mean that the peace of Caesar was not worth having. Even the inner peace of the wise man is described by Epictetus through a military metaphor, albeit a defensive one: The wise man or progressor toward wisdom is at peace with all men, like a well-fortified and well-supplied city that can laugh at besieging armies (*Discourse* 4.5). Seneca recognizes that the philosopher owes a debt to the ruler, who fights wars so that the philosopher can enjoy peace and find his inner freedom (*Epistle* 73.9–10). Stoics believed that even a wise man might fight in a just war. Epictetus, in the same discourse in which he scoffs at false freedom, praises Socrates for doing his military duty (4.1.159). Seneca praises Cato the Younger, a great hero of Roman Stoicism, because Cato fought for true *gloria* in the civil wars, in contrast with the false glory pursued by his contemporaries Caesar, Pompey, and Crassus (*Epistles* 95.37, 69–73; 104.29–33). Elsewhere, it is true, Seneca wonders whether a philosopher like Cato should have entered politics at all (*Epistle* 14.12–14). There was always some ambivalence among Stoics about whether a philosopher should become a ruler, but there was none about the place of just warfare among the duties of a ruler. Even Alexander the Great was not invariably cast as a tyrant. Panaetius mentions him along with Cyrus the Great and Pericles as one of the good rulers (Cicero, *On Duties* 2.5.16). Arrian, who was at least a casual Stoic and a follower of Epictetus, wrote a history of Alexander that brings in the usual moralistic anecdotes in which Alexander suffers rebuke at the hands of Diogenes the Dog and the Hindu sages (*Anabasis of Alexander* 7.1–2), but this does not prevent Arrian from taking a generally favorable view of Alexander's conquests (1.12, 7.28–30).

In short, Stoic "pacifism" consists of a set of moral commonplaces about the dangers of greed and ambition. This traditional rhetoric could sometimes have an effect on policy. During the civil war of A.D. 69, the Senate sent embassies to the rival commanders to persuade them to keep the peace, and one of these included the Stoic philosopher Musonius Rufus, who harangued the troops about the blessings of peace and the hazards of war (Tacitus, *Histories* 3.81), probably using some of the Stoic arguments cited earlier. The fact that he was a noted Stoic may have lent extra credibility to his mission, but there was nothing new about his arguments. As the author of the pseudo-Aristotelian *Rhetoric to Alexander* had advised centuries earlier, any orator who wished to persuade his audience to make peace should harp on these themes. The fact that this was a *civil* war made the arguments for peace particularly cogent. We cannot say that Musonius would not have been equally ready to use the traditional arguments for war had he thought the cause just.

The *Seventh Epode* of Horace, another locus classicus of "antiwar" sentiment, also derives its point from the fact that the poet is addressing the subject of civil war only:

> Why are your hands grasping the swords that have once been sheathed? Has too little Roman blood been shed on field and flood—not that the Roman might burn the proud towers of jealous Carthage, or that the Briton, as yet unscathed, might descend the Sacred Way in fetters, but that, in fulfillment of the Parthians' prayers, this city might perish by its own right hand? Such habit ne'er belonged to wolves or lions, whose fierceness is turned only against beasts of other kinds. (trans. C. E. Bennett)

The contrast between the virtuous beasts and corrupt civilized man is another commonplace, a variant on the golden-age theme. But the lions and wolves are better than men because they do not practice intraspecific conflict, which is here equated with civil war; just warfare is the equivalent of predation and other interspecific conflict, as though Carthaginians and Britons belonged to another species.

This Stoic tradition—as it may loosely be described, though its rhetoric was used by many other writers—was not without effect in curbing warfare, but it is better called an anti-imperialistic rather than an antiwar rhetoric. It encouraged closer scrutiny of the motives for so-called just wars, and it has influenced the literature of pacifism to the present day. In the Renaissance, Erasmus and his followers collected these classical texts and in such satires as the *Complaint of Peace* turned the tradition into a genuine antiwar polemic, not by denying the validity of just warfare in principle but by arguing that in practice almost all wars are unjust. This strategy was suggested to Erasmus by some of the classical authors cited earlier. But in ancient times, the complaint of peace never explicitly went so far as to deny that just wars existed.

The Wall of the World

It is more significant to find this moralistic rhetoric occasionally used to advocate a general policy of defense. There is no doubt that by the second century A.D., some members of the elite were highly suspicious of any further attempt to expand the empire. At this time a new empirewide elite was developing, vociferously claiming to continue the old Roman mores but in reality less and less dominated by the old Roman code of honor and glory. By the reign of Trajan, who was the most ambitious conqueror among the post-Augustan Caesars, some members of this elite were becoming vocal in their opposition to expansion.

The *Fourth Oration* of Dio Chrysostom, *On Kingship*, was probably delivered before Trajan around A.D. 100, when the emperor was about to embark upon his conquest of Mesopotamia.[11] It is another retelling of the Diogenes-Alexander meeting, in which the Cynic reproves Alexander for his insatiable ambition. This is clearly an oblique criticism of Trajan, who openly sought to emulate Alexander; Dio, who sometimes called himself a Cynic, just as openly casts himself in the role of Diogenes. At about the same time, Epictetus, another Stoic teacher with Cynic sympathies, told his audience that wars are among the supreme examples of human folly and ignorance and offered a list of such wars, starting with the Trojan War, which he said was over nothing but a pretty woman, and ending with the current Roman wars against the Getae—an undisguised reference to Trajan's conquest of Dacia (*Discourse* 2.22).

Trajan's successor, Hadrian, abruptly reversed Trajan's policy and withdrew from the new eastern conquests. This policy clearly met with the approval of the imperial bureaucrat Suetonius, who wrote his *Lives of the Caesars* under Hadrian. This is a revisionist account of the history of the principate, which consistently debunks conquest and conquerors. Suetonius does not accept Julius Caesar's justification for the conquest of Gaul. According to him, Caesar actually went about picking quarrels with neighbors, even allies, of Rome on the flimsiest of pretexts; he implies that Caesar was really after money—the invasion of Britain is said to have been motivated by Caesar's greed for pearls (*Life of Julius* 24, 47). Augustus, on the other hand, receives Suetonius's praise on the grounds that he never tried to expand the empire (*Life of Augustus* 21). This was an absurd piece of revisionism, contradicted by Augustus's own *Res gestae*, which was on display on public inscriptions all over the empire; but Augustus was the model emperor, and those who opposed Trajan's expansionism had to claim somehow that it was not in the spirit of Augustus. Among the more recent Caesars, Domitian is criticized for going to war without good cause (*Life of Domitian* 6), and had Suetonius thought it politic to continue his biographies any further, he would doubtless have criticized Trajan on the same grounds.

Hadrian's successor, Antoninus Pius, continued his policy of retrenchment. When the canon of ideal Caesars was fixed in the late second century A.D., it consisted of Augustus, Trajan, Antoninus, and Marcus Aurelius, three of whom spent much of their reigns in warfare; but the absence of military activity in Antoninus's reign did not disqualify him. It should be noted, however, that Antoninus was said to have intimidated his enemies by reputation alone, so that he did not have to go to war (Victor 15.1). The Romans still thought of the peaceable man as the one who, in the words of Isocrates, is always prepared for war.

The traditional rhetoric went on through the Antonine Age, but now there is clear evidence for the spread of a defensive mentality that implicitly rejected the idea of expansion. The most striking literary testimony to this new mentality is the *Roman Oration* that the celebrated Greek rhetorician Aelius Aristides delivered in A.D. 143 to honor the anniversary of the founding of Rome. Here, the universality of Rome is a repeated theme, but the theme of expansion, which had normally accompanied it in the literature of the late republic and early principate, is altogether absent. Instead, the orator uses the recurrent metaphor of a walled city. He speaks as if all the human race lives within the walls of this world-city, by which he means all of the human race that matters. It is acknowledged that there are some peoples left outside the empire (otherwise, of course, there would be no need for a wall around it), but these are not worth including: "There are no sections which you have omitted, neither city nor tribe nor harbor nor district, except possibly some that you condemned as worthless. The Red Sea and the Cataracts of the Nile and Lake Maeotis, which formerly were said to lie on the boundaries of the earth, are like the courtyard walls to the house which is this city of yours" (28).[12] The Roman empire is said to far exceed in size the empires of the Persians and the Macedonians because it extends much farther west than either (the fact that both extended much farther east than Rome ever did goes unmentioned). Rome equally exceeds the earlier empires in justice: "Of all who ever gained empire you alone rule over men who are free" (36). The Athenian and the Spartan empires failed because they did not know "how to rule with justice and with reason" (58).

> What another city is to its own boundaries and territory, this city is to the boundaries and territory of the entire civilized world, as if the latter were a country district and she had been appointed common town. It might be said that this one citadel is the refuge and assembly place of all perioeci or of all who dwell in outside demes. (61)

> You did not forget walls, but these you placed around the empire, not the city. (80)

> An encamped army like a rampart encloses the civilized world in a ring. (82)

> It is right to pity only those outside your hegemony, *if indeed there are any,* because they lose such blessings. (99 [my italics])

This notion that the empire already included all the human race worth ruling was common in the Antonine Age. Pausanias in his *Description of Greece* asserts that the only peoples left outside Roman rule had been deliberately left out owing to their worthlessness (1.9.5). He praises Antoninus Pius because the emperor never went to war unless attacked, in which case he always punished the invaders (8.43.3). Appian of Alexandria, Pausanius's contemporary, presents an even more exaggerated version of Antonine universalism in the preface to his *Roman History:*

> Possessing the best part of the earth and sea they [the Romans] have, on the whole, aimed to preserve their empire by the exercise of prudence, rather than to extend their sway indefinitely over poverty-stricken and profitless tribes of barbarians, some of whom I have seen at Rome offering themselves, by their ambassadors, as its subjects, but the emperor would not accept them because they would be of no use to him. They give kings to a great many other nations

whom they do not wish to have under their own government. On some of these subject nations they spend more than they receive from them, deeming it dishonourable to give them up even though they are costly. They surround the empire with great armies and they garrison the whole stretch of land and sea like a single stronghold. (Preface 7 [trans. Horace White])

All who are outside the Roman empire are assumed to be Roman clients. The notion that the empire already includes everyone worth including implies, of course, that there is no further need for expansion.

As we have seen, the old ideology of expansion nevertheless persisted, and at the end of the second century A.D., some of the Severan emperors attempted new conquests, especially Caracalla, who modeled himself on Alexander the Great and dreamed of seizing Mesopotamia. The historian Cassius Dio, a Roman senator of Greek origin related to the Stoic orator Dio Chrysostom, left an oblique criticism of Caracalla's policies in his *Roman History*. There already existed a tradition that Augustus had been opposed to expansion, and Dio elaborates it: He claims that Augustus left a will explicitly forbidding his successors to enlarge the empire on the grounds that it would become too large to defend (*dysphylakton*) (Dio 54.9, 56.33). He condemns Domitian and other emperors who went to war unnecessarily (67.4). He praises Hadrian for living in peace; but one should note that even Dio must add the traditional qualification—Hadrian was able to live at peace only because he was always prepared for war (69.9).[13]

Notes

1. Not all Stoics believed in human equality. A fragment of Posidonius shows that he accepted the Aristotelian doctrine that some peoples are naturally servile. But there is no reason to think this was intended as a justification for the Roman empire, as some have thought. See *Posidonius,* ed. Ludwig Edelstein and I. G. Kidd (Cambridge, 1988), frag. 60, with commentary; and Peter Gruen, *The Hellenistic World and the Coming of Rome* (Berkeley, 1984), 351. The fragments of the third book of Cicero's *On the Republic* show that it contained a similar doctrine of natural slavery. But no such doctrine appears in the more mature political philosophy of Cicero's *On Duties.*

2. See the full discussion of this problem by Gruen (*Hellenistic World,* 158–200), who concludes it is unlikely that the terminology of patronage was ever applied to interstate relations during the period of Roman ascendancy.

3. Cicero, *Defense of Balbus* 64 (speaking of Caesar); *Defense of Sestus* 67 (of Pompey); *On Catiline* 3.26 (Pompey); and *On the Consular Provinces* 30ff. (Pompey and Caesar).

4. J. H. Collins, "Caesar as Political Propagandist," in *Aufstieg und Niedergang des Römischen Welt* I, vol. 1, ed. Hildegard Temporini (Berlin, 1972), 922–966.

5. P. A. Brunt, *Roman Imperial Themes* (Oxford, 1990), 307. On Roman concepts of empire, see especially Brunt, "Roman Imperial Illusions," and other essays collected in *Roman Imperial Themes;* Benjamin Isaac, *The Limits of Empire: The*

Roman Army in the East (Oxford, 1990); D. C. Earl, *The Moral and Political Tradition of Rome* (Ithaca, 1967), especially the chapter on *gloria.*

6. For the policy of Augustus, see Brunt, *Roman Imperial Themes;* Peter Gruen, "The Imperial Policy of Augustus," in *Between Republic and Empire: Interpretations of Augustus and His Principate,* ed. K. A. Raaflaub and Mark Toher (Berkeley, 1990), 395–416; Josiah Ober, "Tiberius and the Political Testament of Augustus," *Historia* 31 (1982), 306–328. Attitudes toward expansion in the later principate are discussed by J. B. Campbell, *The Emperor and the Roman Army, 31 B.C.–A.D. 235* (Oxford, 1984), 382–401.

7. J. C. Mann, "The Frontiers of the Principate," in *Aufstieg und Niedergang der Römisches Welt,* II, vol. 1 (Berlin, 1974), 508–533.

8. Harry Sidebottom, "Philosophers' Attitudes to Warfare Under the Principate," in *War and Society in the Roman World,* ed. John Rich and Graham Shipley (London, 1993), 241–264. Other discussions of philosophers' attitudes to war include Michael Austin, "Alexander and the Macedonian Invasion of Asia: Aspects of the Historiography of War and Empire in Antiquity," in *War and Society in the Greek World,* ed. John Rich and Graham Shipley (London, 1993), 197–223; and Christopher Pelling, "Plutarch: Roman Heroes and Greek Culture," in *Philosophia Togata: Essays on Philosophy and Roman Society,* ed. Miriam Griffin and Jonathan Barnes (Oxford, 1989), 199–232.

9. Duncan Cloud, "Roman Poetry and Anti-Militarism," in *War and Society in the Roman World,* 113–138.

10. On the Stoic view of Alexander, see Brunt, "From Epictetus to Arrian," *Athenaeum* n.s. 55 (1977), 19–48; and J. R. Fears, "The Stoic View of the Career and Character of Alexander the Great," *Philologus* 118 (1974), 113–130.

11. John Moles, "The Date and Purpose of the Fourth Kingship Oration of Dio Chrysostom," *Classical Antiquity* 2 (1983), 251–278.

12. Translated with commentary by J. H. Oliver, "The Ruling Power. A Study of the Roman Empire in the Second Century After Christ Through the Roman Oration of Aelius Aristides," *Transactions of the American Philosophical Society* n.s. 43, pt. 4 (Philadelphia, 1953).

13. Meyer Reinhold and P. M. Swan, "Cassius Dio's Assessment of Augustus," in *Between Republic and Empire,* 155–173.

Chapter Nine

The Romans and Raison d' Etat

The Trickeries of the Greeks

In A.D. 66, the oppressions of the Roman procurator incited rebellion at Jerusalem. The Jewish prince Agrippa II, a loyal Roman client, made a speech to the crowd in the gymnasium to persuade them not to rise against Rome. Here are the words that the Jewish historian Josephus, who shared Agrippa's pro-Roman views, attributed to him:

> Now, I know that there are many who wax eloquent on the insolence of the procurators and pronounce pompous panegyrics on liberty; but, for my part, before examining who you are and who are this people whom you are undertaking to fight, I would first consider apart two distinct pretexts for hostilities which have been confused. For, if your object is to have your revenge for injustice, what good is it to extol liberty? If, on the other hand, it is servitude which you find intolerable, to complain of your rulers is superfluous; were they the most considerate of men, servitude would be equally disgraceful.
>
> Consider then these arguments apart and how weak, on either ground, are your reasons for going to war. (Josephus, *Jewish War* 2.348–350 [trans. H. St. J. Thackeray])

Agrippa tells his audience not to mix arguments based on justice with arguments based on advantage (in this case, the preservation of freedom, always recognized as the supreme advantage and the strongest argument for war) and then proceeds to mix the two himself, for the rest of his speech is given over to proving that war with Rome would *neither* be just nor advantageous for the Jews. It would not be just because Rome had been, on the whole, a just patron and they should not blame all the Romans for the crimes of one procurator; it would not be advantageous because they would not stand a chance, a point established by listing all the powerful nations the Romans had conquered. The oration is reminiscent of the Mitylenean debate in Thucydides, where both Cleon and Diodotus begin by distinguishing the factors of justice and expediency with a great show of logic chopping, and then each proceeds to conflate the two in support of his own case. The pseudo-Aristotelian *Rhetoric to Alexander* advised political orators to combine arguments from justice with arguments for expediency whenever possible and, when trying to persuade an audience to stay out of war, recommended that they use exactly the line of argument that King Agrippa followed. This was a tradition of political rhetoric that played about considerably with the distinction between justice and expediency. Agrippa mentions this as if it were a well-established principle of rhetoric that would be familiar to some of his audience, and his speech demonstrates some of the tricks that could be played with it. Agrippa insists that justice and expediency be separated only when his opponents try to combine them; for his part, he would have argued on grounds of expediency only if there had been no possible way to defend Roman imperialism on moral grounds.

This tradition was still lively in the Hellenistic world under the Roman principate, though the gradual absorption of Roman client states allowed less and less scope for it. But at Rome itself, it never found a home, and the reasons for this rejection are the subject of this chapter.

Certain traditions were passed down about the early confrontations between Greek and Roman culture that made much of the theme of Greek trickery versus Roman forthrightness. One of the first Romans to beat Greeks at their own game was Marcius Philippus, who, on an embassy in 172 B.C., tricked the Macedonians into believing that Rome was not preparing war. According to Livy, probably following Polybius, a group of old-fashioned senators protested this violation of the Roman code of war, which required declaration by the fetials and open hand-to-hand combat without night attacks, feigned retreats, and other plots (*insidiae*): Greeks and Carthaginians fought with craft (*ars, calliditas*), cunning (*astus*), and trickery (*doli*), thinking it more glorious to dupe (*fallere*) an enemy than to vanquish (*superare*) him; Romans fought with manliness (*virtus*) and piety (*religio*).[1] Nonetheless, a majority of the Senate approved of the Machiavellian diplomacy of Philippus (Livy 42.47).

Even a Greek observer as shrewd and sophisticated as Polybius thought there was some truth to the claims of the senatorial conservatives. He believed that even in his day the Romans, and they alone, preserved some traces of the old Greek code of hoplite warfare, for they preferred open declarations of war and pitched battles with no surprises (Polybius 13.3).

In 155 B.C., a more famous cultural collision occurred. While Carneades, the head of the Platonic Academy (now a stronghold of philosophical skepticism), was on an Athenian embassy to Rome, he delivered a public disputation on the subject of justice: First, he gave a lecture presenting Platonic-

Aristotelian arguments to show that justice is based on objective standards in natural law, then followed it with a second lecture refuting the arguments of the first from the point of view of a skeptic. The story was remembered as the first serious impact of Greek dialectic upon the Roman aristocracy. Plutarch says Carneades drove all the youth of Rome mad with philosophy (*Life of Cato* 22.4–5; compare Quintilian 12.1.35, Pliny, *Natural History* 7.112). But conservatives were alarmed, and Cato the Censor, self-appointed guardian of the old Roman mores, was moved to banish philosophers from Rome lest the youth be corrupted. Some have thought Carneades meant to criticize the Roman empire, but that would have been a highly undiplomatic move on the part of an ambassador; he only meant to dazzle his audience with a display of logic and rhetoric.

Nevertheless, it was obvious that such Greek rhetoric had disturbing implications for the cherished Roman belief in the justice and piety of their empire. In his *On the Republic*, a dialogue set in the year 129 B.C., Cicero set out to remove these doubts. One of the speakers in the dialogue, the ex-consul Furius Philus, is asked to summarize the arguments of Carneades against justice. The arguments that Cicero puts in his mouth probably have little or no resemblance to those of Carneades, who is used here simply as a symbol of Greek sophistry.[2] The surviving fragments of Philus's speech (*Republic* 3.5.8–18.28) show that Philus used standard skeptical arguments to deny that there is any justice in nature, with special reference to the Roman empire. All rulers, he says, seek their own advantage, not the interests of the governed; the dictates of reason and prudence are opposed to those of justice; "no people would be so foolish as not to prefer to be unjust masters rather than just slaves" (3.18.28, trans. C. W. Keyes). Philus admits that the Romans have fought unjust wars under the pretexts of the fetial law and have assembled an unjust empire; if Rome and other empires wished to be just, he argues, they would have to give up all they have taken and withdraw to a life of poverty and misery, but they will not, because justice is irrational and imprudent.

This sounds like cold-blooded Machiavellism, the most extreme statement of that point of view since the Melian dialogue of Thucydides; but unlike the Greeks in that dialogue, Philus is not advocating political realism but playing devil's advocate. The rhetoric is artificial, the cynicism exaggerated. The practical conclusion to be drawn from such a position is withdrawal from this world of hopeless injustice into the inner freedom of the Stoic or the heavenly city of the Christians. Much of Philus's argument has been passed down by Christian writers, who found in it proof of the irredeemable evil of the Roman empire and all other worldly empires:[3]

> For it was a witty and a truthful rejoinder which was given by a captured pirate to Alexander the Great. The king asked the fellow, "What is your idea, in infesting the sea?" And the pirate answered, with uninhibited insolence, "The same as yours, in infesting the earth! But because I do it with a tiny craft, I'm called a pi-

rate: because you have a mighty navy, you're called an emperor." (Augustine, *City of God* 4.4 [trans. Henry Bettenson] = *Rep.* 3.14.24)

This is not, of course, the impression that Cicero intended. The argument of Philus is not there to promote either Thucydidean worldliness or Augustinian otherworldliness. It is an example of Greek sophistry presented for refutation. Another speaker in the dialogue, Laelius, follows it immediately with the defense of just warfare and just imperialism reviewed in the previous chapter—an argument also based on Greek philosophy, but here it is the sound moral teachings of Plato, Aristotle, and the Stoics.

One decade later, Cicero treated the laws of war more fully in *On Duties.* He makes some attempt in this work to follow the common Greek distinctions among the several causes of war, a distinction perhaps found in his Stoic source. There is one kind of war that is fought for survival and freedom and another kind that is fought for hegemony (*de imperio*): The Roman wars against the Celts were of the first type; the Roman wars with Italians, Greeks, and Carthaginians belonged to the second. But in Cicero's opinion, the rules of the just war apply to both kinds of warfare (1.12.38).[4] Later in the treatise, he argues at length (departing from his Stoic source) that there can be no possible conflict between morality (*honestum*) and expediency (*utilitas*). He points out that the Senate has never resorted to tactics such as assassination, regardless of the consequences. The Roman commander in the Pyrrhic War refused a chance to poison King Pyrrhus and instead turned the would-be assassin over to the king for punishment, though the deed would have put an end to a long and destructive war (3.22.86). Many other examples from Roman history are brought up, especially the case of Regulus, the hero of the First Punic War, who surrendered himself to the Carthaginians to keep his oath, although he knew it would mean death by torture (3.29.108). In Cicero's view, Romans who failed to follow this high standard were aberrations or belonged to the corrupt period of the recent civil wars. One such was Scribonius Curio, consul in Cicero's youth, who, in judging the claims of certain colonists, was guilty of uttering the pernicious Greek formula that these claims, though just, were not expedient for the republic (3.22.88).

Cicero is able to prove—to his own satisfaction—that morality and prudence can never diverge; he rehearses commonplaces about how just conduct wins the loyalty of allies and overawes enemies and therefore is both just and expedient. Thus, he claims, it was the strict adherence to the fetial code that Rome displayed even in the dark times after the disaster at Cannae that caused Hannibal to lose heart (3.32.114). We can admit the obvious core of truth in these commonplaces. All ancient orators recognized the supreme importance of morale in wartime and how essential to morale the sense of being in the right is. But Hannibal did not lose heart after Cannae; and that a mind as subtle as Cicero's was so incapable of dealing with hard and obvious questions in this area says much about the Roman aristocratic mentality.

These expressions of contempt for Greek trickery are common in Latin literature.[5] The terms for "trickery" cover a variety of things: diplomatic chicanery, improper motives for warfare, any use of treachery in dealing with enemies such as assassinations or oath breaking, any use of tactical surprise and any kind of battle other than direct frontal assault, and an implicit suspicion of rational strategic planning and utilitarian thinking about warfare at any level. As will become clear, this was not the only Roman military tradition, but it was sufficiently powerful to inhibit the Roman elite from publicly adopting Greek realism in the discussion of foreign affairs.

Roman Historiography[6]

It is therefore not surprising that so little Thucydidean realism is to be found in Latin oratory and Latin historical writing. The peculiar development of Roman historiography is particularly significant, as this was the main genre for the discussion of military affairs.

The tradition of writing history began at Rome in the third century B.C. as an imitation of Greek historiography, and for a long time histories at Rome were written in Greek. But what the Romans adopted was a special variant of Greek historiography: not the epic military history of Herodotus and Thucydides but the local history, or "horography," an account of a single city following a year-by-year chronicle format, hence called *annales* in Latin. The works of the early annalists are lost to us except for fragments, but much of their content has been passed down by Livy and other late historians. It was an inward-looking tradition, focused entirely on the city of Rome, and though it was largely concerned with the wars of Rome, the world was viewed through Roman eyes, without the Greek historians' tradition of impartiality.

Roman historiography focused not only on Rome but also on the Senate. Down to the time of Augustus, it was written entirely by members of the senatorial elite, whereas Greek historiography tended to be written by exiles. This was considered a laudable aristocratic pastime, the self-conscious aim of which was the preservation of the old Roman values. The writers seem to have worked with a limited group of patriotic and didactic themes— the examples of virtue set by great men, the good faith of the Romans in all their dealings with other cities.

Some were aware this was different from what the Greeks usually meant by *historia*. Sempronius Asellio, who wrote a history of Rome in the late second century B.C., wrote that "annals" are different from "histories" in that annals merely record events as they happened, as in a story for children, without inquiry into causes. This suggests that the Roman annals contained none of those discussions of the causes of wars that are such a prominent feature of Greek historiography, except presumably for the recitation of the grievances declared by the fetial priests. Sempronius himself was clearly trying to produce a "history" in the Greek tradition, but he had no intention of departing from the patriotic and moralistic aims of the annalists: In the fragment to which I refer, he says that the deficiency of annals is that they cannot inspire people to fight for their country as history can (Aulus Gellius 5.18.9). The main attraction of Greek historiography was its literary art.

In the Augustan Age, historiography was raised to a higher level by Sallust and Livy, who wrote literary histories in the Greek fashion and created Latin versions of the two main narrative styles of Greek historiography, the Herodotean and the Thucydidean. But both authors remained faithful to the introverted and didactic traditions of the republic.

The prose of Livy resembles the fluid expansive narrative mode of Herodotus, Xenophon (who was particularly popular at Rome for his moralism and didacticism), and many Hellenistic historians. Livy explains in his preface that the function of history is to display models for people to imitate and to avoid, and that Roman history is the best subject, offering as it does the largest number of the first and the fewest of the second. His efforts at historical explanation are mostly concerned with the mental states of his characters, and his concept of causation is practically limited to the motives of the leaders. Livy relies heavily on fictional speeches, the main function of which is psychological characterization, not strategic analysis as in Thucydides. The speeches are imaginative and dramatically effective—the critic Quintilian said that everything in the speeches of Livy is perfectly fitted to the speakers and to their circumstances—but characters remain stereotypes fitted to the expectations of Livy's senatorial audience. He explains the Second Punic War simply by blaming it on Hannibal, ignoring the complex discussion of causation he has read in Polybius. His battle descriptions have exercised a largely malign influence on the rhetoric of military historians to the present day: Each Livian battle is a series of disjunctive actions in which all soldiers act and think in unison, with much emphasis given to their emotional reactions and to the personal achievements of generals, all described in epic and poetic terms, with slight attention paid to topography or tactics.[7]

More might have been expected from the realistic narrative tradition introduced into Latin literature by Sallust, who was called the Roman Thucydides (Quintilian 10.101). The style of Sallust is indeed Thucydidean, terse and epigrammatic, filled with antitheses and unexpected variations. He was drawn to this style because it suggested pessimism, satire, and subversion, in deliberate contrast to the smooth and balanced prose of Livy and Cicero. It was a style fit for a story of imperial decline, with Rome replacing Athens. But the imitation is only stylistic. The decline that Sallust portrays in his *War with Jugurtha* and *War with Catiline* is moral, not political; his main theme is not the struggle of intelligence to master fortune as in Thucydides, but the corruption of virtue by ambition and greed. His adaptation of the great Attic historian is a striking testimony to the general tendency of Roman thought "to represent political crises as moral ones."[8]

In Thucydides, the debates are the hinges of the narrative. In Sallust, there is only one comparable debate, that between Caesar and Cato the Younger in *War with Catiline* (51–52), which is modeled on the Mitylenean debate in Thucydides. As in the Mitylenean debate, the issue is whether rebels should be treated leniently or harshly, with Caesar taking the role of Diodotus and Cato that of Cleon (Sallust had been in Caesar's party in the civil war). But the issue here is a purely domestic matter, the punishment of Roman citizens, not a problem of interstate relations like the Athenians' dealings with Mitylene. Neither speaker makes any distinction between justice and expediency, the keynote of the Mitylenean debate; and when they talk of justice, they make no distinction between justice to Rome's own citizens and justice to other states. All the philosophical subtleties of the Mitylenean debate have disappeared.

The battle descriptions of Sallust may seem less stereotyped than those of Livy and most other Latin historians, but they owe this air of realism partly to the fact that they copy the battle scenes in Thucydides. Two of the battle descriptions in *War with Jugurtha* (60, 101) are based upon the famous account of the battle in Syracuse harbor in the seventh book of Thucydides.

A century later, the style of Sallust was revived by Tacitus, the last of the senatorial historians. His tone is even more censorious and bitter than Sallust's, his tale of decline and corruption even darker. He has relatively little to say about external affairs because he wrote entirely about the principate and his constant theme was the relationship between the Caesars and the Senate. The introspective quality of Roman historiography reaches its peak in Tacitus: The tradition had always focused almost exclusively on the senatorial elite, and the elite had now narrowed to one man. The moralism of the tradition reaches a dead end: Historians were supposed to portray moral examples, but practically all the examples available to Tacitus were bad. "It seems to me a historian's foremost duty is to ensure that merit is recorded, and to confront evil deeds and words with the fear of posterity's denunciations. But this was a tainted, meanly obsequious age [the Julio-Claudian period]" (*Annals* 3.65, trans. Michael Grant). Within this tradition, historians had nothing left to write about.

It is odd, therefore, that this atypical, narrowly focused, unmilitary historian[9] came to be considered in the sixteenth and seventeenth centuries the great classical model of Machiavellian *raison d'état*. This was partly for reasons of style rather than content. To Renaissance humanists, the antithetical style of Sallust and Tacitus connoted truthfulness, candor, the stripping away of pretense and illusion, making the marmoreal perfection of Livy's prose look artificial and empty beside it; it seemed the perfect vehicle for writing about affairs of state in the new Machiavellian manner. But the preference for Tacitus was also due to the simple fact that almost alone of the major classical historians, he wrote about a world of absolute monarchy, which the men of the Renaissance saw as a mirror of their own society. It mattered little that Tacitus wrote almost exclusively about internal affairs: He still provided plenty of pungent maxims and memorable examples illustrating the politics of absolutism, and they could be applied readily to foreign affairs.

Roman Strategies

The fact that the Roman historians record so little high-level strategic discussion raises the question of whether there existed much to record. Here again emerges the problem of the so-called "grand strategy" of Rome.

There are good reasons to think the political culture of the Roman elite was never very conducive to such a thing. Under the republic, the Senate was secretive in its deliberations, and there was no tradition of open debate before assemblies of the people. We know the Senate was always riddled with factions and family rivalries and that military command was regarded as an aristocratic prerogative. Factional politics and family connections—not what we think of as strategic considerations—determined who got the chance to win *laus* and *gloria* in any particular year. Furthermore, all classical city-states were devoted to the principle of amateur leadership, as rotation in office was essential to their notion of citizenship, and none was more determined in its amateurship than the leadership of Rome, which cherished to the end the belief that a Roman gentleman could handle anything in war or peace. Roman commanders were expected to learn the art of war from the examples of their ancestors and on-the-job training, not from books; there was a continuing prejudice against those who spent much time reading Greek treatises on *strategica* and *tactica,* and the like.[10] The short tenures of office would have strengthened these attitudes. Provincial governors, who held the key military positions, were left very much on their own: Their "provinces" were open-ended assignments rather than territories with definite boundaries, and as we have seen, it was more or less expected that they would pick quarrels with their neighbors and try to expand their frontiers. The fact that the Roman republic found it necessary to pass a law (the *lex Julia*) forbidding provincial governors to start wars without authorization by the Senate shows that this was a common practice.[11]

All this changed, of course, with the establishment of the principate. Now there was central and unified control over external relations. The principate had a relatively huge bureaucracy by ancient standards; it had many emperors deeply interested in warfare and expansion, and historians assume that they discussed such questions with their close advisers, mostly drawn from the upper classes.[12] But we do not know what they discussed, nor what terms and arguments were thought cogent when a Caesar asked his counselors if he should go to war that year. The imperial secretariat, though divided into many specialized staffs, never included any group of officials specifically concerned with diplomacy or external relations, or with military affairs, apart from problems of supply. The imperial army never developed any equivalent to the officer corps of a modern European army, which is capable of exercising long-term influence on government policy both in war and peace. To the end of the empire, Roman governors and commanders remained much the same valiant amateurs they had always been. It was a world without experts. In some ways, the elite of the principate seems to have been even less capable of realistic political discussion than that of the republic. If the Senate had any tradition of realistic oratory, it died under Augustus; and what happened to senatorial historiography has already been described.

In addition, we tend to forget how dependent our modern concepts of strategic thinking are upon readily available and precisely detailed maps. It seems doubtful that Roman cartographic techniques were sufficiently advanced to allow large-scale strategies. Generals thought in terms of peoples and cities and armies, not territory. In the civil war of A.D. 68, Vespasian planned to first seize Africa so as to cut off the grain supply of Rome: Tacitus thought it necessary to explain to his readers that this made sense because Africa was "on the same side" of the Mediterranean as Italy (*Histories* 3.48). An even more startling testimony to the vagueness of the Roman geopolitical sense is Tacitus's statement that Ireland lay between Britain and Spain (*Agicola* 24). This was told him by his kinsman Agricola, a brilliant general with long experience in the British Isles, who was then planning the invasion of Ireland on the basis of such data as this.[13]

The Greeks and Romans were accustomed to clear descriptions of battle tactics and, sometimes, of campaign strategies. But they never described anything that we would call a "grand strategy," and those who think they had one are simply assuming "without further ado that the Romans were capable of realizing in practice what they could not define verbally,"[14] by a sort of intuition. This hypothesis is based upon an unspoken parallel with modern army organization and its general staffs and map rooms. This is not to deny that the inner circle of the Senate and the council of the emperor were capable of strategy in the sense of long-term conscious direction of policy, only to doubt that it was very grand and to question whether the principles behind it were as rational and utilitarian as many assume. What looks like a coherent defense system can as easily be explained as the result of a series of ad hoc reactions to crises, and what sound like strategic reflections amount to no more than obvious commonsense maxims, often expressed in moralistic terms.

The hegemonial "strategy" of the republican *imperium,* which was to maintain a cordon of client states around Italy, required no particular theory, reflection, or debate. Most ancient empires started out with such a hegemonial organization because they could do nothing else. They understood well enough what these clients were for. It was said by one of his supporters that Julius Caesar made "friends" of Oriental kings so that they could "guard the provinces" of the Romans.[15] I have argued before that we should not read into such language any distinction between offensive and defensive strategies. The Caesars, like their republican predecessors, were expected to guard the provinces of Rome by taking the offensive whenever possible, and the common motives they gave for going to war were honor and glory.

By Hadrian's time, the Romans did shift to perimeter defense, but again, that was because they had no choice. When the client states were absorbed and became Roman provinces, the Roman frontiers, in J. C. Mann's phrase, "arose by default." The frontiers arose where the legions stopped, not results of a deliberate defense strategy but a frozen line of advance, like a tank that breaks down in the desert and is converted into a blockhouse.[16] We have seen that many of the elite by the Antonine Age did convert to a genuinely defensive mentality, meaning that they thought of the *imperium* as a vast fortification, which was the only way they could conceive of pure defense. But we have also seen how little rationalized this rhetoric is and how indifferent it is to elementary strategic questions such as whether a frontier should follow this line or that.

By Constantine's time, the Romans had abandoned perimeter defense, but once again, that was because they had no choice. The blockhouse had finally been overrun. The empire fell back upon such expedients as were available, all of which had the effect of exposing the provinces to barbarian invasion and abandoning the concept of the unitary territorial empire, ringed by an encamped army like a rampart, as Aelius Aristides had said. This cost the Caesars the loyalty of much of their elite. But to the end, the problem was discussed in the traditional moral terms. Practically the only significant literary comment on the military crisis of the late empire comes from Zosimus, one of the last pagan historians, who accused Constantine of "removing the greater part of the soldiery from the frontiers to cities that needed no auxiliary forces. He thus deprived of help the people who were harassed by the barbarians and burdened tranquil cities with the pest of the military, so that several straightway were deserted" (2.34 [trans. J. J. Buchanan and H. J. Davis]).

Roman Stratagems

The Romans never developed a political culture that made possible realist strategic discussion on the classical Greek level. But they did develop what may be described as a countertradition that persistently undermined the moralistic assumptions of the official ideology. This was the Greek tradition of "stratagems" or *ruses de guerre,* adopted into Latin literature by Frontinus in the Antonine Age.

By the first century B.C., many Romans did not share the anti-intellectual attitudes toward military literature described earlier. Sallust portrayed the famous soldier Marius making a speech in which he attacked the military incompetence of the old nobility: Marius says that they got all their knowledge of war from books, from histories of Rome and Greek military treatises, and that they did not begin to read these until they were elected consul, whereas a "new man" of humble origins like himself had learned the art of war in the field (*War with Jugurtha* 85.12–14). Augustus Caesar combed Latin and Greek literature to find useful precepts with anecdotes attached, and he circulated collections of such passages among his generals (Suetonius, *Life of Augustus* 25, 89). The examples given are precepts such as "I would rather have a safe commander than a rash one," which one imagines the generals found of slight practical value. But there were more practical things in the Greek military literature. There was a revival of interest in it under the principate, and several Greek treatises on *tactica* have survived, all of them derived largely from Polybius.[17] None of these could have been of much use to a Roman general, either, because they are antiquarian exercises concerned with the drill techniques of the Macedonian phalanx, a formation long obsolete. But Greek military literature also included a great deal of information about *stratagemata*. This word was related to *strategika*, or generalship, and originally meant "deeds of generals," though by the Augustan Age it had taken on a different connotation and meant "clever tricks of generals," or *ruses de guerre*. Collections of these had been popular ever since the military encyclopedia of Aeneas the Tactician. In the second century A.D., another such collection of anecdotes with the title *Stratagemata* was written in Greek by Polyaenus and was dedicated to the Stoic emperor Marcus Aurelius. This dedication may seem surprising, because *stratagemata* were well-known examples of the sort of Greek trickery that pious Romans like Marcus were expected to scorn. But that is why the "stratagem" tradition deserves attention here: It provided an avenue through which a sanitized version of *raison d'état* could be made acceptable to Romans.

In the preface to his Latin *Stratagemata*, Frontinus explained that the Greeks used the word *strategika* for all the qualities of a general, whereas *stratagemata* referred to the *sollertia*, the clever plans, of a general. Latin writers did not use *stratagemata* much, but they had a sizable vocabulary of equivalents, which E. L. Wheeler has collected and analyzed: *dolus, fraus, sollertia, insidiae, furtum*, all terms with the connotation of trickery, traps, intrigues, secret actions; but they could also use as equivalents terms like *consilium* (planning or prudence) and *ars* (craft or skill), which did not necessarily suggest deceit except in certain military contexts. In the works of Latin historians, these terms occur frequently and normally suggest the use of deception or surprise in interstate relations. These deceptions might be practiced in peacetime diplomacy or in warfare. In warfare, "stratagems" might be used either in strategy or in tactics, and the commander might use them either to deceive the enemy or to fool his own troops. For the most part, the historians use these terms in a favorable sense, sometimes with allusions to Greek commonplaces about the usefulness of surprise and indirection in warfare (for example, Thucydides 5.9; Xenophon, *Cyrus* 1.6.27). But in view of the Roman traditions noted earlier in this chapter, it is hardly surprising that there is also much ambivalence about trickery.

Valerius Maximus's anthology of *Memorable Deeds and Words* included in the seventh book a collection of stratagems of war, the earliest that has survived in Latin. The anecdotes concern ploys involving surprise, and commanders are unequivocally praised for practicing them, especially when they allow a city to be taken without the need for a costly siege or assault, as when King Tarquin of ancient Rome took a city by sending his own son inside the gates disguised as a refugee ("he thought cunning stronger than weapons," 7.4.2). But in the ninth book, a collection of evil deeds, Valerius assures his readers just as unequivocally that all treachery (*perfidia*) is evil (9.6). *Perfidia* is always a bad word. But the group of words just listed could be used with commendation when speaking of military affairs.

How did the Romans tell the difference between wicked treachery and commendable trickery? Sometimes one suspects that when Greeks acted this way, it was Greek fraud but when Romans did, they were exhibiting Roman prudence. But we can find in Roman authors, if not a serious discussion of this distinction, at least passages suggesting an awareness of tensions.

One approach was to treat stratagems as permissible under certain circumstances but still as contemptible, un-Roman, and greatly inferior to pitched battle. That seems to be the implication of Julius Caesar's rhetoric. In a prebattle oration, he told his troops that the Germans they were about to fight were not as formidable as their reputation: They had won their recent victory over the Gauls not through bravery but merely through a surprise attack, and tricks of that sort, he said, would not work against Romans anyway (*Gallic Wars* 1.40). He describes how a besieged Gallic town tried to counter the bravery of the Romans with siege devices like mines and sorties, but the Romans proved better at such things than the Gauls (7.22). The Romans may affect to despise stratagems, but they know how to use them.

Another approach was to treat stratagems as evil only when they violated the rules of just warfare. In the epitome of Livy written by the second-century historian Florus, Mark Antony is condemned for a surprise attack on the Parthians, but apparently what is blameworthy is not the stratagem itself but the fact that it was not preceded by a declaration of war (Florus 2.20).

Despite this attitude, even a writer as moralistic as Cicero could admit that there were extenuating circumstances when the restrictions of the just war could be lifted. His treatment of the sack of Corinth in *On Duties* is extraordinary. Earlier, in the speech to the Roman assembly quoted in the preceding pages, Cicero had not hesitated to boast of this deed. In a philosophical work like *On Duties,* he is forced to admit that it was totally unjust (1.11.35, 3.11.46). The rules of war do not allow such barbarities unless the enemy has stooped to them: On those grounds, the sack of Carthage might be excused, but the destruction of Corinth the same year could not be. Yet, he suggests that the act might be condoned because of the advantages (*opportunitas*) of the site of Corinth, perched on its isthmus connecting the seas—"the place it-self might someday encourage someone to make war." The Corinthians are blamed not because of any injustice they have practiced but simply for their location (compare 2.22.76, where the conqueror of Corinth is praised). This comment, frankly acknowledging the existence of a kind or degree of advan-tageousness that is totally free of the demands of morality, contradicts every-thing else in *On Duties* on the subject of international relations. Cicero's po-litical thought could not absorb this idea, yet he could not resist expressing it.

Finally, it was possible for the Romans to moralize the stratagems them-selves. The most striking example of this tactic known to me is Seneca's *On Wrath*. Here, we are told that the barbarians are characterized by unthinking rage in warfare, like wild animals. Their rage leads them to violate the laws of nations and start unjust wars, and in battle, it leads them to fall headlong on the enemy without forethought. When they fight Romans, Seneca explains, they are undone by their own anger, for the Romans know that war should not be fought in blind rage. The model of a Roman commander he uses is Fabius Maximus the Delayer, who defeated Hannibal by refusing to give him battle: He was able to conquer Hannibal because he had first conquered his own anger (1.11–12, 3.2). Seneca has turned the usual moralistic rhetoric upside down. The tactics of decisive battle, normally associated with honor and glory in classical literature, are here identified with injustice, bestial rage, lack of self-control, and barbarism; stratagems that avoid battle, often thought wicked and cowardly, are associated with rationality and Stoic virtue.

But there was at least one Roman—an author of great importance for later European military thought—who was unequivocal in his acceptance of stratagems and unusually clearheaded in recognizing their implications. Sex-tus Julius Frontinus (circa A.D. 35–103) had a distinguished ancestry and a distinguished career—three times consul, governor of Britain—but he also had an interest in technical matters unusual in his class. He built roads in Britain and wrote a lost treatise on surveying; he served as water commis-sioner of the City of Rome and wrote an extant treatise *On Aqueducts*, which is one of the most competent technical works to survive from the an-cient world; and his military commands inspired him to become the first Latin military writer of significance. Frontinus produced a theoretical trea-tise called *The Art of War*, which is lost, and followed it with a collection of *Stratagems*, which has survived. The opening passage is worth quoting:

> Since I alone of those interested in military science have undertaken to reduce its rules to system, and since I seem to have fulfilled that purpose, so far as pains on my part could accomplish it [referring to his lost *Art of War*], I still feel under obligation, in order to complete the task I have begun, to summarize in convenient sketches the adroit operations of generals, which the Greeks em-brace under the one name *stratagemata*. For in this way commanders will be furnished with specimens of wisdom and foresight, which will serve to foster

their own power of conceiving and executing like deeds. There will result the added advantage that a general will not fear the issue of his own stratagem, if he compares it with experiments already successfully made.

I neither ignore nor deny the fact that historians have included in the compass of their works this feature also, nor that authors have already recorded in some fashion all famous examples. But I ought, I think, out of consideration for busy men, to have regard to brevity. For it is a tedious business to hunt out separate examples scattered over the vast body of history; and those who have made selections of notable deeds have overwhelmed the reader by the very mass of material. My effort will be devoted to the task of setting forth, as if in response to questions, and as occasion shall demand, the illustration applicable to the case in point. (1.1 [trans. C. E. Bennett])

There is a noticeable self-confident claim to originality here. Frontinus wants to present the lessons of warfare in a more systematic way than anyone before him. He understands, like Thucydides and Polybius but like few Romans, that the point of presenting historical examples is not that they might be directly copied, as though history were to precisely repeat itself, but rather to enlarge the experience and stimulate the imagination. Most anecdotes had been presented haphazardly by previous authors, but Frontinus organizes them by subject ("On leading an army through places infested by the enemy," "On laying and meeting ambushes while on the march," and so on). Most anecdotes gave examples of moral behavior, like those of Valerius Maximus; Frontinus focuses on political causes.

The most original aspect of his method is his practice of organizing examples dialectically, so as to present arguments for and against a particular policy. In Book 1.3, "On Determining the Character of the War," he asks whether a general ought to try to engage the enemy in a pitched battle. On the positive side, he lists the examples of Alexander the Great and Julius Caesar; among the counterexamples, he cites Fabius Maximus, who avoided battle with Hannibal, and Themistocles and Pericles, both of whom took to the sea rather than defend the land of Attica from invaders. The reasons for these decisions are given: Alexander and Caesar only sought decisive battle when they knew they had strong armies; Fabius knew he could not risk battle with Hannibal, and neither could Pericles with the Spartans.

Finally, Frontinus treats moral actions as if they were stratagems. In his section "On Ensuring Loyalty," we read of the chivalry that Alexander and Scipio displayed to captive women and the clemency that Germanicus showed to certain Germans: These acts are commended not because they were noble in themselves (though it is not denied that they were noble) but because they won over the enemy and accomplished more than could have been done by battle. These examples are preceded by several others in which the same end of ensuring loyalty was achieved through treachery and deceit: "Gnaeus Pompey, suspecting the Chaucensians and fearing that they would not admit a garrison, asked that they would meanwhile permit his invalid soldiers to recover among them. Then, sending his strongest men in the guise of invalids, he seized the city and held it" (2.11.2 [trans. Bennett]). The chivalry of Scipio is placed on the same moral level as the treachery of Pompey, and both are commended: Justice happened to be a workable stratagem in Scipio's case, but it would not have worked for Pompey, so he was correct to employ treachery. The acceptance of *raison d'état,* though left implicit, is unmistakable. Other stratagems include the burning of a temple (3.2.4), bad faith in negotiations (3.2.6), and the poisoning of a town's water supply (3.7.6). A whole section is devoted to "On Inducing Treachery" (3.3). The fourth book of the *Stratagems,* probably not by Frontinus but added later by an unknown imitator, contains a chapter "On Justice" (4.4), the political realism of which is as blunt as anything Frontinus wrote. Two examples of justice are offered in the stories of the Roman heroes Camillus and Fabricius, both of whom refused to practice treachery upon an enemy and were rewarded with victory. But in the case of Fabricius we are told that he refused to poison King Pyrrhus because he saw that would not be necessary to achieve victory, implying that if it had been necessary he would have done it. This anecdote came from Cicero's *On Duties* (3.22.86), which attaches to it exactly the opposite interpretation: The expedient thing to do, according to Cicero, would have been to poison Pyrrhus, but Fabricius did the honorable thing at great military cost.

Frontinus's *Stratagems* was probably the most influential text in the transmission of classical realism in war and diplomacy. His method seems to have strongly influenced Machiavelli, who copied the chapter "On Justice" in *Discourses* 3.20 and expanded upon its lessons.[18]

Notes

1. F. W. Walbank, "A Note on the Embassy of Q. Marcius Philippus, 172 B.C.," *Journal of Roman Studies* 31 (1941), 82–93.

2. J. L. Ferrary, "Le discours de Philus (Cicerón, *De Re Publica*, III, 8–31) et la philosophie de Carnéade," *Revue des études latins* 55 (1977), 128–156.

3. Much of the argument is summarized by Lactantius, *Divine Institutes* 5–6.

4. This passage has sometimes been interpreted to mean that wars for glory and hegemony belong in a different category from the just war; see, for example, Anthony Pagden, *Lords of All the World: Ideologies of Empire in Spain, Britain, and France c. 1500–c. 1800* (New Haven, 1995), 96. But it seems clear that Cicero, like Aristotle and most other philosophers, thought of warfare *de imperio* as another type of just war.

5. Passages are collected by E. L. Wheeler, *Stratagem and the Vocabulary of Military Trickery* (Leiden, 1988), a monograph to which this chapter owes much.

6. For Roman historians in general, see Charles Fornara, *The Nature of History in Ancient Greece and Rome* (Berkeley, 1983); *Latin Historians*, ed. T. A. Dorey (New York, 1966); Mark Toher, "Augustus and the Evolution of Roman Historiography,"

in *Between Republic and Empire,* ed. K. A. Raaflaub and Mark Toher (Berkeley, 1990), 139–154.

7. See the comments on the rhetoric of military history in the first chapter of John Keegan's *The Face of Battle* (New York, 1976). He uses Julius Caesar as an example of the Latin tradition, but the features of the stereotyped battle description are common in Latin literature.

8. D. C. Earl, *The Political Thought of Sallust* (Cambridge, 1961), 44. See also T. F. Scanlon, *The Influence of Thucydides on Sallust* (Heidelberg, 1980).

9. Theodor Mommsen called Tacitus the most unmilitary of historians, but for a more positive assessment, see K. Wellesley, "Tacitus as a Military Historian," in *Tacitus,* ed. T. A. Dorey (New York, 1969), 63–98; for a general introduction, see Ronald Mellor, *Tacitus* (New York, 1992), for his political thought, see Ronald Syme, "The Political Opinions of Tacitus," in Syme, *Ten Studies in Tacitus* (Oxford, 1970).

10. Brian Campbell, "Teach Yourself How to Be a General," *Journal of Roman Studies* 77 (1987), 13–29.

11. P. A. Brunt, "Charges of Provincial Maladministration Under the Early Principate," *Historia* 10 (1961), 189–223.

12. On the decisionmaking process of the principate, see Fergus Millar, *The Emperor in the Roman World, 31 B.C.–A.D. 337* (Ithaca, 1977). For Roman provincial administration, see Andrew Lintott, *Imperium Romanum: Politics and Administration* (London, 1993), 22ff., 53.

13. Benjamin Isaac, *The Limits of Empire: The Roman Army in the East* (Oxford, 1990), 372–418. The interpretation of the Roman frontier policy I follow here is based mostly on the work of Isaac and J. C. Mann, "Power, Force and the Frontiers of the Empire," *Journal of Roman Studies* 69 (1979), 175–183 (see n. 16 to follow). For a more positive evaluation on Roman strategy, see E. L. Wheeler, "Methodological Limits and the Mirage of Roman Strategy," *Journal of Military History* 57 (1993), 7–42, 215–240.

14. Isaac, *Limits of Empire,* 374–375.

15. This occurs in the *Alexandrian War* (65.4)—a continuation of Caesar's *Commentaries on the Civil Wars,* written by a Caesarean. A. N. Sherwin-White has called this "the first formal expression in Latin historical literature of the doctrine of the buffer-state" (*Roman Foreign Policy in the East, 168 B.C. to A.D. 1* [Norman, Okla., 1983], 301). But is not the Roman describing a client state rather than a buffer state? "Buffer state" normally means a state that is nobody's client, and Sherwin-White uses the phrase in that sense himself (54).

16. J. C. Mann, "The Frontiers of the Principate," in *Aufstieg und Niedergang der Römisches Welt,* II, vol. 1 (Berlin, 1974), 513ff.

17. A. M. Devine, "Aelian's Manual of Hellenistic Military Tactics: A New Translation from the Greek with an Introduction," *Ancient World* 19 (1989), 31–64.

18. Neal Wood, "Frontinus as a Possible Source for Machiavelli's Method," *Journal of the History of Ideas* 28 (1967), 243–248, suggested this thesis to me.

Chapter Ten

Warfare and the Roman Constitution

Metus Hostilis

Much Greek political thought was devoted to the place of warfare in the constitution, originally focusing on the obvious question of which type of constitution was best at war. The Romans never doubted that theirs was, and those who were drawn to the Greek sort of constitutional speculation found a ready-made explanation in Polybius: Rome had produced the perfect mixed constitution. Cicero tried to develop this idea in *On the Republic,* but few members of the Roman elite were interested in such theorizing. Despite all the borrowing of Greek terms, Roman political discourse was fundamentally different in quality. As T. A. Sinclair put it, the Roman state

> depended for its working not on what the Greeks called *nomoi,* but on such notions as *imperium, consilium, auctoritas,* notions not indeed foreign to Greek thought, but having little or nothing to do with constitutions of any type. Personal rule, personal influence, personal dependence of the lesser folk on the great—these were the things that counted in Roman political life. Hence Roman political thought expressed itself in such terms.[1]

As has been discussed, Roman historiography never became an instrument for the exploration of political or constitutional issues. It did, however, develop its own terms for explaining constitutional developments, and one of its major organizing concepts deserves attention here. In brief, it was widely believed that Rome had been kept united and virtuous by war and had declined in peacetime: Hence, the end of republican expansion was thought to mark the beginning of decline in the Roman constitution, with particular significance attached to the date 146 B.C., when Carthage was destroyed.

About that time, there were many who feared foreign contact was rotting the moral fiber of Rome. Polybius believed that the decline began with the importation of Greek luxuries following the conquest of Macedon in 168 B.C. (31.25). In the years before the Third Punic War (149–146 B.C.), there was a running debate in the Senate between Cato the Censor, who urged that Carthage be destroyed, and Scipio Nasica, who wanted Carthage preserved on the grounds that Rome needed enemies: He "would have had the fear of Carthage to serve as a bit to hold the contumacy of the multitude" (Plutarch, *Life of Cato* 27, Dryden trans.; compare Appian 8.10.69, Florus 1.3.5). After the destruction of Carthage in 146, Scipio's prediction seemed fulfilled, for Rome soon fell into recurrent civil strife. During the last century of the republic, the main subject of the Roman historians and annalists was not glorious foreign war but tragic domestic upheaval, and Roman moralists had to find some way to explain this disaster.

One explanation, already dealt with in a previous chapter, emphasized Rome's relations with the allies: It was claimed that before the sack of Carthage, Rome had treated its allies justly but afterward became a harsh tyrant. This idea seems to have been popularized by the *Histories* of the Stoic Posidonius, circa 100 B.C. It stems from traditional Greek notions about just and unjust hegemonies.[2]

But the more influential and more Roman version, adopted by Sallust around 40 B.C., emphasized domestic affairs rather than foreign: Before 146, Rome had enjoyed harmony but, after the removal of Carthage, fell into civil war.

> Now the institution of parties and factions, with all their attendant evils, originated at Rome a few years before this [the war with Jugurtha, which began in 111 B.C.] as the result of peace and an abundance of everything that mortals prize most highly. For before the destruction of Carthage the people and senate of Rome together governed the republic peacefully and with moderation. There was no strife among the citizens either for glory or for power: fear of the enemy preserved the good morals of the state ["metus hostilis in bonis artibus civitatem retinebat"]. But when the minds of the people were relieved of that dread, wantonness and arrogance naturally arose, vices which are fostered by prosperity. Thus the peace for which they had longed in time of adversity, after they had gained it proved to be more cruel and bitter than adversity itself. For the nobles began to abuse their position and the people their liberty, and every man for himself robbed, pillaged, and plundered. Thus the community was split into two parties, and between these the state was torn to pieces. (*War with Jugurtha* 41 [trans. J. C. Rolfe])

> But when our country had grown great through toil and the practice of justice, when great kings had been vanquished in war, savage tribes and mighty peoples subdued by force of arms, when Carthage, the rival of Rome's sway, had perished root and branch, and all seas and lands were open, then Fortune began to grow cruel and to bring confusion into all our affairs. Those who had found it easy to bear hardship and dangers, anxiety and adversity, found leisure and wealth, desirable under other circumstances, a burden and a curse. Hence the lust for money first, then for power, grew upon them; these were, I may say, the root of all evils. (*War with Catiline* 10 [trans. Rolfe])

Now the idea that warfare is good for the citizen body was known to the Greeks. It was in fact the essence of the civic militarist ideal. But the Greeks expressed this differently. Plato in the *Laws* writes that fear of the enemy had united Athens in the Persian Wars, but he makes it clear that it would have been far better if the Athenians could have been united by fear of their own laws, and in his own ideal state, the citizens will have no need of the first sort of fear (*Laws* 3.698–699). Aristotle is even more suspicious of those who rely on fear of the enemy, claiming it is a weakness in military states like Sparta that they need warfare to preserve morale and in peacetime lose their temper like an unused blade (*Politics* 1334a). Polybius makes a comment that is closer to the view of Sallust when he says that as a general rule, constitutions tend to decay once they are freed from external threats; but he does not regard this process as inevitable and hopes that a mixed constitution like the Roman can escape this tendency (6.18, 57). No Greek writer seems to have said that the constitution *needs* fear of the enemy. Taken literally, this seems a contradiction: If virtue must be imposed by external threats, how can it be virtue? Yet the Sallustian doctrine of the *metus hostilis* (the epigram just quoted, that the city was kept in good character by fear of the enemy) became axiomatic among Romans.

It is interesting that Sallust's descriptions of moral corruption at Rome are modeled upon Thucydides' well-known passages describing the stasis on Corcyra (Thucydides 3.82–83). Sallust's epigrams express the same sense of the corruption of language: "But in very truth we have long since lost the true names for things. It is precisely because squandering the goods of others is called generosity, and recklessness in wrong doing is called courage, that the republic is reduced to extemities" (*War with Catiline* 52 [trans. Rolfe]). He delights in Thucydidean antitheses contrasting moral appearances with base realities:

> Against these men [the popular party] the greater part of the nobles strove with might and main, ostensibly in behalf of the senate but really for their own aggrandizement ["senatus specie pro sua magnitudine"]. For, to tell the truth in a few words, all who after that time assailed the government used specious pretexts, some maintaining that they were defending the rights of the commons, others that they were upholding the prestige of the senate; but under the pretence of the public welfare each in reality was working for his own advancement ["bonum publicum simulantes pro sua quisque potentia certabant"]. (*Catiline* 38 [trans. Rolfe])

But in Thucydides's Corcyra, *stasis* was caused by war. In Sallust's Rome, it is caused by peace.

This nostalgia for the expansionist republic was continued by Livy and Tacitus and became a dominant theme of Roman historiography. These authors saw the history of Rome as essentially a story of decline, explained in moral terms that helped to block realistic political analysis; at the same time, the assumption that virtue and solidarity had been the results of, and dependent upon, constant warfare imparted to the Roman version of civic militarism an open aggressiveness unknown to the Greeks.

Many Greeks, especially Stoics, did not, of course, accept the *metus hostilis* theory: They continued to speak of civil strife as something associated with war, not peace, and deplored both foreign war and civil war as aspects of the same greed and ambition. Dio Chrysostom, in an address to the Rhodians, praised them for the courage they had shown in their wars of the past, but he did so only to make the point that now they could display the same virtue in peacetime (*Oration* 31; compare Dio, *Oration* 17.10; Epictetus, *Discourse* 1.22).

The *metus hostilis* theme did not always emphasize civil war. Sometimes it was Roman virtue, rather than Roman solidarity, that was ruined by peace. A locus classicus is Juvenal's Sixth Satire:

> In the old days poverty
> Kept Latin women chaste: hard work, too little sleep,
> These were the things that saved their humble homes from corruption—
> Hands horny from carding fleeces, Hannibal at the gates,
> Their menfolk standing to arms. Now we are suffering
> The evils of too-long peace. Luxury, deadlier
> Than any armed invader, lies like an incubus
> Upon us still, avenging the world we brought to heel.
> (287ff. [trans. Peter Green])

The glorification of war is stronger in the Latin—*nunc patimur longae pacis mala* (now we suffer the evils of long peace).

The Legacy of Vegetius

Under the principate, civic militarism naturally became an ideal associated with the long-vanished republican past. A vestige of it survived in the frequent complaints, especially from writers who favored expansion, that the army, now a standing professional army recruited largely from noncitizens, needed the discipline of war. Peace was thought to be bad for the soldiers. Tacitus wrote that at the start of Nero's Parthian war, the Syrian legions were so demoralized by years of peace that many soldiers owned no helmets or armor and found ramparts and ditches novelties (*Annals* 13.35). One of the reasons for praising an emperor who sought conquests was the belief that this revived the morale of the troops.[3]

But the most important contribution of the Latin tradition to the ideal of civic militarism came at the very end of the western empire. In the late fourth or early fifth century A.D., a Christian bureaucrat named Publius Flavius Vegetius Renatus wrote *Epitome of Military Affairs (Epitoma rei militaris),* which has been called the "most influential military work written in the western world" before the nineteenth century.[4] It was the only classical military treatise that remained continuously popular throughout the Middle Ages, and its reputation increased in the Renaissance. Vegetius wrote after the disastrous Roman defeat at Adrianople in A.D. 378—not long after, if the emperor to whom the epitome is addressed was Theodosius the Great, as many think—and though Vegetius himself was a civil rather than a military bureaucrat, he hoped to promote desperately needed reforms in the Roman army, which was increasingly composed of barbarian mercenaries. The influence of this treatise in later centuries owes much to the fact that it is a piece of deliberate antiquarianism that holds up an idealized picture of the ancient Roman army as a model for military reform.

Vegetius claims that what he describes is the military organization of the Roman republic, based on sources going back to the time of Cato the Elder, who wrote the first Latin treatise on the art of war in the second century B.C.:

> So once the recruits have been tattooed the science of arms should be shown them in daily training. But neglect due to long years of peace has destroyed the tradition of this subject. Whom can you find able to teach what he himself has not learned? We must therefore recover the ancient custom from histories and (other) books. But they wrote only the incidents and dramas of wars, leaving out as familiar what we are now seeking. The Spartans, it is true, and the Athenians and other Greeks published in books much material which they call *tactica,* but we ought to be inquiring after the military system of the Roman People, who extended their Empire from the smallest bounds almost to the regions of the sun and the end of the earth itself. This requirement made me consult competent authorities and say most faithfully in this opuscule what Cato the Censor wrote on the system of war, what Cornelius Celsus, what Frontinus thought should be summarised, what Paternus, a most zealous champion of military law, published in his books, and what was decreed by the constitutions of Augustus, Trajan, and Hadrian. (1.8 [trans. N. P. Milner])

> Cato the Elder, since he was unbeaten in war and as consul had often led armies, thought he would be of further service to the State if he wrote down the military science. For brave deeds belong to a single age; what is written for the benefit of the State is eternal. Several others did the same, particularly Frontinus, who was highly esteemed by the deified Trajan for his efforts in this field. These men's recommendations, their precepts, I shall summarise as strictly and faithfully as I am able. For although both a carefully and a neglectfully ordered army costs the same expense, it is to the benefit of not only the present but of future generations also if, thanks to Your Majesty's provision, August Emperor, both the very strongest disposition of arms be restored and the neglect of your predecessors amended. (2.3 [trans. Milner])

Vegetius may have known these earlier writers only through epitomes like his own, and the organization he describes is in fact a hodgepodge containing elements from several different periods.

Nevertheless, he grasped correctly the essential fact about the republican army: It had been a heavy infantry army whose secret lay in intensive discipline and drill. He saw correctly that the problem with the Roman army of his day was the neglect of heavy infantry and of discipline. "In every battle it is not numbers and untaught bravery so much as skill and training that generally produce the victory. For we see no other explanation for the conquest of the world by the Roman People than their drill-at-arms, camp-discipline and military expertise" (1.1 [trans. Milner]). Vegetius notes that the Roman infantry wore heavy armor from the founding of Rome down to the reign of Gratian (died 383) but had now abandoned it:

> On this subject [armor] ancient practice has been utterly destroyed. For despite progress in cavalry arms thanks to the example of the Goths, and the Alans and Huns, the infantry is well-known to go unprotected ... Why else was the infantry army called a "wall" among the ancients [perhaps *Iliad* 4.299], if not because the serried ranks of legions shone in their shields, cataphracts [cuirasses] and helmets? (1.20 [trans. Milner])

Vegetius was right in thinking that the tradition of disciplined heavy infantry had been lost, but he was just as important for what he got wrong. He did not understand that the republican army was a citizen army. He knew that recruitment was as essential as training, that heavy-infantry discipline could never be revived unless soldiers were recruited from the right population; but he thought that it would be sufficient to recruit the troops from "Romans," that is, from free inhabitants of the empire, virtually all of whom were citizens in his time, rather than from barbarians outside the frontiers, as was increasingly the case after Adrianople:

> A sense of security born of long peace has diverted mankind [from military service] ... Thus attention to military training obviously was at first discharged rather neglectfully, then omitted, until finally consigned long since to oblivion ... Therefore recruits should constantly be levied and trained. For it costs less to train one's own men in arms than to hire foreign mercenaries. (1.28 [trans. Milner])

Because Vegetius did not understand that Roman citizenship in the Christian empire meant something very different from what it had meant in the Rome of Cato, the imaginary army he described for posterity was more a national than a civic army, the army of a monarchy rather than a republic. For this reason, Vegetius would seem immediately relevant to Renaissance Europe. He showed how the military ideals of the classical city republics, the disciplined heavy-infantry tactics, might be adapted to a world of national monarchies and professional armies.

A final point about the legacy of Vegetius: He was not a great supporter of the offensive in either tactics or strategy. He was cautious about the decisive battle, recognizing that it offered the chance for total victory, yet advising generals not to risk this unless the odds were highly favorable (3.9, 3.11). The most famous maxim in Vegetius is "He who desires peace, let him prepare for war" (3, preface). This is another turn on the ancient commonplace that one must be both warlike and peaceable, but earlier versions of it assume that being always prepared for war entails actually going to war on occasion (for example, Thucydides 4.92). Vegetius seems to imply that if one is sufficiently well prepared for war one may never have to go to war: "No one dares challenge or harm one whom he realises will win if he fights" (3, preface); "no one dares to challenge to war or inflict injury on a kingdom or people whom he knows is armed and ready to resist and revenge any attack" (4.31 [trans. Milner]). These statements do not deny the possibility of preventive strikes, and even Vegetius can fall into the ancient rhetoric of imperialism—he tells his readers that the art of war not only preserves their liberty but *extends their frontiers* (3.10). But in fact, this was a farcical thing to say in the crumbling empire he lived in, and the republican ideology behind it was alien to him. The passages quoted herein are among the clearest statements of a theory of deterrence to be found in classical literature, and on the whole, Vegetius probably acted as a moderating influence on the classical cult of the offensive.

Notes

1. T. A. Sinclair, *A History of Greek Political Thought*, 2d ed. (Cleveland, 1968), 280.

2. Diodorus of Sicily (34/35.33.5–6, in a section based on Posidonius), says Rome became harsh to its allies after the fall of Carthage. See Peter Gruen, *The Hellenistic World and the Coming of Rome* (Berkeley, 1984), 351 ff.

3. J. B. Campbell, *The Emperor and the Roman Army, 31 B.C.–A.D. 235* (Oxford, 1984), 190ff., 300ff., 409ff.

4. T. R. Phillips, *Roots of Strategy* (Harrisburg, Pa., 1940), 67. See the commentaries by L. F. Stelten, ed., *Flavius Vegetius Renatus Epitoma Rei Militaris* (New York, 1990), and N. P. Milner, trans., *Vegetius* (Liverpool, 1993).

Part Four

The Classical Legacy

Our mindes must be so confirmed and conformed, that we may bee at rest in troubles, and have peace even in the midst of warre.

—Justus Lipsius, *Of Constancie* (trans. Sir John Stradling, 1584)

Chapter Eleven

Warfare in Medieval Thought

Early Christianity

Soon after Vegetius wrote, the western empire collapsed. For a thousand years to come, warfare in western Europe would be interpreted by theologians and jurists: Vegetius, Sallust, and other Latin secular writers never ceased to be read, but those who read and commented on them were mostly monks and clerics, whose basic assumptions about warfare came from the church fathers. Of the three ancient traditions surveyed in this book, the moral had virtually swallowed the realistic and the constitutional. Nevertheless, there was more continuity in the classical legacy than we often think, for Christian thought about warfare was totally dominated by a just war doctrine[1] that was itself of pagan Greco-Roman origin.

Christians had no choice but to take over the classical legacy in this area because it was impossible to extract any coherent theory of warfare from the sacred books of Christianity. This literature contains two absolutely contradictory traditions. There is the Old Testament tradition of the War of Yahweh, which has been described in Chapter 2. The historical and legal books portrayed the early Hebrews going to war at the express command of God, who ordered them to exterminate all the pagans of the Holy Land and reduce to servitude all living outside it. Whether the real early Hebrews ever did either is open to doubt, but few early Christians doubted it. The New Testament, by contrast, taught a doctrine of extreme nonviolence. It is true that the New Testament also taught obedience to worldly authority, but it offered no obvious way to reconcile the two principles. Jesus said to resist not evil but also to render unto Caesar that which is Caesar's; Paul told the Christians of Rome to leave vengeance to the Lord but also to honor the powers that be. Still, the main impression left by the passages on war in the New Testament is as irenic as the impression left by the Old is sanguinary. During the early centuries, many Christians shunned military service as sinful, many apologists condemned the Roman empire and all its works, and none saw any useful political model in the holy wars of the Old Testament, which were assigned to a former dispensation or sometimes allegorized out of existence.

The Byzantine Tradition

When the church made its alliance with the empire in the fourth century A.D., this contradictory heritage provided no way to explain the new relationship. The Judaic side of it contained no relevant theory of statecraft; the Christian side contained no statecraft at all. Constantine's bishops perforce adopted, with greater or lesser hesitation, the traditional Roman ideas about warfare and imperialism surveyed in previous chapters—aided, of course, by the fact that the Roman tradition had always been sententiously ethical and religious in tone. The tradition was now given a Christian flavor, which sometimes smacked of the New Testament and sometimes more of the Old. The Christian versions of just war have always tended toward either one or the other.

Among the patristic writers of the Christian empire, the Old Testament influence generally predominates over the New. The emperor was regarded as deputy of God and protector of the faith. The concept of the universal empire was revived and took on a new dimension, for the Roman people were now also the people of Christ, and the universal claims of Rome merged with the equally universal claims of the church. The barbarian enemies of Rome were conflated with the pagan and heretical enemies of the church, and military service to protect the Christian empire from both became a pious Christian duty. The New Testament precepts of nonviolence were interpreted as referring to an inner disposition and in their literal sense were thought to be binding only on the clergy and monks. Some bishops mingled the pagan rhetoric of righteous and triumphal imperialism with Old Testament language about holy war. St. Ambrose's *On Duties,* an adaptation of Cicero's *On Duties* for Christian clergy, did not omit military duties, though acknowledging that some would find this unfit for priests. St. Ambrose pointed out that Old Testament heroes like Joshua, Samson, and David had won glory in war, and he even suggested that what Cicero, Panaetius, Aristotle, and other pagans had said about this subject had been borrowed from the Hebrew Scriptures (*Duties* 1.35; Christians liked to claim that everything that was of any value in the pagan classics had been stolen from the Scriptures, which they imagined to be of vastly greater antiquity).

> For courage, which in war preserves one's country from the barbarians, or at home defends the weak, or comrades from robbers, is full of justice. (1.27.129)

> Here, then [in the example of the Maccabees] is fortitude in war, which bears no light impress of what is virtuous and seemly upon it, for it prefers death to slavery and disgrace. (1.41.211 [trans. H. de Romestin])

In the Byzantine empire the tradition of triumphal rulership continued throughout the Middle Ages. But its imagery did not begin to appear in the Greek liturgy until the seventh century, a tardiness that suggests that even at Constantinople there persisted a sense of anomaly about praising warfare in Christian services.[2]

Augustine

Western Christianity became dominated by a different tradition. The early collapse of the western empire did not allow Byzantine triumphal rulership to take root; and St. Augustine, who wrote his *City of God* to explain the sack of Rome in A.D. 410, deliberately set the Latin churches on a separate track. Throughout the Middle Ages, the writings of Augustine remained the most important influence on western European thinking about warfare.[3] His concepts and imagery reflect the Gospels far more than the Books of Joshua and Maccabees. He firmly rejected the ideals of triumphal rulership then gaining acceptance in the East and refused to identify the *civitas Dei,* the invisible community of the saved, or even the visible organization of the church, with the Roman empire or with any earthly city.

In A.D. 382, the Christian emperor Gratian had the ancient statue of the goddess Victory removed from the Roman Senate, and the defenders of paganism claimed this resulted in the sack of 410. In the *City of God,* Augustine asks satirically why they did not also have a god named Empire, and continues with a sustained assault on the Roman tradition of just imperialism.

> I would . . . have our adversaries consider the possibility that to rejoice in the extent of empire is not a characteristic of good men. The increase of empire was assisted by the wickedness of those against whom just wars were waged. The empire would have been small indeed, if neighbouring peoples had been peaceable, had always acted with justice, and had never provoked attack by any wrong-doing. In that case, human affairs would have been in a happier state; all kingdoms would have been small and would have rejoiced in concord with their neighbours. There would have been a multitude of kingdoms in the world, as there are a multitude of homes in our cities. To make war and extend the realm by crushing other peoples, is good fortune in the eyes of the wicked; to the good, it is stern necessity. But since it would be worse if the unjust were to lord it over the just, this stern necessity may be called good fortune without impropriety. Yet there can be no shadow of doubt that it is greater good fortune to have a good neighbour and live in peace with him than to subdue a bad neighbour when he makes war. It is a wicked prayer to ask to have someone to hate or to fear, so that he may be someone to conquer.
>
> So if it was by waging wars that were just, not impious and unjust, that the Romans were able to acquire so vast an empire, surely they should worship the Injustice of others as a kind of goddess? For we observe how much help "she" has given toward the extension of the Empire by making others wrong-doers, so that the Romans should have enemies to fight in a just cause and so increase

Rome's power . . . With the support of those two goddesses, "Foreign Injustice" and Victory, the Empire grew, even when Jupiter took a holiday. (*City of God* 4.15 [trans. Henry Bettenson])

Augustine admits that Rome brought universal peace and fellowship,

but think of the cost of this achievement! Consider the scale of those wars, with all that slaughter of human beings, all the human blood that was shed! . . . But the wise man, they say, will wage just wars. Surely, if he remembers that he is a human being, he will lament the fact that he is faced with the necessity of waging just wars; for if they were not just, he would not have to engage in them, and consequently there would be no wars for a wise man. For it is the injustice of the opposing side that lays on the wise man the duty of waging wars; and this injustice is surely to be deplored by a human being, since it is the injustice of human beings, even though no necessity for war should arise from it. (19.7 [trans. Bettenson])

No Stoic had seen so clearly the fundamental hypocrisy of Roman imperialism, its unholy eagerness to exploit the "injustices" of foreigners. Yet Augustine never questions that just wars must be fought, so long as they are fought in the spirit he describes in this quotation, or that the earthly peace they bring is anything but good, even if it is not heavenly peace. War, like other social and political evils, is a punishment for original sin, but it is also a restraint upon sin, the instrument through which the just curb the wicked. Behind it all there is God's providential plan, directing the rise and fall of empires, but this plan is mysterious to us; he says we cannot tell why God allowed the fall of the Christian Roman Empire or any other state, and it is presumptuous to think that we can see the unfolding of the divine plan in the rise of any state. This Augustinian historical vision is reminiscent in some ways of the cosmic law of Herodotus, except that the Herodotean vision, however pessimistic, did inspire an interest in the rise and fall of states, which to Augustine has become a repetitious and unimportant phenomenon whose study can only distract us from contemplation of that heavenly city that is our true home.

The Augustinian attitude toward warfare is therefore deeply pessimistic and unwilling to assign positive value to it. The paradoxical result of this pessimism is that it made Augustine's view of just war *more* vindicative than the traditional pagan view. To Augustine, a just war is permissible only if carried out for motives of charity. There is an obligation to go to war to resist *any* kind of immorality, and the insistence that we can only fight for the purest of motives tends to remove restraint. Those who fight for love may be more ruthless than those who fight for glory or land. Augustine said nothing to suggest that a just war should not be offensive, so long as our motives are pure; and he provided an explicit justification for offensive war in his commentary on Numbers 21.21–25, where the Israelites start war simply because their neighbors would not give them right of passage through their country, proving that denial of any right is a just cause (*Questions on the Heptateuch* 4.44). Augustine defined a just war simply as a war to avenge injuries (*Heptateuch* 6.10), a definition that was to enter the medieval canon law and become the classic statement of this view.

It should be emphasized, however, that this is a peculiarly Augustinian brand of moral vindication: Warfare, in this perspective, is undertaken to avenge the whole moral order, but there is everywhere in Augustine's works so much awareness of the ineffability of God's plan that it is difficult to identify just warfare with any particular state or ruler, as the pagan Romans and the Christian Byzantines did in their different ways. Also, the moral criteria for a just war seem so exacting that they raise the question of whether there had ever been one, apart from the wars of Yahweh in the Old Testament— which Augustine thought were simply just wars, not particularly "holy" wars, differing from other just wars only in that we happen to *know* those were just by revelation. With those exceptions in the distant past, Augustine provided ample reasons to doubt the justice of any war, to those who read him carefully. Isolated quotations from Augustine about the vindictiveness of war could have the opposite effect.

The Medieval Just War Doctrine[4]

The continuous history of just war doctrine began about 1140 with the *Decretum* of Gratian, the basic compilation of canon law (the laws of the church), which discusses the morality of warfare in its *Causa* 23. Gratian quoted there the definitions of a just war by Cicero (through Isidore of Seville) and by Augustine: The first is Roman and emphasizes the need for formal declaration; the second is Christian and emphasizes vindicative purpose, but it is a matter of emphasis. Gratian synthesized the two in his comment on these passages: "A just war is waged by an authoritative edict to avenge injuries" (*Causa* 23, *quaestio* 2, *dictum post canonum* 2 [trans. F. H. Russell]).

Commentaries on this section by the canon lawyers of the later twelfth and thirteenth centuries stayed within Gratian's definition and generally followed his lines of interpretation; and the theologians followed the lead of the canonists. (Discussion of warfare was dominated by canon lawyers throughout the Middle Ages because the basic text of the canon law, Gratian's *Decretum*, included a section on warfare, whereas the texts studied by theologians passed over the problem; hence the legalistic tone of this discussion.) Today the best-known medieval treatment of the ethics of war is that of Thomas Aquinas in the *Summa Theologiae* (2.2. *quaestio* 40), who laid down three requirements for a just war: It must have right cause, right intention, and right authority. The major medieval contributions to the theory may be conveniently divided into these three areas.

Not much of substance was added to the ancient theory of just cause. Medieval discussions commonly recognize the causes mentioned in Gratian: A just war must repel or avenge injuries or recover goods. All seem to assume a just war may take the offensive, citing Augustine on the Israelites' right of passage in Numbers 21. But it is significant that both jurists and theologians pay little attention to the crusade. Gratian did not even mention crusades. The papal bulls authorizing crusades were not included in the collections of papal decretals that were added to Gratian. When canonists did discuss crusading, they generally defined it as simply a special type of just war: the just warfare of the church, declared by the pope for the protection of the Christian faith, subject to the same rules as any other just war. Some said crusades must be confined to the Holy Land, for they were intended to recover the lands of the church. In any case, they had to be justified as responses to some injury to the church committed by infidels. As usual, the concept of injury was flexible. For example, it could include attempts to interfere with the work of Christian missionaries. Still, few thought infidels could be attacked simply for their infidelity. To the end of the Middle Ages, Christian thought continued to balk at the notion of a genuinely holy war, fought for religious reasons alone, without secular justification.

The problem of right intentions produced the most lasting medieval contribution to just war theory. The Augustinian principle that wars must be fought in a spirit of charity, without hatred for the enemy, compelled the canonists and theologians to pay far more attention to the *jus in bello,* the rules for the conduct of warfare, than had ever been done in antiquity. They focused on noncombatant immunity. By the thirteenth century, the canon law recognized a lengthy list of persons who were supposed to be exempt from violence in wartime—clergy, monks, women, peasants, merchants, indeed everyone but the fighting class of knights and soldiers. Such concerns were unknown in the classical world; they constitute the main specifically Christian and Augustinian element in the modern theory of just warfare. Modern attempts to limit warfare have generally followed the same strategy of making clear distinctions between combatants and noncombatants and insisting on the immunity of the latter, though in the twentieth century this distinction has become increasingly difficult to enforce.

As for the problem of right authority, it was peculiar to the Middle Ages, and discussion of it then has little relevance to any time before or since. No one in antiquity gave much thought to the question of who was authorized to declare a war because the answer was nearly always obvious. But it was not obvious over much of western Europe in the Middle Ages, where authority was fragmented within a confusing network of imperial, royal, clerical, and feudal jurisdictions, so the canonists found themselves spending much time on the problem of who possessed the authority to declare a just war. Until around the year 1250, many said that only the Holy Roman Emperor could declare a just war, except for a crusade, which had to be declared by the pope. After that time, it was generally conceded that just wars could be proclaimed by any prince who was supreme in his own kingdom. But another category of permissible warfare was also recognized: the war of self-defense. It was a principle of Roman law that anyone had the right to repel force with force. This right applied only to private persons, but the canonists applied it to warfare and recognized that any knight could rightfully defend himself if attacked. This was distinct from the just war, which required a higher authority, and it was a strictly circumscribed right: The attack had to come first, the response had to be immediate, the violence used had to be proportionate to the danger. The unintended effect was to introduce into the just war tradition for the first time a clear definition of a purely defensive type of warfare distinct from vindicative just war in the traditional sense.

By the later Middle Ages, there was general agreement in western Europe on the rules of warfare. A synthesis had developed that was essentially based on the work of twelfth- and thirteenth-century canonists and theologians. It incorporated the principles just described but added elements from the revived study of Roman law, the revived study of Aristotle, and the knightly code of chivalry.[5] The synthesis was propagated by works like *The Tree of Battles* by the monk Honoré Bovet (1387) and *The Book of Deeds of Arms and of Chivalry* by the poetess Christine de Pisan (1410), both written in French for a lay and knightly audience. It was universally recognized that any prince had the right to wage just wars, but there was strong emphasis on the obligation of every prince to respect the common law of Christendom, to never pick wars for selfish or frivolous reasons, and to conduct wars in a spirit of Christian love and knightly chivalry, paying particular attention to the immunity of women and other noncombatants. This common law of Christendom was an amalgam of all the elements mentioned earlier and could be described in different ways: Theologians and canonists of the old school spoke of it as a divine law revealed in Scripture, theologians influenced more by Aristotle than Augustine preferred to call it a natural law imposed by human reason, and the glossators on the Roman law called it the *jus gentium,* the law of nations, that body of customs observed by all men and imposed by common consent. But these were differences in terminology: Divine law, natural law, and the law of nations were regarded as aspects of the same universal order, founded on revelation, reason, and custom.

The study of historical and military literature was considered valuable for the art of war. In the late Middle Ages, Vegetius was translated into the vernacular languages and read by increasing numbers of literate laymen. Frontinus, Caesar, Sallust, and Valerius Maximus were also popular. About 1350, the king of France commissioned a French translation of Livy to assist princes to "defend and govern their lands, possess and conquer in proper manner foreign ones, injure their enemies, defend their subjects and help their friends."[6] But they made no distinction between classical historians and more recent writers and read them all in the same spirit, with little awareness that

Roman wars had been different from their own. Christine de Pisan was unusual in perceiving that warfare in her day relied much more on cavalry than the armies of Vegetius, but she did not follow up on the observation. Medieval historical writing was not so obsessed with theology as we are sometimes told, but the influence of Christianity and chivalry combined to keep it from becoming an instrument for the exploration of politics and strategy.

One classical tradition that fitted uneasily into the medieval synthesis was that of stratagem. In the eighth chapter of Joshua a feigned retreat and ambush carried out by Joshua against the city of Ai is described, and on this basis, St. Augustine remarked that deceptions were allowed by God in a just war. This contradicted the principle that good faith (*fides*) must be kept with the enemy in wartime, an observation also found in the works of Augustine and other church fathers. In *Causa* 23, Gratian tried to resolve the contradiction by concluding that stratagems were allowable only if good faith had *not* been promised, and later canonists wrestled inconclusively with the problem. There was a general sense that stratagems were permissible in a just war, but this was not an area that the medieval mind wished to explore.[7]

Early Renaissance Florence:
The Rebirth of Civic Militarism

The first crack in the medieval synthesis appeared in Italy around 1400, with the rise of "civic humanism."[8] The magistrates and governing elite of the Florentine republic began to imitate both the literary form and content of classical Latin historiography and oratory. The new style appeared full blown in the early years of the fifteenth century in the Ciceronian orations and Livian historical works of Leonardo Bruni, later chancellor of Florence and the first of a succession of Florentine humanist magistrates who soon spread the new genres over Italy. Unlike earlier humanists like Petrarch and Boccaccio, these men sought to copy the thought, as well as the expression, of Cicero and Livy. They identified themselves with the ancient Romans and absorbed ancient Roman attitudes toward politics and war, as they understood them.

The Romans with whom they identified themselves were the Romans of the republic, not the principate. They bought the interpretation of Roman history they found in the Roman historians: The key to that history was the decline of republican virtue, above all, military virtue. The keynote of the new rhetoric was the ideal of "liberty," meaning participation in politics, which was seen as the source of all virtue because it inspired heroic achievement. Bruni had picked up a comment by Tacitus at the beginning of his *Histories:* Virtue only flourishes in liberty, and therefore it declined under the Caesars. This provided a political explanation for the decay of Roman virtue recorded by Sallust and Livy. Bruni and his circle learned from Tacitus that the principate had dealt republican liberty and virtue their death blow.

They knew from Sallust that the decline had begun much earlier with the coming of peace. They learned from most Roman authors a glorification of war uninhibited by Christian misgivings.

The Florentine breakthrough was the result of several factors: the consolidation of a tight oligarchy bent on building a centralized state in Tuscany; the weak position of the papacy during the Great Schism, which left humanist circles uniquely free of clerical interference during the early fifteenth century; and the long wars between the Florentine republic and the princely state of Milan between 1390 and 1402, which inspired the Florentine oligarchs to identify themselves with classical Rome and Athens and with classical republican ideals in opposition to monarchy. They were attracted to the military aspect of that tradition because it held out hope that an army of free citizen soldiers would be invincible in war over armies of mercenaries, who were then taking over Italian warfare. The core of the humanist program was revival of the communal militia of Florence—an anachronistic ideal, for these medieval militias were rapidly becoming obsolete in an Italy increasingly dominated by despots and condottieri.

In many ways, this was a limited breakthrough. Bruni's *History of the Florentine People,* the great monument of Livian history in the Renaissance, revived all the limitations of Livy: the moralistic biographical approach to history, the lack of interest in causation, the unquestioned dogmas about the justice of Roman warfare and Roman imperialism. Bruni believed that Florence had been founded not by Julius Caesar, as tradition said, but by the Roman republic, for it was essential to the new ideology to make Florence the heir of the republic and not the principate; and he thought this an adequate reason to claim that all the wars of Florence were just, like the wars of the Roman republic, and that Florence had inherited Rome's just dominion over the world.[9] He seriously attempted to trace the origins of the Guelph Party to republican Rome and that of their Ghibelline opponents to the Caesars. In his *On War* (*De militia*), he attempted to trace the origins of European knighthood and chivalry to ancient Rome and Sparta. But he never understood how different ancient warfare was from medieval war and placed no special importance upon infantry.

In short, civic humanism was more medieval than it looked. Outside Florence, its rhetoric was imitated more than its ideas, and even at Florence, it was dying in the later fifteenth century under the rule of the Medici. But the humanists had given currency to certain seminal concepts about politics and war that eventually bore fruit in the work of Machiavelli.

Notes

1. For a survey of the just war tradition, see J. T. Johnson, *Ideology, Reason, and the Limitation of War: Religious and Secular Concepts, 1200–1740* (Princeton, 1975), and *Just War Tradition and the Restraint of War* (Princeton, 1981).

2. Michael McCormick, *Eternal Victory: Triumphal Rulership in Late Antiquity, Byzantium, and the Early Medieval West* (Cambridge, 1986).

3. The issues touched on here are discussed in nearly all the vast literature on Augustine's political thought; see especially C. N. Cochrane, *Christianity and Classical Culture: A Study of Thought and Action from Augustus to Augustine* (New York, 1957).

4. F. H. Russell, *The Just War in the Middle Ages* (Cambridge, 1975), is comprehensive. There are discussions of medieval theories of warfare in Hans Delbrück, *History of the Art of War,* 4 vols., trans. W. J. Renfroe, Jr. (Westport, Conn., 1975–1985), vol. 3, *Medieval Warfare,* and Philippe Contamine, *Warfare in the Middle Ages,* trans. Michael Jones (Oxford, 1984).

5. M. H. Keen, *The Laws of War in the Late Middle Ages* (London, 1965).

6. Contamine, *Warfare,* 214.

7. Consult the index in Russell's *Just War* under "ambush."

8. Hans Baron's *The Crisis of the Early Italian Renaissance: Civic Humanism and Republican Liberty in an Age of Classicism and Tyranny,* 2 vols. 2d ed. (Princeton, 1966) gives the classic interpretation of the origins of modern republicanism. Its military aspects are studied by C. C. Bayley, *War and Society in Renaissance Florence: The "De Militia" of Leonardo Bruni* (Toronto, 1961).

9. Bruni, "Panegyric to the City of Florence," in *The Earthly Republic: Italian Humanists on Government and Society,* ed. B. G. Kohl and R. G. Witt (Philadelphia, 1978), 150.

Chapter Twelve

Warfare in Renaissance Thought

Machiavelli[1]

In 1494, the French invasion turned Italy into the battleground of the new centralized monarchies and their professional mercenary armies. One by-blow of the invasion was the overthrow of the Medici at Florence and the temporary restoration of the republic. Niccolò Machiavelli, who served the republic in diplomatic and military affairs throughout its history, organized a communal militia based on infantry; but it proved no match for the Spanish professionals, who brought back the Medici in 1512 and put an end both to the republic and to Machiavelli's political career. He devoted his retirement to the study of the classical authors—chiefly the Romans, though by his time most of the major Greek historians were available in Latin translation—and to the attempt to understand and reconstruct the classical art of war. There were two main aspects to Machiavelli's achievement, both revolutionary. Firstly, he succeeded in reviving civic humanism. Without him, republicanism would have been an episode in the intellectual history of Florence, confined to one nostalgic generation. Machiavelli made it one of the enduring themes of European political thought. Secondly, he revived the classical principle of *raison d'état,* formulating it more lucidly and systematically than it ever had been by the classical authors.

Like the earlier Florentine humanists, he took the Roman republic for his ideal constitution but carried the glorification of warfare even further. He offered an original explanation for why republics are best suited for warfare: The democratic element in a republican constitution opens up resources of manpower and morale, which forces the state to conquer and expand. He thought an imperialistic popular government like that of the Roman republic was preferable to a stable oligarchy like Sparta's or to the contemporary republic of Venice. It is true that democracy produces civil strife, but Machiavelli thought that tolerable: Unlike any of his contemporaries and unlike any classical author whose work survives, he thought competition between social classes essential to liberty. This is perhaps his single most original notion.

> If therefore you wish to make a people numerous and warlike, so as to create a great empire, you will have to constitute it in such manner as will cause you more difficulty in managing it; and if you keep it either small or unarmed, and you acquire other dominions, you will not be able to hold them, or you will become so feeble that you will fall a prey to whoever attacks you. And therefore in all our decisions we must consider well what presents the least inconveniences, and then choose the best, for we shall never find any course entirely free from objections. Rome then might, like Sparta, have created a king for life, and established a limited senate; but with her desire to become a great empire, she could not, like Sparta, limit the number of her citizens ... If anyone therefore wishes to establish an entirely new republic, he will have to consider whether he wishes to have her expand in power and dominion like Rome, or whether he intends to confine her within narrow limits. In the first case, it will be necessary to organize her as Rome was, and to submit to dissensions and troubles as best he may; for without a great number of men, and these well armed, no republic can ever increase ... I believe it therefore necessary rather to take the constitution of Rome as a model than that of any other republic (for I do not believe that a middle course between the two can be found), and to tolerate the differences that will arise between the Senate and the people as an unavoidable inconvenience in achieving greatness like that of Rome. (*Discourses on Livy* 1.6 [trans. Luigi Ricci])

In his *Art of War* published in 1521, he suggested that the Roman decline began after the Punic Wars, when the republic made the mistake of switching from a citizen army to mercenaries, a process completed under the Caesars.

But Machiavelli was pessimistic about the possibility of imitating the Roman republic, and he thought republics were rare in history. The very success of Rome had killed most of the ancient republics, and Christianity had killed the rest. Even the Florentine republic had been no more than a poor copy of the Roman. In *The Art of War,* the principal speaker in the dialogue concludes glumly: "For seeing that there is now such a proportion of *virtù* [military virtue] left among mankind that it has but little influence in the affairs of the world—and that all things seem to be governed by *fortuna*—they think it is better to follow her train than to contend with her for superiority" (*Art of War* 80 [trans. Ellis Farneworth]).

The author of *The Prince* knew that republicanism was an ideal and that he lived in a world of monarchies. He meant his military advice to be useful to princes as well as republics, and he advised princes also to avoid reliance upon mercenaries and to recruit armies from their numerous and loyal subjects (*Discourses* 1.21, 43; *The Prince* 12–13). Any state could thus imitate some of the advantages of the popular republican army, though not its unique dynamism.

If the interpretation of Roman history I advanced earlier is right, then Machiavelli exaggerated the democratic element in the Roman constitution. But he perceived correctly the reason for the military success of classical republics in general and explained it in institutional rather than the conventional moral terms. The effect was to strengthen the connection between republicanism and militarism.

Even more significant than Machiavelli's revival of classical republicanism was his rediscovery of classical realism. The main sources of this "Machiavellian" philosophy seem to be Frontinus and Xenophon.

Frontinus suggested to Machiavelli the vision of politics as an amoral power struggle, in which ethical considerations, if they appear, are adopted for calculating reasons. Probably it was Frontinus, too, who suggested to him one of the most fruitful ideas to be found in the realistic historiographical tradition, namely that such calculations should be guided by the systematic study of historical examples. Frontinus may even have given him the notion of a commentary on Livy as a vehicle; as Wood pointed out, Frontinus drew more of his anecdotes from Livy than from any other source. Many of Frontinus's stratagems are repeated in *The Art of War* (see also *Discourses* 3.20).

Another important source was the Latin translation of Xenophon's *Cyropaedia*—in Machiavelli's time the most widely read of all Greek historical works, judging from the number of editions and translations published in Latin Europe.[2] Citing Xenophon as his authority, Machiavelli justified the practice of bad faith by comparing warfare to the hunting of beasts (*Discourses* 2.13, 3.39). He qualifies this counsel by adding that it does not justify such perfidies as treaty breaking (3.40) but then qualifies that, concluding that anything is permissible where freedom is as stake (3.41–42), and refers the reader to the notorious eighteenth chapter of *The Prince*, "In What Way Princes Must Keep Faith." There the reader learns that a prince must be both man and beast (again the imagery suggests Xenophon) and in his beast form must be both lion and fox; when it is necessary to play the fox, he will practice bad faith, while keeping up the pretense of good faith.

Xenophon had not gone so far, and Frontinus had been less candid. The originality of Machiavelli lay in his perception that good faith is a publicity device. He had laid bare the real world behind the moralisms of Livy. Disregarding totally the Roman historiographical tradition, he attributed to the Roman republic a deliberate strategy of conquest. He did not deny that the Romans always kept good faith, which is to say, observed the formalities; but he was convinced that behind that good faith there was bad faith, for the Romans cultivated allies for the purpose of reducing them to dependency and expanding their dominion. I think he misunderstood Roman religion, but he was correct about the expansionary nature of the Roman state. He did not blame the Romans, because the real world he had exposed was a world of constant struggle, in which the best bulwark against fortune was to organize the state for war and expansion like the Roman republic: "We see therefore that the Romans in the early beginning of their power already employed fraud, which it has ever been necessary for those to practise who from small beginnings wish to rise to the highest degree of power; and then it is less censurable the more it is concealed, as was that practised by the Romans" (*Discourses* 2.13 [trans. Ricci]).

Machiavelli's spokesman in the *Art of War* remarks at the end of the work that the inordinate thirst for dominion exhibited by Alexander and Caesar cannot be commended; but in fact, expansion is commended in many passages in that dialogue, as well as in Machiavelli's other works. Preventive warfare is explicitly approved: "War is not to be avoided, and can be deferred only to the advantage of the other side" (*Prince* 3 [trans. Ricci]). Thus Rome fought the Hellenistic kings in Greece so as not to have to fight them in Italy. And one must always seek out decisive battles. Rome is especially praised for bringing all its wars to a quick conclusion.

> When these indolent princes or effeminate republics [of modern times] send a general with an army into the field, the wisest order they think they can give him is never to risk a battle, and above all things to avoid a general action. In this they think they imitate the salutary prudence of Fabius Maximus, who by delaying battle saved the Roman republic; but they do not understand that in most cases such a commission is either impracticable or dangerous . . . A thousand examples attest the truth of what I have advanced. (*Discourses* 3.10 [trans. Ricci])

Through the fog of his sources, Machiavelli had grasped correctly the basic principles behind Greco-Roman military success: The disciplined army of heavy infantry, recruited from its own soil, is best used to seek decisive battle where its mass and morale can be used to best advantage; and it is the indispensable instrument to carry out what would soon be described in Italy as *ragione di stato*.

Holy War

Machiavelli was an aberration in an intellectual world where notions of imperialism and war were still dominated by theology. But the medieval theological synthesis was breaking apart in the early sixteenth century into several rival theories. The Reformation and the wars of religion produced for a time an extreme version of holy war doctrine based on the Old Testament. This was found in all denominations, but especially among Calvinists, because they rejected the canon law traditions that formed the basis of medieval just war doctrine and tried to return to the Scriptures, where the Old Testament had far more to say on this subject than the New. About 1640, a New England assembly is said to have adopted the following resolutions:

1. The earth is the Lord's and the fullness thereof. Voted.
2. The Lord may give the earth or any part of it to his chosen people. Voted.
3. We are His chosen people. Voted.[3]

To people with this mentality, wars were not merely permitted by God as in medieval theology but commanded by God, not merely justifiable but "justified" in the Protestant sense. Such wars could only be fought for religious purposes and were free of the restraints of secular warfare: They were offensive almost by definition, since the usual purpose of this biblical rhetoric was to call for attack upon God's enemies, as when English Puritan preachers demanded war against Spain for the defense of the true faith; and sometimes they rejected the *jus in bello*, demanding that holy war be prosecuted with the methods used by Joshua against the Canaanites. This was a phenomenon peculiar to the age of religious war. Most Christians, both Protestant and Catholic, did not accept this doctrine even then, and it disappeared totally, except in the minds of a few fanatics, with the end of the wars of religion in 1648. The tradition is of interest here chiefly because this was the only time in Christian history when the Old Testament idea of war broke completely free from the restraints of the classical tradition. The medieval crusade, as we have seen, was normally interpreted as a variant of just war.

Aristotle and Natural Slavery

At the same time, there appeared another doctrine of offensive warfare, based not on Deuteronomy but on Aristotle.[4] The discovery of America had forced Europeans to confront the question of whether the medieval just war doctrine, with its easy assumptions about the universality of the law of nations, really applied to peoples as strange as the Aztecs and Incas. How could the Spanish conquests be justified, and how were the conquered Indian populations to be treated? Some scholars of the early sixteenth century revived Aristotle's theory that barbarians, being slaves by nature, could be conquered and enslaved without further justification. In 1550, there was a famous disputation at Valladolid between the Dominican friar Bartolomé de Las Casas and the humanist jurist Juan Ginés de Sepúlveda on the status of the Native Americans. Sepúlveda argued that the Indians were natural slaves, as was proven by their human sacrifices and other crimes against nature. Therefore, they could not conduct just wars and were fair game for conquest and enforced servitude; and if they resisted this fate, they should be destroyed. He referred to the conquests of the Greeks and Romans as examples of this type of warfare (quite incorrectly in the case of the Romans, who had been little affected by Aristotle's racial prejudices). Las Casas argued that there may have been natural slavery in Aristotle's time, but if so, it had been replaced by Christian equality, and the Christian laws of war applied to all men. This debate continued for a long time in Spain and its empire. The racist doctrines of Sepúlveda were often repeated, usually in a modified form. Some claimed that natural slavery applied to wild forest Indians but not to civilized peoples like the Incas. But in Europe as a whole, educated opinion generally accepted the basic humanity of the Americans, as defended by Las Casas and his influential order. One permanent effect of the debate was to cause the Spanish Dominicans and other theologians to refine the traditional notions of just warfare and the law of nations, as will be seen shortly.

Erasmus

The three theories summarized thus far were all attacks on the medieval idea of the just war, but they emanated from very different quarters. The doctrines of the Puritans and the Aristotelians were of limited scope, meant to apply only to certain types of war—the first to wars fought for religion, the second to the Spanish conquests in America—and had no permanent effect on what Europeans thought about normal European warfare. The doctrine of Machiavelli was to have permanent and corrosive effects, but it would be a long time before these became obvious.

Finally, a fourth critique of the just war appeared in the early sixteenth century. The northern humanist circles led by Desiderius Erasmus revived the ancient Stoic antiwar themes.[5] As has been discussed, the Stoics had never denied the principle of the just war but had excoriated most real wars as examples of greed and folly. In works like *The Praise of Folly* (1511) and *The Complaint of Peace* (1517), Erasmus followed the same strategy but took it a step further. He did not deny the principle of just war, which would have been heresy—and he was accused of this—but he managed to suggest that for all practical purposes just wars were as rare as the Stoic wise man. In *The Education of a Christian Prince* (1516), he advises the future emperor Charles V that war causes "the shipwreck of all that is good": "A good prince should never go to war at all unless, after trying every other means, he cannot possibly avoid it." The prince should reflect on how evil war is "even if it is the most justifiable war—if there really is any war which can be called 'just'" (Chap. 11 [trans. L. K. Born]). Augustine and other Fathers may approve of war in "one or two places," but far more often speak of it with abhorrence, and the New Testament invariably condemns it.

> We will not attempt to discuss whether war is ever just; but who does not think his own cause just? Among such great and changing vicissitudes of human events, among so many treaties and agreements which are now entered into, now rescinded, who can lack a pretext—if there is any real excuse—for going to war? . . . even if there are some [wars] which might be called "just," yet as human affairs are now, I know not whether there could be found any of this sort—that is, the motive for which was not ambition, wrath, ferocity, lust, or greed. (Chap. 11 [trans. Born])

This is as close to pacifism as any writer had ever come, and probably as close as anyone could dare in the sixteenth century. But Erasmus could not challenge the assumptions of the just war doctrine. He does not deny the vindicative purpose of war, and though his language may suggest that wars should only be fought in self-defense, he does not explicitly say so. In the end, he can only urge the prince to examine his conscience carefully before going to war. He probably foresaw how much restraint that would place on the conduct of the emperor Charles V.

The Renaissance Just War Doctrine

All the critiques of the just war described here may be called reactions to the several crises that transformed European interstate relations in the early sixteenth century. Machiavelli and Erasmus were reacting, in opposite ways, to the new destructiveness of Renaissance warfare; Sepúlveda, to the discovery and conquest of the New World; the holy war preachers, to the Reformation and the wars of religion. But the just war tradition survived all these attacks. It remained the central doctrine of European thought about interstate relations. In the early sixteenth century, the doctrine was systematized and revised by Catholic theologians, particularly by the Spanish Dominican Francisco de Vittoria, to take account of the new developments I have sketched. What emerged was a doctrine less biblical and theological, more secularized, based more on natural than on divine law. The idea of holy war was now emphatically rejected. Vittoria denied that even the Old Testament wars had been ordered by God for religious purposes: He claimed that the wars of the Jews had been ordinary just wars, fought because heathens had refused them right of passage or committed other offenses recognized as just causes for war by the law of nature or the law of nations, still regarded as much the same thing. Warfare had to be explained in Aristotelian terms as an act arising from the nature of the human community. But one set of Aristotelian terms that Vittoria rejected just as emphatically as holy war was that of natural slavery: All human communities were equal, all were subject to the laws of nature and of nations in warfare. Those laws declared the *jus ad bellum* and the *jus in bello*. The distinction between just and unjust war was vigorously reasserted against both Erasmus and Machiavelli; and though their subversive influence continued to allure some, the principles summarized here commanded general assent in faculties of theology and law throughout Catholic and Protestant Europe.

The Early Modern Synthesis

I cannot attempt here to trace the entire history of the classical tradition, but it seems useful to continue this story a stage further. In the late sixteenth and early seventeenth centuries, the western European elite achieved widespread agreement on principles of warfare and interstate relations. There emerged what may be described as an early modern intellectual synthesis, comparable to the late medieval synthesis, whose influence lasted into the nineteenth century. It was a combination of the just war doctrine and Machiavellianism, a dialectic between humanity and necessity, all of it secularized and based upon the classical authors.[6]

In 1589 Giovanni Botero published a treatise called *Ragione di Stato*, which popularized this phrase in European languages. He tried to make Machiavelli, heretofore regarded throughout Europe as a diabolical villain, respectable and compatible with Christian values by distinguishing between a good and a bad type of *raison d'état*. The bad kind, which he blamed on Machiavelli, was exercised by tyrants for selfish motives; the good kind, which he preferred to associate with Tacitus to give it classical dignity, was used by monarchs for the good of their people. Political realism thus became one of the prerogatives of absolute monarchy. The civic militarism of Machiavelli was also adapted to absolute monarchy: Machiavelli's preference for republics went unmentioned, but there was much emphasis on the value of war for promoting unity and virtue within a kingdom, and princes were advised to recruit and train disciplined and loyal national armies. Botero was widely translated and imitated, and his recommendations soon became commonplaces.

Botero and his school had suggested the outlines of a synthesis that might embrace everything that seemed useful in the Western tradition. The work was completed mostly by northern, humanistically trained jurists—the Frenchman Jean Bodin, the Fleming Justus Lipsius, the Dutchman Hugo Grotius. The most influential contribution was perhaps Lipsius's *Politics* (1589), a collection of maxims from classical authors and anecdotes from ancient history intended as a commonplace book for princes. The doctrine of just war as systematized by sixteenth-century theology, the sanitized Machiavellianism or "Tacitism" then being popularized by Botero, and the need for national armies based on disciplined infantry—all were reiterated by Lipsius, supported with abundant classical references, and made to seem compatible with absolute monarchy. Like Machiavelli, Lipsius advised the prince to be both lion and fox. He insisted that the prince should never go to war without just cause and should keep faith with other princes; but the absolute sovereignty of the prince and his right to declare war in what he saw to be his own interest were taken for granted. Furthermore, the prince could practice deceit for the good of the realm. Lipsius even found a good word to say for Machiavelli, calling him "the Italian fault-writer (who poor soule is layde at of all hands)" (*Politics* 4.13, trans. William Jones [London, 1594]). The prince, Lipsius maintained, should keep up an active diplomacy and meddle in the affairs of his neighbors—"trouble others, rather than undo thyself" (4.9). He should recruit and train a disciplined, patriotic national army consisting largely of infantry. Lipsius did recommend a cautious brand of Machiavellianism, for he was hesitant about the strategy of decisive battle and found much in his classical sources that favored Fabius over Caesar; it was obvious by his time that gunpowder created many more problems for the offensive than Machiavelli had foreseen. Lipsius was suspicious of preventive strikes and saw the fallacy in Cicero's justification for Roman imperialism:

And this [the traditional just cause] is right and lawful defence: herein onely do thou persist, and neyther move hand nor foote under this couler and pretext, to seaze upon other men's goods; which the flowre of Romane eloquence doth confesse the Romaines them selves have done, when he sayth "Our Nation in defending our confederates are become Lords of the whole earth." I allow it not, neither do thou follow their example. (5.3 [trans. Jones])

Nevertheless, his concept of "right and lawful defence" is still vindicative and entirely in the hands of the prince.

Lipsius's *Politics* became the bible of princely humanism. In 1625, Hugo Grotius presented substantially the same ideas fortified with more classical citations in *The Laws of War and Peace,* which became the universal authority in the Western world on the laws of warfare and diplomacy. Little was added to it during the seventeenth and eighteenth centuries. In fact, the neoclassical synthesis summarized herein survived essentially intact through that entire period, though thinkers of the Enlightenment propagated an increasingly critical attitude toward princes and their just wars and often preferred to say that the laws of war were based upon concepts like "humanity" or "civilization" rather than "nature."

Notes

1. Felix Gilbert, "Machiavelli: The Renaissance of the Art of War," in *Makers of Modern Strategy: Military Thought from Machiavelli to Hitler,* ed. E. M. Earle (Princeton, 1943), 3–25 (reprinted in rev. ed., Peter Paret, 1986); Neal Wood, introduction to *The Art of War* (New York, 1965); Michael Mallet, "The Theory and Practice of Warfare in Machiavelli's Republic," and other papers in *Machiavelli and Republicanism,* ed. Gisela Bock, Quentin Skinner, and Maurizio Viroli (Cambridge, 1990).

2. Peter Burke, "A Survey of the Popularity of Ancient Historians, 1450–1700," *History and Theory* 5 (1966), 135–152.

3. Quoted in Garrett Mattingly, *Renaissance Diplomacy* (Baltimore, 1965), 251.

4. Anthony Pagden, *Lords of All the World: Ideologies of Empire in Spain, Britain, and France c. 1500–c. 1800* (New Haven, 1995). Only in Spain was there any prolonged controversy over the legitimacy of conquest. The English and French in North America cultivated a myth that they had settled an almost vacant continent with the consent of the natives. J. H. Parry, *The Spanish Theory of Empire in the Sixteenth Century* (New York, 1940); Lewis Hanke, *Aristotle and the American Indians: A Study of Race Prejudice in the Modern World* (London, 1959).

5. Ronald Musto, *The Catholic Peace Tradition* (Maryknoll, N. Y., 1986); R. P. Adams, *The Better Part of Valor: More, Erasmus, Colet, and Vives on Humanism, War, and Peace* (Seattle, 1962).

6. On the school of Botero, Friedrich Meinecke's *Machiavellism: The Doctrine of Raison d'Etat and Its Place in Modern History,* trans. Douglas Scott (New Haven, 1957); on the school of Lipsius, Gerhard Oestreich, *Neostoicism and the Early Modern State,* trans. David McLintock (Cambridge, 1982); and on the revival of Tacitus, *Tacitus and the Tacitean Tradition,* ed. T. J. Luce and A. J. Woodman (Princeton, 1993).

Chapter Thirteen

Conclusion

It seems appropriate to complete this survey with a few comments on the fate of the classical tradition. The neoclassical synthesis of early modern times began to fall apart some two hundred years ago. What destroyed it was the death of civic militarism. By the time of the American and French Revolutions, many enlightened thinkers had come to distrust the fierce bellicosity of the classical ideal of citizenship and to prefer a humane, peaceful, and commercial model of republicanism. Many were suspicious even of the primacy of politics in the classical republics, for modern liberals tended to be distrustful of the state and centralized power. Most would have agreed with John Adams, who in the course of the debate over the American Constitution in 1787, castigated Aristotle for excluding merchants from his ideal constitution: "It is of infinitely more importance to the national happiness, to abound in good merchants, farmers, and manufacturers, good lawyers, priests, and physicians, and great philosophers, than it is to multiply what are called great statesmen and great generals."[1]

Worse than the classical authors' fascination with political life was their obsession with war. In 1791, a clergyman preached to the General Court of New Hampshire that "no aera since the creation of the world" was "so favourable to the rights of mankind as the present." He criticized harshly the "imperfect civilization" of "the Grecian and Roman nations":

> They who are acquainted with the true history of Greece and Rome, need not be informed, that the cruelty they exercised upon their slaves, and those taken in war, is almost beyond the power of credibility. The proud and selfish passions have always endeavoured to suppress the spirit of Freedom. Even Rome herself, while she pretended to glory in being free, endeavoured to subject and enslave the rest of mankind.—But no longer shall we look to antient histories for principles and systems of pure freedom. The close of the eighteenth century, in which we live, shall teach mankind to be truly free.[2]

Some Renaissance humanists had been uneasy at the way the classical authors associated freedom with hegemony, but at the close of the eighteenth century, that association seemed a blatant and intolerable contradiction. True freedom could never lead to a desire to dominate other peoples. Classical and modern republicanism had nothing in common. As Alexander Hamilton put it in *The Federalist,* "The industrious habits of the people of the present day, absorbed in the pursuits of gain, and devoted to the improvements of agriculture and commerce are incompatible with the condition of a nation of soldiers, which was the true condition of the people of those [ancient Greek] republics" (8 [47]).

There was a growing conviction that warfare could be legitimately practiced only for motives of safety, never gain or glory—that is, for immediate self-defense against aggression, not for the larger aims of self-preservation assumed in the traditional idea of "defense." There was a growing hope that warfare might vanish entirely with the spread of republicanism, commerce, and civility. Land-based empire was now perceived as an unmitigated evil, destructive even to the imperial power itself. New European empires were to arise overseas, but from this time on they would be justified not as imitations of imperial Rome but as the peaceful diffusion of European science and progress over a grateful globe. The new language of nineteenth-century imperialism was heard as early as 1794 in the influential *Sketch for a Historical Picture of the Progress of the Human Mind* by the Marquis de Condorcet, who convinced himself that the peoples of Africa and Asia were "waiting only to be civilized and to receive from us the means to be so, and find brothers among the Europeans to become their friends and disciples."[3]

Everything the classics had to say about war and statecraft now seemed of questionable value. The hold of the classical tradition on Western thought about those matters, and others, began slowly but inexorably to weaken. Soon the influence of the classical historians was replaced by the new scientific history of Niebuhr, and that of the classical treatises on the art of war was eclipsed by the new military science of Jomini and Clausewitz.

Civic militarism was quite dead, but in ethical and strategic thought, the influence of the classics lingered for a long time. Many military thinkers continued to find something especially paradigmatic about the ancient military experience. As late as World War I, the German war plan was based on the tactics of Hannibal at Cannae; but that war showed that the twentieth-century military experience had become different indeed, and it rendered the final blow to the ancient ideal of glory.

This was the second great intellectual watershed that doomed the classical tradition. In the late eighteenth century, the Western world began to lose faith in militarism; in the late nineteenth, it began to lose faith in morality. The classical and neoclassical traditions had always been based on a universal belief in natural law. Ideas about the functions and justifications of warfare commanded assent because they were supposed to reflect eternal truths about human nature. The existence of these has seemed increasingly questionable since Darwin, and in this century, natural law has become an almost unintelligible notion to the great majority of intellectuals. Parts of Grotius's neoclassical synthesis survive in contemporary international law, but they have lost their philosophical coherence. This is why the moral and strategic vocabularies of war have drifted apart, producing the mutual incomprehension described in my introduction to this book.

Is there any reason they should not remain apart? I suggest that there is. Neither the ethical tradition nor the strategic tradition by itself seems an adequate instrument for the discussion of war. Consider the current state of the ethics of war, about which there has been a notable revival of interest among late twentieth-century philosophers and theologians. There are three main contemporary approaches. Firstly, there is pacifism, or the belief that all war is evil. Secondly, there is defensivism, which holds that wars are justifiable only when undertaken for immediate self-defense against aggression. Thirdly, there is the traditional just war in various revised forms.[4] Since the collapse of natural law, each of these positions is usually defended by utilitarian arguments. Pacifists commonly argue that at least under modern conditions no war can be worth the cost—an argument more plausible in the case of nuclear war and succinctly summarized by the slogan Better Red than dead. Defensivists think that those risks are sometimes worth taking for the survival of the state or culture, but since the only cause they recognize is self-defense, they are faced with the problem of defining "aggression." And believers in the just war are unwilling to give up entirely the ancient vindicative concept of war, while recognizing how much it has been abused in the past; they think war can still be a valid moral instrument of collective security, pursued for the protection of the innocent and the punishment of the wicked, and it cannot serve that function if states must wait until they are attacked themselves. Each of these moral positions is also a strategic position; the utilitarian arguments all rest upon cost-benefit analyses that cannot be attempted without adopting the strategic vocabulary. It seems equally obvious that the vocabulary of strategy cannot work in isolation: Military goals make no sense except as instruments of political goals, which, on the highest level at least, involve the ethical choices mentioned previously. The modern divorce between military thought and larger philosophical questions produced the body of literature known as "nuclear strategy," which may be described as the reductio ad absurdum of the decisive battle.

There is much in the classical tradition that we are well rid of. But we cannot afford to ignore its lessons. War will not go away. There is need for a new synthesis that can make possible an informed public discourse about these matters in terms that are both realistic and responsible.

Notes

1. John Adams, *A Defence of the Constitutions of Government of the United States of America,* in *The Works of John Adams,* ed. C. F. Adams (Boston, 1850–1856), vol. 4, 526.

2. Quoted in P. A. Rahe, *Republics Ancient and Modern: Classical Republicanism and the American Revolution* (Chapel Hill, N.C., 1992), 568. The other citations from American authors I also owe to Rahe.

3. Quoted by Anthony Pagden, *Lords of All the World: Ideologies of Empire in Spain, Britain, and France c. 1500–c. 1800* (New Haven, 1995), 10. I know of no comprehensive study of Enlightenment thought about war, but see Kingsley Martin, *French Liberal Thought in the Eighteenth Century: A Study of Political Ideas from Bayle to Condorcet*, ed. J. P. Mayer (New York, 1963); Peter Gay, *The Enlightenment: An Interpretation*, vol. 2 (New York, 1969). J.G.A. Pocock, *The Machiavellian Moment: Florentine Political Thought and the Atlantic Republican Tradition* (Princeton, 1975).

4. Representatives of these several schools include: for pacifism, D. A. Wells, "How Much Can 'the Just War' Justify?" *Journal of Philosophy* 66 (1969), 819–829; for defensivism, F. R. Struckmeyer, "The 'Just War' and the Right of Self-Defense," *Ethics* 82 (1971), 48–55; and for the just war, Michael Walzer, *Just and Unjust Wars: A Moral Argument with Historical Illustrations* (New York, 1977).

Bibliography

This select bibliography is intended as a guide to further reading and includes only books. Articles are cited in full in the notes.

General

Ceadel, Martin. *Thinking About Peace and War.* Oxford, 1987.

Clark, Ian. *Waging War: A Philosophical Introduction.* Oxford, 1988.

Delbrück, Hans. *History of the Art of War.* 4 vols. Trans. W. J. Renfroe, Jr. Westport, Conn., 1975–1985.

Howard, Michael, G. J. Andreopoulos, and M. R. Shulman, eds. *The Laws of War: Constraints on Warfare in the Western World.* New Haven, 1994.

Keegan, John. *A History of Warfare.* New York, 1993.

Paret, Peter, ed. *Makers of Modern Strategy: From Machiavelli to the Nuclear Age.* Princeton, 1986.

Walzer, Michael. *Just and Unjust Wars: A Moral Argument with Historical Illustrations.* New York, 1977.

Wright, Quincy. *A Study of War.* 2d ed. Chicago, 1965.

Primitive Societies

Dennen, J.M.G. Van der, and V. Falger, eds. *Sociobiology and Conflict: Evolutionary Perspectives on Competition, Cooperation, Violence, and Warfare.* London, 1990.

Durham, W. H. *Coevolution: Genes, Culture, and Human Diversity.* Stanford, 1991.

Eibl-Eibesfeldt, Irenäus. *The Biology of Peace and War: Man, Animals, and Aggression.* Trans. Eric Mossbacher. New York, 1979.

Ferguson, R. B., ed. *Warfare, Culture, and Environment.* Orlando, Fla., 1984.

Ferguson, R. B., and N. L. Whitehead, eds. *War in the Tribal Zone: Expanding States and Indigenous Warfare.* Santa Fe, N. Mex., 1992.

Fried, M. H., Marvin Harris, and R. F. Murphy, eds. *War: The Anthropology of Armed Conflict and Aggression.* Garden City, N.Y., 1968.

Haas, Jonathan, ed. *The Anthropology of War.* Cambridge, 1990.

Harris, Marvin. *Our Kind: Who We Are, Where We Came From, Where We Are Going.* New York, 1988.

Nettleship, M. A., and R. D. Givens, eds. *Discussions on War and Human Aggression.* The Hague, 1975.

Nettleship, M. A., R. D. Givens, and A. Nettleship, eds. *War: Its Causes and Correlates.* The Hague, 1975.

Price, T. D., and J. A. Brown, eds. *Prehistoric Hunter-Gatherers: The Emergence of Cultural Complexity.* Orlando, Fla., 1985.

Rapaport, Roy. *Pigs for the Ancestors: Ritual in the Ecology of a New Guinea People.* New Haven, 1968.

Turney-High, H. H. *Primitive War: Its Practices and Concepts.* 2d ed. Columbia, S.C., 1971.

Wilson, E. O. *On Human Nature.* Cambridge, Mass., 1978.

The Ancient Middle East

Claessen, H.J.M., and Peter Skalnik, eds. *The Early State.* The Hague, 1978.

Cohen, Ronald, and E. R. Service, eds. *Origins of the State: The Anthropology of Political Evolution.* Philadelphia, 1978.

Drews, Robert. *The End of the Bronze Age: Changes in Warfare and the Catastrophe ca. 1200 B.C.* Princeton, 1993.

Ferrill, Arther. *The Origins of War: From the Stone Age to Alexander the Great.* London, 1985.

O'Connell, R. L. *Ride of the Second Horseman: The Birth and Death of War.* New York, 1995.

Otterbein, K. F. *The Evolution of War: A Cross-Cultural Study.* N.p., 1970.

Yadin, Yigael. *The Art of Warfare in Biblical Lands in the Light of Archaeological Discovery.* London, 1963.

The Greeks

Adcock, F. E. *The Greek and Macedonian Art of War.* Berkeley, 1957.

Anderson, J. K. *Military Thought and Practice in the Age of Xenophon.* Berkeley, 1970.

Connor, W. R. *Thucydides.* Princeton, 1984.

Dover, K. J. *Greek Popular Morality in the Time of Plato and Aristotle.* Berkeley, 1974.

Edmunds, Lowell. *Chance and Intelligence in Thucydides.* Cambridge, Mass., 1975.

Evans, J.A.S. *Herodotus: Explorer of the Past.* Princeton, 1991.

Fornara, Charles. *The Nature of History in Ancient Greece and Rome.* Berkeley, 1983.

Garlan, Yvon. *War in the Ancient World: A Social History.* Trans. Janet Lloyd. Ithaca, 1975.

Gould, John. *Herodotus.* Oxford, 1989.

Gruen, Peter. *The Hellenistic World and the Coming of Rome.* Berkeley, 1984.

Hanson, Victor. *The Western Way of War: Infantry Battle in Classical Greece.* New York, 1989.

———, ed. *Hoplites: The Classical Greek Battle Experience.* New York, 1991.

Hornblower, Simon. *Thucydides.* Baltimore, 1987.

Kennedy, George, ed. *Aristotle on Rhetoric: A Theory of Civic Discourse.* New York, 1991.

Ober, Josiah. *Fortress Attica: Defense of the Athenian Land Frontier, 404–322 B.C.* Leiden, 1985.

Pritchett, W. K. *The Greek State at War.* 5 vols. Berkeley, 1971–1991.

Rich, John, and Graham Shipley, eds. *War and Society in the Greek World.* London, 1993.

Romilly, Jacqueline de. *The Rise and Fall of States According to Greek Authors.* Trans. Philip Thody. Ann Arbor, Mich., 1977.

Sacks, K. S. *Polybius and the Writing of History.* Berkeley, 1981.

Starr, Chester. *The Influence of Sea Power on Ancient History.* New York, 1989.

Wheeler, E. L. *Stratagem and the Vocabulary of Military Trickery.* Leiden, 1988.

Whitehead, David, ed. *Aeneas the Tactician: How to Survive Under Siege.* Oxford, 1990.

Woodman, A. J. *Rhetoric in Classical Historiography.* London, 1988.

The Romans

Adcock, F. E. *The Roman Art of War Under the Republic.* Cambridge, 1960.

Brunt, P. A. *Roman Imperial Themes.* Oxford, 1990.

Campbell, J. B. *The Emperor and the Roman Army, 31 B.C.–A.D. 235.* Oxford, 1984.

Dorey, T. A., ed. *Latin Historians.* New York, 1966.

Earl, D. C. *The Political Thought of Sallust.* Cambridge, 1961.

———. *The Moral and Political Tradition of Rome.* Ithaca, 1967.

Ferrill, Arther. *The Fall of the Roman Empire: The Military Explanation.* London, 1986.

Harris, W. V. *War and Imperialism in Republican Rome, 327–70 B.C.* Oxford, 1979.

Hopkins, Keith. *Conquerors and Slaves.* Cambridge, 1978.

Isaac, Benjamin. *The Limits of Empire: The Roman Army in the East.* Oxford, 1990.

Keppie, J. F. *The Making of the Roman Army.* Totowa, N. J., 1984.

Lintott, Andrew. *Imperium Romanum: Politics and Administration.* London, 1993.

Luttwak, Edward. *The Grand Strategy of the Roman Empire from the First Century A.D. to the Third.* Baltimore, 1976.

Mellor, Ronald. *Tacitus.* New York, 1992.

Millar, Fergus. *The Emperor in the Roman World, 31 B.C.–A.D. 337.* Ithaca, 1977.

Milner, N. P., ed. *Vegetius: Epitome of Military Science.* Liverpool, 1993.

Rich, John, and Graham Shipley, eds. *War and Society in the Roman World.* London, 1993.

The Classical Legacy

Adams, R. P. *The Better Part of Valor: More, Erasmus, Colet, and Vives on Humanism, War, and Peace.* Seattle, 1962.

Baron, Hans. *The Crisis of the Early Italian Renaissance: Civic Humanism and Republican Liberty in an Age of Classicism and Tyranny.* 2 vols. 2d ed. Princeton, 1966.

Bayley, C. C. *War and Society in Renaissance Florence: The "De Militia" of Leonardo Bruni.* Toronto, 1961.

Bock, Gisela, Quentin Skinner, and Maurizio Viroli, eds. *Machiavelli and Republicanism.* Cambridge, 1990.

Contamine, Philippe, *Warfare in the Middle Ages.* Trans. Michael Jones. Oxford, 1984.

Hanke, Lewis. *Aristotle and the American Indians: A Study of Race Prejudice in the Modern World.* London, 1959.

Johnson, J. T. *Ideology, Reason, and the Limitation of War: Religious and Secular Concepts, 1200–1740.* Princeton, 1975.

———. *Just War Tradition and the Restraint of War.* Princeton, 1981.

Mattingly, Garrett. *Renaissance Diplomacy.* Baltimore, 1965.

Meinecke, Friedrich. *Machiavellism: The Doctrine of Raison d'Etat and Its Place in Modern History.* Trans. Douglas Scott. New Haven, 1957.

Musto, Ronald. *The Catholic Peace Tradition.* Maryknoll, N.Y., 1986.

Pagden, Anthony. *Lords of All the World: Ideologies of Empire in Spain, Britain, and France c. 1500–c. 1800.* New Haven, 1995.

Parry, J. H. *The Spanish Theory of Empire in the Sixteenth Century.* New York, 1940.

Pocock, J.G.A. *The Machiavellian Moment: Florentine Political Thought and the Atlantic Republican Tradition.* Princeton, 1975.

Rahe, P. A. *Republics Ancient and Modern: Classical Republicanism and the American Revolution.* Chapel Hill, N.C., 1992.

Russell, F. H. *The Just War in the Middle Ages.* Cambridge, 1975.

About the Book and Author

What is the source of the uniquely Western way of war, the persistent militarism that has made Europe the site of bloodshed throughout history and secured the dominance of the West over the rest of the world? The answer, Doyne Dawson persuasively argues in this groundbreaking new book, is to be found in the very bedrock of Western civilization: ancient Greece and Rome.

The Origins of Western Warfare begins with an overview of primitive warfare, showing how the main motivations of prehistoric combat—revenge and honor—set the tone for Greek thinking about questions of war and morality. These ideas, especially as later developed by the Romans, ensured the emergence of a distinctive Western tradition of warfare—dynamic, aggressive, and devastatingly successful when turned against non-Western cultures.

Dawson identifies key factors that led Western culture down this particular path. First, the Greeks argued that war could be justified as an instrument of human and divine justice, securing the social and cosmic order. Second, war was seen as a rational instrument of foreign policy. This, probably the most original contribution of the Greeks to military thought, was articulated as early as the fifth century B.C. Finally, Greek military thought was dominated by the principle of "civic militarism," in which the ideal state is based upon self-governing citizens trained and armed for war.

The Roman version of civic militarism became thoroughly imperial in spirit, and in general, the Romans successfully modified these Greek ideas to serve their expansionist policies. At the end of antiquity, these traditions were passed on to medieval Europe, forming the basis for the just war doctrines of the church. Later, in early modern Europe, they were fully revived, systematized, and founded on natural law—to the benefit of absolute monarchs. For centuries, this neoclassical synthesis served the needs of European elites, and echoes of it are still heard in contemporary justifications for war.

Providing a careful reconsideration of what the classical sources tell us about Western thinking on fundamental questions of war and peace, *The Origins of Western Warfare* makes a lasting contribution to our understanding of one of the most persistent and troubling aspects of Western culture.

Doyne Dawson received his Ph.D. from Princeton University and is the author of *Cities of the Gods: Communist Utopias in Greek Thought.* He lives in Greensboro, North Carolina.

Index